Social Indicators Research Series

Volume 84

This series provides a public forum for authored and edited volumes on social indicators research. It is a companion series to the journal Social Indicators Research. The book series deals with problems associated with the quality of life from a broad perspective. It welcomes research on a wide range of substantive areas, including health, crime, housing, education, family life, leisure activities, transportation, mobility, economics, work, religion and environmental issues. The topics represented in this series cover and involve a variety of segmentations, such as social groups, spatial and temporal coordinates, population composition, and life domains. The series presents empirical, philosophical and methodological studies that cover the entire spectrum of society and are devoted to giving evidence through indicators. It considers indicators in their different typologies, and gives special attention to indicators that are able to meet the need of understanding social realities and phenomena that are increasingly more complex, interrelated, interacted and dynamic. In addition, it presents studies aimed at defining new approaches in constructing indicators. An international review board for this series ensures the high quality of the series as a whole.

Available at 25% discount for International Society for Quality-of-Life Studies (ISQOLS). For membership details please contact: ISQOLS; e-mail: office@isqols.org

More information about this series at https://link.springer.com/bookseries/6548

Paolo Corvo • Fabio Massimo Lo Verde
Editors

Sport and Quality of Life

Practices, Habits and Lifestyles

Springer

Editors
Paolo Corvo
University of Gastronomic Sciences
Pollenzo, Italy

Fabio Massimo Lo Verde
University of Palermo
Palermo, Italy

ISSN 1387-6570 ISSN 2215-0099 (electronic)
Social Indicators Research Series
ISBN 978-3-030-93091-2 ISBN 978-3-030-93092-9 (eBook)
https://doi.org/10.1007/978-3-030-93092-9

This Springer imprint is published by the registered company Springer Nature Switzerland AG.
The registered company address is: Gewerbestrasse 11, 6330 Cham, Switzerland

Contents

Chapter 1
Introduction

Fabio Massimo Lo Verde and Paolo Corvo

In the last 30 years, the sport has taken on a significant meaning in people's lives and, even if with considerable differences, both in advanced economic development and developing countries.

At the individual level, it constituted an area of *identity investment*. It can assume the shape of "sports spectacle" to be enjoyed, fueling the practice of cheering and fandom or representing the model of a winning lifestyle. But also, when the sport took the form of free time practice through which to keep fit, making grow, in this case, the diffusion of a culture of health and well-being.

These are two ways of approaching the consumption of sports by spectators and actors, and the two ways of use can be strongly related to the perception and assessment of peoples' quality of life. However, the "semantic universes" that connote sport and "free time sports" have often appeared polarized.

On the one hand, commercial sport and sports professionalism are intertwined with the institutions of economics, politics, and culture, which, above all, stress its "spectacularity" to capture, first and foremost, the audience. On the other hand, sports practices in leisure time are linked to the actions of the institutions of economics, politics and culture, with the difference that this stress, above all, its "healthy value", aimed at the "healthy and rational" investment of time in an activity which improves the quality of life in the short, medium and long period.

This polarization between the consumption of sports *entertainment*—commercial sport—and the consumption of sport as a *leisure activity*—the sport for all—has become increasingly interconnected because of the increased need for collective

F. M. Lo Verde
University of Palermo, Palermo, Italy
e-mail: fabio.loverde@unipa.it

P. Corvo (✉)
University of Gastronomic Sciences, Pollenzo, Italy
e-mail: p.corvo@unisg.it

P. Corvo, F. M. Lo Verde (eds.), *Sport and Quality of Life*, Social Indicators Research Series 84, https://doi.org/10.1007/978-3-030-93092-9_1

identity *via* sport. In other words, we have witnessed the spread of sports expressions that recall their importance for psychophysical well-being, for integration and social participation, for the reduction of social inequalities, ethnic and cultural differences. However, the importance assumed by sports was weakened in the show from agonism, from the competition, from the physical confrontation between two contenders or two teams. A sport in which we act *with* competitors as well as *against* competitors. And, at the same time, we have gradually witnessed the "spectacularization" of sports in our free time, to the point that the sharing of the results, obtained through the declination of a competitive spirit that presents itself as directed no longer against *other contenders*, but *against its performance limits*, it has become how each person makes part of his or her own life spectacular, the one he often considers *most authentic*.

This work aims to describe how the relationship between the commercial/professional dimension of sports and its playful/recreational practice is fueled by the demand and the offer of *social identity* that characterizes these two "semantic universes".

All of the contributions in this volume are on one of two sides, but all of them look at the relationship between sport, well-being, and quality of life. Contributions refer both to the individual or collective practice of sport and to the enjoyment of the sporting spectacle. In this second case, the enjoyment of the sporting spectacle becomes a means to build identity and community through the collective sharing of emotions.

The text is aimed at young scholars and students who intend to study the theme of sport as a set of "finite provinces of meaning", quoting Schutz, which helps us to clarify the concept of "good quality of life" through an "active life". But also observing the relationship between sports practice, enjoyment of the sports show, participation, and quality of life. For this reason, the text is divided into four parts that collect:

1. theoretical and the questions of definitions regarding the theme of the relationship between sport, well-being, and quality of life (Part I);
2. the description of how the sport is practiced and the enjoyment of the sports show in some Italian urban and local realities (Part II);
3. the more general issues that are encountered at the international level and which concern the articulation of inequalities in sports and inclusion policies for the quality of life through sport (Part III);
4. the issues related to fitness culture concerning—aging—sports, and quality of life (Part IV).

Despite what is usually presented in many books concerning these themes, the vision we applied in it is clearly "sociological" and not "psychological" or "philosophical". Therefore, we observe specific phenomena concerning sociological literature and sociological research to isolate the more specifically social connotations that contribute to the construction of socially shared meanings of well-being and quality of life concerning the consumption of sport practiced and enjoyed in the forms of show and show entertainment.

1.1 Part I

In the first contribution **Marco Ciziceno** presents a literature review entitled *The conceptions of quality of life, wellness and well-being*. During the last years, questions related to the nature of the "good life" have gained the attention of governments, experts, and public opinion. Terms as wellness, well-being or happiness have become popular both in the scientific and in the everyday language. However, as the interest in these topics grows, the disagreement among scholars about what wellness or well-being means grows simultaneously. The author aims to provide clear identification of existing theoretical models of wellness and well-being in social sciences. Starting from the differences in physical and mental well-being, he looks inside the internal dimensions of wellness and subjective well-being, suggesting future directions for research on these topics.

In the contribution entitled *Sports participation, physical activity, life satisfaction, and quality of life. Evidence from EU microdata data*, **Maurizio Esposito and Ciprian Panzaru** analyse the relationship between sports and physical activity and quality of life. The authors used secondary data from Eurobarometer "Fairness, inequality and inter-generational mobility, Sport and physical activity, and EU citizens". Moreover, data from Eurobarometer are valuable because they contain information about all EU states. The authors built the study on two main directions. In the first stage, descriptive statistics were used to illustrate the main aspects of sport participation in the European Union. In the second stage, regression analyses were employed for the European Union and in five countries, separately. In the third contribution**, Antonio Mussino** presents the importance of monitoring participation in sports and physical activities in a country and, in a coordinated way, in different countries. The paper *Conceptual and operational problems in monitoring participation in sports* are divided into two parts: the first section deals with the problems researchers face when they have to standardize definitions, plan a questionnaire and a survey strategy, and produce comparable indicators. In the second part, data from Eurobarometer 472 (December 2017) are processed in an original way to present trends, including their main determinants, of participation in sports and physical activities in the European Union countries.

Bruno Barba, with the contribution entitled*football: no, nothing will be some as before*, asserts that professional football was taking a dangerous slope: the power of TV, marketing, and money seemed to overturn ancient, loved, and chivalric logic. There are two fundamental questions: who knows if this grave moment of crisis by Corona Virus will not reconsider calendars, wages, passions, participation; and who knows if, once the storm is over, we will not be able to return for football its "noble" role of total social fact.

1.2 Part II

The second part of this book describes how sports phenomenon, including sport practice, sports participation, is represented in some Italian urban and local realities.

Fabio Massimo Lo Verde and **Vincenzo Pepe,** analyze three categories of urban sports: running and skateboard (Lo Verde) and cycling (Pepe). Studying the sport in the city, the so-called "urban sports," constitutes an emerging area of sociological research. Recently, an increasing number of people enjoy urban sports or interact with the urban environment. Many of them are hybrid forms of sports adapted to the urban context. This phenomenon has important implications for studying the relationships between metropolitan cities, their spaces, and sports activities. In this chapter, authors starting from the urban population theory highlights how the urban environment has been recoded to meet peoples' needs for physical and spiritual well-being. Moreover, the authors reflect on the reorganization of urban spaces in response to the growing demand for sports functionality and new sports technologies.

Giovanna Russo and Stefano Martelli, in the paper entitled *From whom comes the new question of well-being in Italy? Practitioners of sport and physical activity* analyze the theme of promoting sport for health and well-being in Italy through the evolution of types of Italian people who practice sport and physical activity, with specific attention to those who practice for health reasons (quantitative comparison through national statistics data). In short, the authors aim to highlight the leading and recent trends taking place in sports and physical activity in Italy.

Football is one of the most popular sports globally and is an excellent source of collective feelings and emotions. In Italy, football is the national sport and moves passion and interests at all social and economic life levels, even political in certain circumstances. Some teams represent large cities, and others represent smaller towns. In the smaller cities, fans come mainly from the province. The contributions of **Paolo Corvo**, *Atalanta, a contemporary myth that challenges the big football clubs,* investigates the case of one of these so-called provincial teams, Atalanta, from Bergamo, in Lombardy, because it significantly highlights the link between the identity and history of a territory and its footballing declination. In recent years, Atalanta has achieved great results nationally and internationally, conquering unexpected goals. However, a part of the big European clubs seems willing to exclude provincial teams from the most prestigious international competitions, creating a Super League, aiming at large television and advertising contracts.

Nico Bortoletto addresses the question of authenticity in sport tourism activity. The contribution entitled *authenticity as an element of connotation in sport tourism activity. Some empirical aspects from the Italian arena* demonstrate that one of the main difficulties that the researcher faces is the definitory one. Where are the boundaries of a sport tourist? The athletes coming from around the world join the New York (or the Rome) marathon are easy to identify, but what about people in Rimini or Nizza that choose to spend the classical two-weeks sea holidays couple of days on a racing bike exploring the outback? The author considered the Italian situation using evidence provided by the Outdoor Sports Tourism Observatory for stressing the increasing relevance of the sector, even declined in a mere socioeconomic way.

Loredana Tallarita analyzes the impact of social capital on the integration of immigrants. Moreover, the author explores the significance of the football game on social inclusion pathways. The contribution is entitled *Social capital and paths of inclusion through sports practice. A closer look at immigration in Italy* looks at the relational networks with which immigrants interact in sports environments promote new forms of solidarity. The research has been conducted in Sicily in the towns of Ragusa and Vittoria (RG). There were 60 in-depth interviews with the refugee center's operators, football school instructors, and immigrants. From the interviews, there have emerged the *symbolic meanings* of the experiences built by immigrants in the host countries.

1.3 Part III

The third part of this book focuses on social representation and articulation of disabilities and inequalities in sports and the international policies aimed at improving quality of life through sports activity.

Bernardeau-Moreau analyzes the progress in the representation of people with disabilities during social interaction situations. These social interactions are fundamental points that inhibit or facilitate access to work for this specific part of society. The aim of the contribution *Social representations of physical disability in professional environments. The example of disabled employees high-performance athletes in a service company* is to provide some elements for reflection on physical disability in the workplace.

Ailton Fernando Santana de Oliveira presents the contributions entitled *Physical and sports activities diagnosis in Brazil: methodology to support policies to improve the population's quality of life.* The author developed a diagnostic study that would allow identifying, knowing, and explaining the reality of physical and sports activities and the profile of practitioners and non-practitioners of the Brazilian population. The data found by the research may contribute to understand the development and the reality of this area, support the decision making by the managers, for the strengthening of actions, programs and projects, within the scope of physical and sports activity, focused on health, leisure or social inclusion that improves the quality of life of children, young people and the elderly.

1.4 Part IV

Finally, part four of this book addresses the question of physical activity and quality of life, including issues related to fitness culture, aging, and sports.

Parkrun is one of the world phenomena that testify to the change in the sports scene today. It is a *big digital* community that brings together lovers of running and is characterized by social networks and digital gaming applications for fitness and health purposes. **Loredana Tallarita** with the contribution entitled *Social Fitness and gamification. The impact on body health and physical activity* explores the most significant changes in the Italian Parkrun community and *the provinces of meaning* through the interview with the manager of Parkrun in Italy: Giorgio Cambiano, an engineer and ex-marathon runner. It has allowed examining the characteristics of the phenomenon and the changes that occurred due to the COVID-SARS-19.

Michele Filippo Fontefrancesco look at the experience of joggers to understand further the relationship between sports and quality of life in an exceptional context, such as the one of the Covid-19 pandemic in Italy. In particular, the paper *A running enemy: Jogging at the time of Covid-19 pandemic*, explores the impact of the lockdown (March–April 2020) on the sportive experience among joggers in North-western Italy and how this change transformed their understanding of the urban surrounding, impacting on their quality of life. By focusing on the history of the life of the joggers, authors explore the impact of the lockdown in changing the very understanding of the urban environment in a novel context of villainization of the sportive practice.

Aging and quality of life in the elderly: the role of physical activity is the title of the contribution of **Ivana Matteucci.** She assesses the relationship between physical activity and quality of life in the elderly by examining a sample population in a province of the Marche region in Italy. In particular, the contribution focused on possible variations in the relationship between physical activity and quality of life based on gender and age. Significant associations between the indicators were found, pointing to a positive general correlation between the amount of physical activity performed and quality of life indicators. Primarily, a correlation was found between physical activity related to walking, light sports, housework, and satisfaction with social participation measured by satisfaction with using one's time, the level of activities carried out, and opportunities to participate in community life.

Luca Benvenga and **Elisabetta Trinca**, with the contribution *Physical activity as a daily practice, "Active aging" between social needs, technology, and quality-of-life improvement,* aim to understand how physical activity ensures individual and social well-being. The key points on which the observation is focused are (a) the daily actions that promote a regular behavior pattern improving the quality of life and public health; (b) the daily practice of motor activity as an opportunity for aggregation and socialization; (c) the state of the art of national and EU policies aimed at creating a value chain for the elderly people who "embrace a complex and multifaceted idea of life and the aging process". The contribution stems from a micro-sociological observation: in the current world, more and more groups of people share a set of practices that redefine daily activities and social communities.

The recent events related to the Co-Vid 19 pandemic have certainly changed the social meaning considerably that sports entertainment and leisure time sports practice have assumed. In the first case, the void in the supply of sports entertainment has made the perception of the danger and seriousness of the moment humanity was experiencing even more alarming. An "absence of normality" was also perceived as the absence of the routine that sports spectacle activates. The "emotions of sport" were "frozen" and took on a nostalgic dimension, even if for a short period. In the second case, on the other hand, the practice of sports seemed like a real liberation, the possibility of accessing spaces that at the time of the lockdown were forbidden to all. The sport was practiced for physical well-being. But above all, for the mental one, to breathe the air of freedom that is the air of everyday life. Never before have sports, quality of life, and well-being been so intertwined as in this period. And overall, because the risk of losing all this "everyday life" has become palpable. And we believe that this condition should be used as a warning concerning the importance of well-being, quality of life, and the sporting experience.

This project was conceived in the period preceding the Covid19 pandemic. During the writing of this book we have experienced moments of great difficulty on a global level. Now it is hoped that the situation improves and that sport also returns to a new normal. Unfortunately, a member of the group of editors, prof. Stefano Martelli, passed away. He was a dear colleague who has contributed significantly with his studies and publications to the diffusion and development of the sociology of sport. It is a great honor for us to host your latest writing. We will always remember him with gratitude and affection.

Part I
General Themes

Chapter 2
The Conceptions of Quality of Life, Wellness and Well-Being: A Literature Review

Marco Ciziceno

2.1 Introduction

Over the last decades, research on wellness, well-being, and quality of life has increased in importance in social sciences (Hagerty et al., 2001; Mayer, 2011; Michalos, 2004). This is because questions related to the nature of the "good life", including the pursuit of happiness (Ryan & Deci, 2001), the balanced lifestyles (Christiansen & Matuska, 2006), or the physical wellness (Brady et al., 2018) have gained the attention of scholars, experts and public opinion. According to Roscoe (2009), the new perspective of health introduced by the World Health Organization (WHO, 1967) has imposed a more comprehensive and global evaluation of human life, which included mind, body, spirit, and social interactions (Helliwell, 2006; Ryff & Singer, 2006; Travis & Ryan, 1988).

For these reasons, quality of life, wellness and well-being have become popular in the scientific debate and they have also captured the interest of governments, that collect information about the perceived well-being of their citizens in order to address health programs or guide their policy decisions (Austin, 2016).

Scholars, across disciplines, have proposed several theoretical models in order to explain the concepts of wellness (Adams et al., 1997; Greenberg, 1985; Lafferty, 1979; Renger et al., 2000), well-being (Dieneret al., 1985; Ryan & Deci, 2001) and quality of life (Michalos, 2004; Michalos et al., 2000). Moreover, a multitude of well-being measures has been developed to conduct survey or specific questionnaire assessments on those topics. As a consequence, empirical research has grown significantly and the disagreements (among scholars) about what these terms actually mean have increased accordantly (Lent, 2004). In practice, the current usage of such terms is limited by some conceptual and methodological concerns

M. Ciziceno (✉)
Department of Economics, Business and Statistics, University of Palermo, Palermo, Italy
e-mail: marco.ciziceno@unipa.it

P. Corvo, F. M. Lo Verde (eds.), *Sport and Quality of Life*, Social Indicators Research Series 84, https://doi.org/10.1007/978-3-030-93092-9_2

(Fernández-Ballesteros, 2011), with scholars that often use them as synonyms or equivalent and studies that measure the same concept in different ways (Diener & Seligman, 2002). Although these misalignments have been stressed by researchers, a clear definition of wellness, well-being or quality of life is not available in the current literature.

In this review, a better identification of existing theoretical models of wellness, well-being and quality of life is provided. For an exhaustive conceptualization of these terms, the next sections describe the main agreed definitions and the conceptual frameworks upon which they are based.

Improving our understanding of wellness, well-being and quality of life is a crucial question for several reasons: first, because a well-defined formulation of such terms contributes to the improvement of their theoretical ground; second, increases the conceptual clarity of these concepts may enhance their correct application in several fields (e.g., clinical and counseling in the case of wellness, or sociology in the case of well-being). Finally, implications and insights for counseling, experts and practitioners are discussed.

2.2 Concepts and Theories of Wellness in the Scientific Literature

In the aftermath of the Second World War, the health conditions in general populations experienced important progress. The medical advances introduced after the years of conflict were available to a larger number of peoples, with the consequent reduction of mortality rates through the massive uses of vaccines and antibiotics (Seaward, 2002). During those years, infectious diseases declined, but new and mysterious disorders, so-called "diseases of civilization" began to emerge (Susser, 1985, p. 2). Many severe chronic-health problems, such as heart disease, diabetes, and obesity affect large population samples. Epidemiological studies establish associations between poor health conditions and many different, interacting factors, including environmental causes (e.g., living and working conditions) and lifestyle factors (e.g., sedentary, smoking and alcohol abuse) (Millar & Hull, 1997).

The prevalence of lifestyle-related diseases has imposed a critical reflection on what makes peoples well. Hence, governments start to introduce public policies and specific evidence-based interventions aimed at reducing unhealthy behaviors and promoting more adequate lifestyles (Miller, 2005).

In this context, the World Health Organization (WHO, 1967) provides a new definition of "health" as: *a state of complete physical, mental and social well-being and not merely the absence of disease or infirmity*. Previous conceptualizations of health were limited to the diagnosis and treatment of physical illness (Larson, 1999; Lerner, 1973). The patient was considered exclusively in relation to its body, according to a narrow physiological paradigm (McSherry & Draper, 1998). In the early 1970s, the "wellness movement" (Miller, 2005) completely transformed the notion of health and it introduced a more comprehensive and holistic perspective of human functioning (Larson, 1999).

Namely, wellness includes all the positive attributes of health, and, more important it exalts the harmony of the mind, body and spirit. Scholars often attribute to Dunn (1961, p. 4) the first modern conceptualization of wellness, defined as the maximization of health through an integrated method of functioning oriented towards one's potentials. According to Neilson (1988), wellness consists of the strength and the ability to overcome illness. High levels of wellness include a complete integration of both mental, psychical and emotional individuals' components. Egbert (1980) founds in the sense of identity and the integrated personality the basis of wellness.

Other authors have described wellness in terms of optimal physical functioning (Ardell, 1977; Greenberg, 1985; Hettler, 1980) self-responsibility (Dunn, 1961; Leafgren, 1990) and one's motivation (Clark, 1996). However, such definitions generally emphasize one or more aspects of wellness, but they fail in the aim to provide an integrated and accepted definition at once (Miller, 2005; Roscoe, 2009).

The Holistic Wellness Model (HWM) introduced by Witmer and Sweeney (1992) and later by Myers et al. (2000) is one of the most popular model of wellness and prevention in the existing literature. It proposes a multidisciplinary approach to the treatment of mental and physical disorders over the life course. Five tasks depicted in a wheel[1] (see Adams et al., 1997), are interrelated and connected and they include spirituality, self-regulation, work, friendship, and love. The subsequent revision of this model (Myers et al., 2000), provides a set of 12 tasks to achieve wellness, based on clinical research findings. Those tasks comprise: (1) sense of control, (2) sense of worth, (3) emotional awareness and coping, (4) realistic beliefs, (5) problem-solving and creativity, (6) sense of humor, (7) self-care, (8) stress management, (9) nutrition, (10) exercise, (11) gender identity, and (12) cultural identity. The evolution of the WoW model into the 5F-Wel (Myers et al., 2004), involves five factors (creative, coping, social, essential, and physical); whereas in its latest released version the 5F-Wel has been integrated by the physical, cognitive-emotional, relational, and spiritual areas of wellness. The seminal paper of Lafferty (1979), provides a reliable conceptual framework for wellness. By applying an holistic perspective of individuals, wellness is viewed as a dynamic process through which peoples be aware and assume positive health attitudes in the physical, social, intellectual, and spiritual dimensions of their life. Similarly, Greenberg (1985), Depken (1994) and Adams et al. (1997) conceptualize high-levels of wellness as the balanced integration of those areas. Over the past two decades, the concept of wellness has developed towards a more comprehensive interpretation, that acknowledges the inclusion of several life domains. For example, Hettler (1980), Leafgren (1990) and Crose et al. (1992) introduced the occupational dimension of wellness, in which the fulfillment gained by which one's work allows the expression of personal values. Anspaugh et al. (2004) and Renger et al. (2000) added the environmental dimensions of

[1] The Wheel of Wellness (WoW).

wellness. Instead, they emphasize the impact that the external context has on one's life and the existence of an important inter-correlation between individuals, others (e.g., social interaction/relationships) and nature. In recent years, Ryff and Singer (2006) have refined the role of some key aspects of psychological wellness and they have provided empirical findings of the factorial structure of well-being (see Ryff's six-factor model of well-being).

Scholars have described wellness in several ways that interact with each other in a complex manner. Despite the number of dimensions mentioned above and summarized in Table 2.1, an integrated and commonly accepted definition has not been reached yet. This in part due to the subjective nature of the construct (Kelly, 2000). General agreements about wellness include that it is a multidimensional concept (Adams et al., 1997; Dunn, 1961), that those dimensions are interconnected (Hettler, 1980), and that wellness is more similar to a dynamic continuum, rather than a state (Clark, 1996; Lafferty, 1979; Lorion, 2000; Sarason, 2000). However, scholars have outlined that, in some cases, the sum of wellness' dimensions are more complex than the concept actually is (Adams et al., 1997; Clark, 1996; Crose et al., 1992) and, for this reason, investigations should be focused to its *rationale*. In the next sections, dimensions of wellness mentioned so far are explored separately.

2.2.1 Physical Wellness

Cooper (1970, 1977) is generally considered the pioneer of physical wellness, since his studies on the relationship between physical exercises, health and longevity, in particular in heart disease patients, have inspired the creation of the modern fitness industry. Improving cardiovascular fitness, and ensuring the flexibility and strength of own' body, are essential components of physical wellness (Hettler, 1980). However, conceptualizations of physical wellness are not limited to maintaining good body indices (e.g., muscle tone, cholesterol level) and following healthy behaviors (e.g., physical exercises, diet regime).

Adams et al. (1997) have focused their definition of wellness on the perception people have about their body and health status. This perspective emphasizes the internal (and subjective) signs of the body in response to daily events. Thus, accepted conceptualizations of physical wellness also include the evaluations of personal health status and the acceptance of one's body image. The physical wellness emphasizes primarily the adoption of healthy lifestyles, even if scholars have also included in such dimension the competence of keeping under control owns' physical limits (Durlak, 2000) and the appropriate use of medicine and medical services (Hettler, 1980).

Table 2.1 Dimensions of Wellness in literature (from 1979 to 2006)

	Physical	Psychological emotional	Social	Intellectual	Spiritual	Occupational	Environmental
1. Lafferty (1979)	X	X	X	X	X		
2. Hettler (1980)	X	X	X	X	X	X	
3. Greenberg (1985)	X	X	X	X	X		
4. Travis and Ryan (1988)	X	X	X	X	X	X	X
5. Leafgren (1990)	X	X	X	X	X	X	
6. Crose et al. (1992)	X	X	X	X	X	X	
7. Depken (1994)	X	X	X	X	X		
8. Adams et al. (1997)	X	X	X	X	X		
9. Renger et al. (2000)	X	X	X	X	X		X
10. Durlak (2000)	X		X	X			
11. Anspaugh et al. (2004)	X	X	X	X	X	X	X
12. Myers et al. (2004)	X	X	X	X	X	X	X
13. Ryff and Singer (2006)	X	X	X		X		X

2.2.2 Psychological and Emotional Wellness

Psychological and emotional wellness are conceptually similar (Roscoe, 2009). Indeed, some conceptualizations of psychological wellness often include emotions and *vice versa*. This is because emotions and human feelings have been traditionally object of study of the psychologists. Over the years, psychological wellness has become central in positive psychology (see Ryan & Deci, 2001; Seligman & Csikszentmihalyi, 2000; Travis & Ryan, 1988), and it has found reliable applications in the counseling assessments. A notable example is given by the Ryff's Psychological Well-Being Scale (see Ryff, 1989), a valid instrument uses for human functioning' assessment. Psychological wellness is a broader and complex concept, that implies both the fulfillment of basic psychological needs, such as self-actualization and self-competence (Ryan & Deci, 2001), and the management of a wide range of feelings (e.g., happiness or life satisfaction) (Diener et al., 1985; Diener & Seligman, 2002).

The emotional wellness defined by Adams et al. (1997) is the control of ones' emotions, the adoption of a positive worldview, and the individuals' ability to use coping strategies to facing life circumstances. Hettler's (1980) definition of psychological wellness also includes many aspects mentioned by Adams et al. (1997). Given these similarities, several authors often considered psychological and emotional wellness closely related (Adams et al., 1997; Crose et al., 1992; Leafgren, 1990).

2.2.3 Social Wellness

The notion of social wellness is usually referred to the quality (and frequency) of interactions whit the others and the nature. It comprises the active support of one's community, such as the volunteer work (Leafgren, 1990), but also the extent and the quality of social relationships (Crose et al., 1992). Hettler (1980) defines social wellness in terms of accountability towards the external environment. Its definition includes mutual respect for others and the assumption of cooperative behaviors. According to Renger et al. (2000) social wellness focuses on the respect of the nature and the contribution that each individual may offer their community. Research findings confirm the importance of social networks and social relations for peoples' wellness. For example, Helliwell (2006) has found that social capital, whose social relations are an essential component, determines higher levels of subjective well-being both in national and international samples. Other studies have demonstrated the importance of social support in reducing psychological disorders, anxiety symptoms, and suicide rates (Andrews & Withey, 1976; Leavy, 1983).

2.2.4 Intellectual Wellness

Intellectual wellness reflects some aspects of the psychological ones, since it involves the cognitive functioning by which people may change their behaviors. An optimal level of intellectual wellness includes the commitment to long-life learning and the constant acquisition of knowledge. According to Renger et al. (2000), intellectual wellness is a combination of personal growth, education achievements, and one's sense of creativity. Hatfield and Hatfield (1992) have stressed the notion of creativity, considered by the authors the ability to acquire critical thinking. Other conceptualizations of intellectual wellness are presents in Hettler (1980), Anspaugh et al. (2004), and Durlak (2000) and they include the improvement of personal skills and knowledge and the abilities to achieve a more satisfying life.

2.2.5 Spiritual Wellness

Spiritual wellness is maybe one of the most debated and controversial components of wellness (Roscoe, 2009). This is because it has been often associated with the definitions of spiritual well-being (Ellison, 1983) and spiritual health (Banks, 1980; Bensley, 1991). Several conceptualizations of spiritual wellness suggested that it primarily consists in the sense of meaning and purpose in life (Adams et al., 1997; Leafgren, 1990). Spiritual wellness has been viewed as a dynamic process that includes a clear sense of identity and coherence, and the full connectedness to one's self. Further conceptualizations of spiritual wellness defined it as the inner harmony with others and the universe, as well as the research of a positive balance between mind, spirit, and body (Hettler, 1980). According to Renger et al. (2000), the achievement of wellness implies the positive use of one's mind and awareness of spiritual needs. However, other theories indicate religion as the favorite channel by which individuals implement their spirituality. According to Ellison (1983), spiritual wellbeing is a two-faceted concept, with a horizontal component specifically referred to peoples' relation with religion and God, and a horizontal dimension that is represented by the sense of meaning in life. Results from Ellison's researches have led to the implementation of the Spiritual Well-Being Scale, a measure of both religious and existential dimensions of well-being.

2.2.6 Occupational Wellness

Occupational wellness taps several aspects of the relation between individuals and their work (paid and unpaid). These include, for example, motivational elements, such as the organizational commitment or the employee identification with their job, and professional elements (e.g., autonomy, professional competence) (Van Horn et al., 2004). However, many authors have defined occupational wellness in relation to satisfaction with one's work (i.e., job satisfaction) and the extent to which individuals can express their potential by the means of their occupation. Another important aspect of occupational wellness is given by the work-life balance (Leafgren, 1990). Other conceptualizations also include the use of personal skills and talents in support of one's community (Crose et al., 1992).

2.2.7 Environmental Wellness

Environmental wellness has been conceptualized as a broad dimension that looked at the individuals' relationship with the environment (e.g., the local community and the nature) (Anspaugh et al., 2004). According to Renger et al. (2000), environmental wellness is based on reciprocal interaction between the individual and their external environment. This interaction reflects the influence of the ecological theories of well-being (see Dolan et al., 2008) and includes the need to respect nature with concrete actions, such as the involvement in recycling, the community clean-up effort, the protection of natural resources, and the awareness of the individual's impact on the environment.

2.3 Subjective Well-Being, Life Satisfaction and Quality of Life

The origin of the term well-being can be traced back to ancient Greek philosophy (Clark, 2014; Gillett-Swan & Sargeant, 2015; McMahan & Estes, 2011). According to Aristotle, Epicurus, and Plato's theoretical assumptions, a life well-lived and the achievement of happiness were the ultimate goals in life. However, what exactly it means to experience life positively is a disputed question among scholars (Gillett-Swan & Sargeant, 2015; La Placa et al., 2013). Indeed, over time, well-being has been conceptualized in a variety of manners (MacLeod, 2015). Some of these include feelings of happiness or a protracted state of contentment, whereas other meanings compared it with wellness and having good physical and mental health. However, none of these definitions are incorrect *per se*, but they describe part of it and are far from the whole (Tov, 2018). So far, the main development in this field has been the acceptance that well-being is a multifaceted construct (King et al., 2014). Considering that a complete conceptualization of the term has not been established yet (Dodge et al., 2012), numerous definitions of well-being are available in the current literature.

McLeod (MacLeod, 2015, p. 1076) asserts that "well-being refers to the aspect of a life that defines it as good for the person who is living it". According to Gillett-Swan & Sargeant (2015, p. 13), it is "an individual's capacity to manage overtime, the range of inputs that can, in isolation, affect a person's emotional, physical and cognitive state in response to given context". Clark (2014, p. 834) claims that "well-being is a state which covers happy, healthy, o prosperous condition of a person or group".

However, in the absence of a complete recognition about well-being, it continues to be associated with correlated expressions or synonyms, such as health, wellness, quality of life, life satisfaction, or happiness (Eger & Maridal, 2015). These terminological misuses have been reported in Maffioletti et al. (2014), whom alert about the reliability of measurements that came from terminological concerns. According to Forgeard et al. (2011, p. 81), "some researchers have preferred to ignore the multifaceted nature of well-being and equate it with one construct (often life satisfaction), leading to the unfortunate omission of their important aspects of well-being".

In the last few years, interest in well-being has grown dramatically in social sciences, especially in positive psychology (McMahan & Estes, 2011). Current research in this field draws from two standing approaches on well-being: hedonic and eudemonic. These two views originate from Aristotle and Epicurus's categories of hedonia and eudemonia (see Ryan & Deci, 2001).

The first approach of well-being (hedonic) exalts the seeking of pleasure attainment and minimizes the pain. It is based on the personal satisfaction of own life as a whole, or whit specific life domains (e.g., work, relations, family). Such judgment generally includes both cognitive and emotional experiences and is named subjective well-being (SWB) (Lindert et al., 2015; Kapteyn et al., 2015; McMahan & Estes, 2011). The introduction of this term in the scientific debate has been first provided by E. Diener (see Diener et al., 1985, 1999). Empirical research describes subjective well-being as the combination of three essential elements: life satisfaction (LS), positive affect (PA) and negative affect (NA) (Andrews & Withey, 1976; Diener et al., 1999). According to the *Encyclopedia of quality of life and well-being research* (Michalos, 2014, p. 6437), SWB "is the personal perception and experience of positive and negative emotional responses and the specific cognitive evaluations of satisfaction with life". Lucas et al. (1996) have explored the internal structure of SWB and they have found that life satisfaction (i.e., a component of SWB) was a separable construct that could be analyzed independently. This is because, according to them, life satisfaction expresses the cognitive trait of SWB and for this reason, it is less sensitive to cultural differences (see for example Ciziceno & Travaglino, 2019) and it tends to remain more stable over time than emotions (Fujita & Diener, 2005). As a result, empirical research often uses life satisfaction as a brief measure of SWB.

According to the eudaimonic approach, the satisfaction of certain needs is fundamental to one's psychological growth. In this perspective well-being is essentially a psychological state that comes not only from pleasant feelings (Ryan & Deci, 2001), but it consists of the complete fulfillment of one's potential. Huta and Waterman (2014) have compared eudemonia to an ethical theory that roots around the notions of personal growth, meaning, authenticity, and excellence. Ryff (1989), starting from Erikson, Jung, and Maslow's theories, has developed a theoretical model of Psychological Well-Being (PWB). The Ryff's six-factor model is based on

Table 2.2 Components of Subjective Well-Being, Life Satisfaction and Psychological Well-Being

Approach	Concept	Author(s)	Main component(s)
Hedonic	Subjective well-being/ SWB	Diener et al. (1985, 1999) Andrews and Withey (1976)	1. Life satisfaction (LS) 2. Positive affect (PA) 3. Negative affect (NA)
	Life satisfaction/LS	Diener et al. (1985) Lucas et al. (1996)	1. Life satisfaction
Eudaimonic	Psychological well-being/ PWB	Ryff (1989) Ryan & Deci (2001)	1. Autonomy 2. Positive relations with others 3. Environmental mastery 4. Self-acceptance 5. Purpose in life 6. Personal growth

some key features that operate as drivers for well-being achievement. Such features include individuals' autonomy (1), the ability to be trusting with others (positive relations) (2), the constructive management of external stressors (environmental mastery) (3), having a positive attitude towards themselves (self-acceptance) (4), having purposes and goals in life (5), and facing positively the everyday circumstances (personal growth) (6).

There are no doubts that both hedonic and eudaimonic approaches are very similar in some of their aspects, however, scholars have noted that none of them supports a holistic perspective of well-being (Gillett-Swan & Sargeant, 2015). Moreover, because of the existence of numerous different conceptualizations, a variety of proxies attempt to measure well-being in national and international surveys (Lindert et al., 2015). For this reason, scholars often suggest mixed-model approaches as an advisable method for empirical well-being research (Ryan & Deci, 2001; Maggino, 2015). In Table 2.2, the essential components of subjective well-being, life satisfaction, and psychological well-being, mentioned above, are summarized.

The concept of quality of life (QOL) is generally used to measure, and sometimes describes, the structures and the evolution patterns of world societies (Costanza et al., 2007). Social policies aimed at increasing people's living standards need to be constantly evaluated and, eventually, improved. Moreover, it is not rare that the impacts of these policies on people's lives are also evaluated directly by them. This situation implies the use of specific indicators for policy goals, generally called quality of life indicators (Cummins, et al., 2003; Land & Michalos, 2018). The QOL (Quality of Life) concept is based on the seminal works of Bauer (1966), Campbell (1976), and Land (1983), considered the pioneers of quality of life indicators and founders of social indicators movement (for a review see Land & Michalos, 2018). Furthermore, there has been notably the contribution of Allardt (1976) in the exploration of welfare dimensions in Scandinavian societies and the studies of OECD on "social well-being" (see Christian, 1974). However, the origin of the term is probably attributable to the economist Pigou (1920), who first used the expression "qualité de vie".

Quality of Life includes subjective/objective indicators to assess peoples' perceptions about the effectiveness of social policies or to measure certain standards of living (Costanza et al., 2007; Haas, 1999). Objective indicators, for example, including measures of economic production (i.e., GDP), literacy rates and life expectancy and are often combined in indices as the Human Development Index (UNPD 1998), whereas subjective indicators of QOL generally encompass subjective evaluations about one's life and circumstances (e.g., subjective well-being (SWB) or life satisfaction), but also they measure immaterial conditions as the sense of freedom, justice or confidence in public institutions (see Helliwell, 2006). In a seminal paper, Hagerty et al. (2001) have reviewed 22 of the main famous QOL indexes around the world, in order to improve their usefulness. The authors have drawn to the conclusion that most of the indexes they analyzed fit with their policy purposes, however, they addressed some recommendations to researchers. These include a clear distinction of the concepts of input, throughput, and output to improve their application and the creation of domain structures for the validation of the results.

Because of its political significance, the concept of QOL has raised the attention of public opinion, and especially it has reached the interest of policymakers. The theoretical appeal of the QOL concept is in part due to its importance in inform politicians about the needs of their citizens and support them in tracing new directions for long-term prosperity. Nevertheless, scholars have outlined that Quality Of Life, as a multidimensional concept, is not universal and it largely depends on the socio-economic contexts and the cultural characteristics of individuals (Schwarz & Strack, 1999).

Hence, QOL can be defined as a broad concept involving different components and those components vary in importance according to specific demographic characteristics (e.g., age, gender, or ethnic group), population parameters, or social-economic ones (Costanza et al., 2007; Fernández-Ballesteros, 1998). As a result, main QOL assessments are limited to specific life situations, or population samples (e.g., patients with chronic diseases).

However, despite the growing importance of the QOL concept in social and medical sciences, scholars have paid little attention to provide a clear and explicit definition (Michalos, 2004) and investigations on this direction are limited. One few exception is given by Fernández-Ballesteros (2002) who has investigated the ingredients of QOL in elderly people by asking to Spanish sample what was essential for their quality of life. Results from this study have led to the isolation of nine components of QOL: health (1), functional abilities (2), economic conditions (3), social relationships (4), activity (5), to have good social and health services (6), quality in the home and the environment (7), life satisfaction (8), cultural and educational opportunities (9).

With the accumulated body of research on QOL measures around the world, several important themes emerge to the forefront. Foremost, a central part of QOL's future development, it may be constituted by the combination of existing social, economic, and environmental indicators to monitoring and implementing social changes (Michalos, 1997). A coherent theoretical platform upon which defining Quality Of Life as a concept, is also required, to encompass existing theories and models to a unique spectrum of research.

2.4 Conclusions and Directions for Research

So far, concepts of wellness, subjective well-being, and quality of life have been conceptualized ambiguously in social sciences, and scholars have often reduced to a single term-umbrella (i.e., well-being) their complexity. Nevertheless, questions concerning what they mean, what measures are advisable for them and which dimensions are important for people it remains, apart from few exceptions, quite clear. This review has highlighted how those terms, although seem very similar, differ in their essence. The term wellness includes all the positive attributes of health and, over time, it has been expanded by other dimensions (e.g., mental health, social relations). Despite the concept of wellness shared most of its attributes whit subjective well-being (SWB) and quality of life (QOL), all these terms refer to different mental categories, are measured with different methods, and are employed in different fields of research.

The first conclusion that can be drawn from this review is that, over the last years, promising advances have been realized in well-being research. Institutions, governments, and scholars aware of the importance to include subjective well-being and quality of life measures in the evaluations of their public policies. Experts and counselors often rely on wellness assessments to support their psychological treatments or improve clinical trials. However, these terms continue to be abstract and the achievement of a clear definition across disciplines represents the main challenge for researchers. Nevertheless, scholars have paid more attention to improve new measurement techniques, rather than provide a solidly grounded theory of well-being. Further theoretical investigations are strongly recommended to consolidate the conceptual frameworks upon which wellness, subjective well-being, and quality of life are based. Moreover, a better conceptualization of those terms may enhance their reliability tools.

The second implication of this review regards the use of a cross-disciplinary approach to the study of such concepts (and their facets). Hitherto, research has been characterized by opposite perspectives among social sciences and low collaboration across disciplines. These oppositions often have revolved around the dichotomy between qualitative and quantitative methods to their measurement. Both approaches (i.e., qualitative and quantitative) present attractive features, but taken alone they do not explain the complexity of wellness, well-being, and quality of life.

Although several conceptual questions remain unanswered yet, the growing body of literature on well-being research (in a broader sense) suggests a promising future for its development in social sciences. A priority for policymakers should be ensuring the long-term well-being of their citizen. Findings came from QOL and

SWB research may be used by them as drivers to address or evaluate their public choices and implement evidence-based interventions. Counselors and experts may adopt wellness models as a means of structuring their therapy or guide counselor's work with clients. Furthermore, experts need to stress the idea that wellness is not just the absence of illness and it includes a multitude of aspects (Roscoe, 2009). Finally, further advances in those areas may be realized when a solid and coherent theoretical framework will be defined.

References

Adams, T., Bezner, J., & Steinhardt, M. (1997). The conceptualization and measurement of perceived wellness: Integrating balance across and within dimensions. *American Journal of Health Promotion, 11*, 208–218.

Allardt, E. (1976). Dimensions of welfare in a comparative Scandinavian study. *Acta Sociologica, 19*(3), 227–239.

Andrews, F. M., & Withey, S. B. (1976). *Social indicators of well-being: Americans' perceptions of life quality*. Plenum.

Anspaugh, D., Hamrick, M., & Rosato, F. (2004). *Wellness: Concepts and applications* (6th ed). McGraw Hill.

Ardell, D. B. (1977). *High level wellness: An alternative to doctors, drugs, and disease*. Rodale Press.

Austin, A. (2016). On well-being and public policy: Are we capable of questioning the hegemony of happiness? *Social Indicators Research, 127*(1), 123–138.

Banks, R. (1980). Health and the spiritual dimension: Relationships and implications for professional preparation programs. *The Journal of School Health, 50*(1), 195–202.

Bauer, R. A. (1966). Social indicators and sample surveys. *Public Opinion Quarterly, 30*(3), 339–352.

Bensley, R. J. (1991). Defining spiritual health: A review of the literature. *Journal of Health Education, 22*, 287–290.

Brady, K. J., Trockel, M. T., Khan, C. T., Raj, K. S., Murphy, M. L., Bohman, B., et al. (2018). What do we mean by physician wellness? A systematic review of its definition and measurement. *Academic Psychiatry, 42*(1), 94–108.

Campbell, D. T. (1976). Focal local indicators for social program evaluation. *Social Indicators Research, 3*(2), 237–256.

Christian, D. E. (1974). International social indicators: The OECD experience. *Social Indicators Research, 1*(2), 169–186.

Christiansen, C. H., & Matuska, K. M. (2006). Lifestyle balance: A review of concepts and research. *Journal of Occupational Science, 13*(1), 49–61.

Ciziceno, M., & Travaglino, G. A. (2019). Perceived corruption and individuals' life satisfaction: The mediating role of institutional trust. *Social Indicators Research, 141*(2), 685–701.

Clark, C. C. (1996). *Wellness practitioner: Concepts, research, and strategies*. Springer.

Clark, D. A. (2014). Defining and measuring human well-being. *Global Environmental Change, 1*, 833–855.

Cooper, K. H. (1970). Guidelines in the management of the exercising patient. *Journal of the American Medical Association, 211*(10), 1663–1667.

Cooper, K. H. (1977). *The aerobics way*. Evans.

Costanza, R., Fisher, B., Ali, S., Beer, C., Bond, L., Boumans, R., et al. (2007). Quality of life: An approach integrating opportunities, human needs, and subjective well-being. *Ecological Economics, 61*(2–3), 267–276.

Crose, R., Nicholas, D. R., Gobble, D. C., & Frank, B. (1992). Gender and wellness: A multidimensional systems model for counseling. *Journal of Counseling & Development, 71*, 149–156.
Cummins, R. A., Eckersley, R., et al. (2003). Developing a national index of subjective wellbeing: The Australian Unity wellbeing index. *Social Indicators Research, 64*, 159–190.
Depken, D. (1994). Wellness through the lens of gender: A paradigm shift. *Wellness Perspectives: Research, Theory, and Practice, 10*, 54–69.
Diener, E., Emmons, R. A., Larsen, R. J., & Griffin, S. (1985). The satisfaction with life scale. *Journal of Personality Assessment, 49*(1), 71–75.
Diener, E., & Seligman, M. E. P. (2002). Very happy people. *Psychological Science, 13*, 81–84.
Diener, E., Suh, E. M., Lucas, R. E., & Smith, H. L. (1999). Subjective well-being three decades of progress. *Psychological Bulletin, 125*(2), 276–302.
Dodge, R., Daly, A., Huyton, J., & Sanders, L. (2012). The challenge of defining wellbeing. *International Journal of Wellbeing, 2*(3), 222–235.
Dolan, P., Peasgood, T., & White, M. (2008). Do we really know what makes us happy? A review of the economic literature on the factors associated with subjective wellbeing. *Journal of Economic Psychology, 29*, 94–122.
Dunn, H. L. (1961). *High level wellness*. R. W. Beatty.
Durlak, J. (2000). Health promotion as a strategy in primary prevention. In D. Cicchetti, J. Rappaport, I. Sandler, & R. Weissberg (Eds.), *The promotion of wellness in children and adolescents* (pp. 221–241). Child Welfare League Association Press.
Egbert, E. (1980). Concept of wellness. *Journal of Psychiatric Nursing and Mental Health Services, 18*(1), 9–12.
Eger, R. J., & Maridal, J. H. (2015). A statistical meta-analysis of the well-being literature. *International Journal of Wellbeing, 5*(2), 45–74.
Ellison, C. W. (1983). Spiritual well-being: Conceptualization and measurement. *Journal of Psychology and Theology, 11*(4), 330–338.
Fernández-Ballesteros, R. (1998). Quality of life: Concept and assessment. In J. G. Adair, D. Bélanger, & K. L. Dion (Eds.), *Advances in psychological science (Vol. 1. Social, personal, and cultural aspects*, pp. 387–406). Psychology Press/Erlbaum (UK) Taylor & Francis.
Fernández-Ballesteros, R. (2002). Social support and quality of life among older people in Spain. *Journal of Social Issues, 58*(4), 645–659.
Fernández-Ballesteros, R. (2011). Quality of life in old age: Problematic issues. *Applied Research in Quality of Life, 6*(1), 21–40.
Forgeard, M. J. C., Jayawickreme, E., Kern, M., & Seligman, M. E. P. (2011). Doing the right thing: Measuring wellbeing for public policy. *International Journal of Wellbeing, 1*(1), 79–106.
Fujita, F., & Diener, E. (2005). Life satisfaction set point: Stability and change. *Journal of Personality and Social Psychology, 88*(1), 158.
Gillett-Swan, J. K., & Sargeant, J. (2015). Wellbeing as a process of accrual: Beyond subjectivity and beyond the moment. *Social Indicators Research, 121*(1), 135–148.
Greenberg, J. S. (1985). Health and wellness: A conceptual differentiation. *Journal of School Health, 55*, 403–406.
Haas, B. K. (1999). A multidisciplinary concept analysis of quality of life. *Western Journal of Nursing Research, 21*, 728–742.
Hagerty, M. R., Cummins, R., Ferriss, A. L., Land, K., Michalos, A. C., Peterson, M., Sharpe, A., Sirgy, J., & Vogel, J. (2001). Quality of life indexes for national policy: Review and agenda for research. *Bulletin of Sociological Methodology/Bulletin de Méthodologie Sociologique, 71*(1), 58–78. https://doi.org/10.1177/075910630107100104
Hatfield, T., & Hatfield, S. R. (1992). As if your life depended on it: Promoting cognitive development to promote wellness. *Journal of Counseling and Development, 71*, 164–167.
Helliwell, J. F. (2006). Wellbeing, social capital and public policy: What's new? *The Economic Journal, 116*(510), C34–C45.

Hettler, B. (1980). Wellness promotion on a university campus: Family and community health. *Journal of Health Promotion and Maintenance, 3*, 77–95.

Huta, V., & Waterman, A. S. (2014). Eudaimonia and its distinction from Hedonia: Developing a classification and terminology for understanding conceptual and operational definitions. *Journal of Happiness Studies, 15*(6), 1425–1456.

Kapteyn, A., Lee, J., Tassot, C., Vonkova, H., & Zamarro, G. (2015). Dimensions of subjective well-being. *Social Indicators Research, 123*(3), 625–660.

Kelly, J. G. (2000). Wellness as an ecological enterprise. In D. Cicchetti, J. Rappaport, I. Sandler, & R. P. Weissberg (Eds.), *Promotion of wellness in children and adolescents* (pp. 101–131). CWLA Press.

King, M. F., Renó, V. F., & Novo, E. M. L. (2014). The concept, dimensions and methods of assessment of human well-being within a socioecological context: A literature review. *Social Indicators Research, 116*(3), 681–698.

La Placa, V., McNaught, A., & Knight, A. (2013). Discourse on wellbeing in research and practice. *International Journal of Wellbeing, 3*(1), 116–125.

Lafferty, J. (1979). A credo for wellness. *Health Education, 10*, 10–11.

Land, K. C. (1983). Social indicators. *Annual Review of Sociology, 9*(1), 1–26.

Land, K. C., & Michalos, A. C. (2018). Fifty years after the social indicators movement: Has the promise been fulfilled? *Social Indicators Research, 135*(3), 835–868.

Larson, J. S. (1999). The conceptualization of health. *Medical Care Research and Review, 56*(2), 123–136.

Leafgren, F. (1990). Being a man can be hazardous to your health: Life-styles issues. In D. Moore & F. Leafgren (Eds.), *Problem solving strategies and interventions for men in conflict* (pp. 265–311). American Association for Counseling and Development.

Leavy, R. L. (1983). Social support and psychological disorder: A review. *Journal of Community Psychology, 11*(1), 3–21.

Lent, R. W. (2004). Toward a unifying theoretical and practical perspective on wellbeing and psychosocial adjustment. *Journal of Counseling Psychology, 51*(4), 482–509. https://doi.org/10.1037/0022-0167.51.4.482

Lerner, M. (1973). Conceptualization of health and social well-being. *Health Services Research, 8*(1), 6.

Lindert, J., Bain, P. A., Kubzansky, L. D., & Stein, C. (2015). Well-being measurement and the WHO health policy health 2010: Systematic review of measurement scales. *The European Journal of Public Health, 25*(4), 731–740.

Lorion, R. P. (2000). Theoretical and evaluation issues in the promotion of wellness and the protection of "well enough." In D. Cicchetti, J. Rappaport, I. Sandler, & R. P. Weissberg (Eds.), *Promotion of wellness in children and adolescents* (pp. 1–27). CWLA Press.

Lucas, R. E., Diener, E., & Suh, E. (1996). Discriminant validity of well-being measures. *Journal of Personality and Social Psychology, 71*(3), 616.

MacLeod, A. K. (2015). Well-being: Objectivism, subjectivism or sobjectivism? *Journal of Happiness Studies, 16*(4), 1073–1089.

Maffioletti, A., Maida, A., & Scacciati, F. (2014). More terminological and methodological problems in measuring happiness, life satisfaction and well-being: some first empirical results. In V. Giorgino (Ed.), *The pursuit of happiness and the traditions of wisdom* (pp. 13–21). Springer International Publishing.

Maggino, F. (2015). Subjective wellbeing and subjective aspects of wellbeing: Methodology and theory. *Rivista Internazionale di Scienze Sociali, 1*, 89–121.

Mayer, C.-H. (2011). *The meaning of sense of coherence in trans-cultural management*. Waxmann.

McMahan, E. A., & Estes, D. (2011). Measuring lay conceptions of well-being: The beliefs about well-being scale. *Journal of Happiness Studies, 12*(2), 267–287.

McSherry, W., & Draper, P. (1998). The debates emerging in the literature surrounding the concept of spirituality as applied to nursing. *Journal of Advanced Nursing, 27*(4), 683–691.
Michalos, A. C. (1997). Combining social, economic and environmental indicators to measure sustainable human well-being. *Social Indicators Research, 40*(1–2), 221–258.
Michalos, A. C. (2004). Social indicators research and health-related quality of life research. *Social Indicators Research, 65*(1), 27–72.
Michalos, A. C. (Ed.) (2014). *Encyclopedia of quality of life and well-being research.* Springer Netherlands.
Michalos, A. C., Zumbo, B. D., & Hubley, A. (2000). Health and the quality of life. *Social Indicators Research, 51*(3), 245–286.
Millar, J. S., & Hull, C. (1997). Measuring human wellness. *Social Indicators Research, 40*(1–2), 147–158.
Miller, J. W. (2005). Wellness: The history and development of a concept. *Spektrum Freizeit, 1*, 84–102.
Myers, J. E., Luecht, R. M., & Sweeney, T. J. (2004). The factor structure of wellness: Reexamining theoretical and empirical models underlying the wellness evaluation of lifestyle (WEL) and the five-factor Wei. *Measurement and Evaluation in Counseling and Development, 36*(4), 194–208.
Myers, J. E., Sweeney, T. J., & Witmer, J. M. (2000). The wheel of wellness: A holistic model for treatment planning. *Journal of Counseling & Development, 78*, 251–266.
Neilson, E. (1988). Health values: Achieving high level wellness-origins, philosophy, purpose. *Health Values, 12*, 3–5.
Pigou, A. C. (1920). *The economics of welfare*. Macmillan and Co.
Renger, R. F., Midyett, S. J., Mas, F. G., Erin, T. E., McDermott, H. M., Papenfuss, R. L., Eichling, et al. (2000). Optimal living profile: An inventory to assess health and wellness. *American Journal of Health Promotion, 24*, 403–412.
Roscoe, L. J. (2009). Wellness: A review of theory and measurement for counselors. *Journal of Counseling & Development, 87*(2), 216–226.
Ryan, R. M., & Deci, E. L. (2001). On happiness and human potentials: A review of research on hedonic and eudaimonic well-being. *Annual Review of Psychology, 52*(1), 141–166.
Ryff, C. D. (1989). Happiness is everything, or is it? Explorations on the meaning of psychological well-being. *Journal of Personality and Social Psychology, 57*, 1069–1081. https://doi.org/10.1037/0022-3514.57.6.1069
Ryff, C. D., & Singer, B. H. (2006). Best news yet on the six-factor model of well-being. *Social Science Research, 35*, 1103–1119.
Sarason, S. B. (2000). Porgy and Bess and the concept of wellness. In D. Cicchetti, J. Rappaport, I. Sandler, & R. P. Weissberg (Eds.), *Promotion of wellness in children and adolescents* (pp. 427–437). CWLA Press.
Schwarz, N., Strack, F., (1999). Reports of subjective well-being: Judgmental processes and their methodological implications. In: Kahneman, D., Diener, E., Schwarz, N. (Eds.), *Well-being: The foundations of hedonic psychology* (pp. 61–84). Russell Sage Foundation,
Seaward, B. L. (2002). *Managing stress: Principles and strategies for health and wellbeing*. Jones and Bartlett.
Seligman, M. E. P., & Csikszentmihalyi, M. (2000). Positive psychology: An introduction. *American Psychologist, 55*(1), 5–14.
Susser, M. (1985). Epidemiology in the United States after world war II: The evolution of technique. *Epidemiologic Reviews, 7*(1), 147–177.
Tov, W. (2018). Well-being concepts and components. In E. Diener, S. Oishi, & L. Tay (Eds.), *Handbook of well-being*. DEF Publishers. nobascholar.com
Travis, J. W., & Ryan, R. S. (1988). *Wellness workbook.* Ten Speed Press.
UNDP. (1998). Human development report 1998: Consumption for human development. http://www.hdr.undp.org/en/content/human-development-report-1998

Van Horn, J. E., Taris, T. W., Schaufeli, W. B., & Schreurs, P. J. (2004). The structure of occupational well-being: A study among Dutch teachers. *Journal of Occupational and Organizational Psychology, 77*(3), 365–375.
Witmer, J. M., & Sweeney, T. J. (1992). A holistic model for wellness and prevention over the life span. *Journal of Counseling & Development, 71*, 140–148.
World Health Organization. (1967). Constitution of the World Health Organization.
World Health Organization. (1998). The World health report: 1998: Life in the 21st century: a vision for all: executive summary (No. WHO/WHR/98.1). World Health Organization.

Chapter 3
Sports Participation, Physical Activity, Life Satisfaction and Quality of Life: Evidence from EU Microdata

Maurizio Esposito and Ciprian Panzaru

3.1 Introduction

Sport is an important part of daily human life. For instance, one of the best evidences is provided by the ancient tradition of the Olympic Games, first written records dating from about 2700 years ago. However, it is not necessary to go back so far to highlight the role of sport in human life. The lockdowns due to the COVID-19 pandemic generated anxiety and boredom, since people were deprived of doing sport and denied regular access to sport facilities and events.

Confined in modernity in a space of leisure for the upper and wealthy classes, specific sports activities have only recently been recognized as an extraordinary social driver; as a privileged environment where social relationships are built; as a real space capable of transmitting and sedimenting values and rules. Specifically, according to this paradigm, sport is characterized as a social and competitive relationship, in which values are achieved independently of the social environment and with particular effects on the production of quality of life, in terms of individuals' psycho-physical and relational well-being (Martelli and Porro, 2013, p. 37). The body and the movement connected to it have thus been recognized as means by which man improves not only his performing abilities, but also the construction of his own identity. In the practice of sport, individuals express not only the representation of their subjectivity, but above all interact with each other to create harmonious solutions in which intelligence manifests itself as a body dimension. The mind thus becomes an extension of the body.

M. Esposito (✉)
University of Cassino and Lazio Meridionale, Cassino, FR, Italy
e-mail: m.esposito@unicas.it

C. Panzaru
Department of Sociology, West University of Timisoara, Timisoara, Timis, Romania
e-mail: ciprian.panzaru@e-uvt.ro

P. Corvo, F. M. Lo Verde (eds.), *Sport and Quality of Life*, Social Indicators Research Series 84, https://doi.org/10.1007/978-3-030-93092-9_3

In this context, the postmodern individual (Bauman, 1997) has become increasingly aware and informed of this relationship by continuously trying to simultaneously improve his emotional and playful sphere, by accumulating the greatest number of significant experiences in this sense, and by increasing the spheres of one's individuality and sociality. In this regard, there is a strengthening of the link between body, physical experiences and lifestyle, which is represented as a kind of lifetime value (Rifkin, 2000).

Moreover, if in modernity, sport was oriented towards the body with the goal of exalting physical beauty, with the advent of the post-modern era the body, through physical activity, becomes part of a more articulated cultural paradigm, where the broader idea of good health conveyed through sport expands at the level of the person's quality of life and psycho-social well-being. The discovery of psycho-physical balance, sweet gymnastics, conscious nutrition and care for one's own well-being, is an expression of a renewed culture of body, in which practices to improve the quality of individual life coexist.

Therefore, it is not surprising that the term "Quality of Life" (QL) is increasingly used today in common language and in the media, a practice that began in the 1960s of the last century, when the Social Indicators Movement was born in the United States. It was formed by a group of scholars interested in overcoming the exclusive use of economic indicators to estimate people's well-being, introducing social indicators in this calculation, aimed at improving the analysis of social conditions and their change over time, and assessing the degree of satisfaction of living conditions of the community through quality of life and well-being indices. According to this approach, social indicators detect psychological satisfaction, happiness and well-being perceived by individuals; a "subjective" reality, therefore, as opposed to the "objective" one.

Consequently, the concept of quality of life in relation to sports takes on a twofold perspective: firstly, it relates to individual health and above all, to the possibility of preventing certain pathologies and chronic diseases; secondly, it involves the entire social sphere of the person in her relationship with the state of physical and mental well-being. In this perspective, the concept of well-being takes on a particularly additive meaning (Secondulfo, 2011), the concept of health also following in this evolution. It is no longer sufficient to remove the negative experiences that make persons' enjoyment difficult, but it is necessary to continually add positive factors to reinforce and support their individuality. Well-being thus becomes a condition that can only be reached through the creation of experiential tools aimed at improving one's living conditions: in this respect, sports practice is a fundamental issue.

The rediscovery of the relational and psychosocial aspects of sport generates attention to the implementation of interventions specifically aimed at promoting and generating an improvement in people's QL. Only in this way sport, as the right of citizenship, experimentation of quality of life and health prevention, will become the main object of social and health policies, fully enrolling in the community welfare regime.

Referring to more recent times, in 2007, the WHO proposed a new definition of HEPA (Health Enhancing Physical Activity), which refers to the weekly frequency of opportunities to participate in activities and their duration. Physical activity should be carried out every day for at least 30 minutes to bring health benefits: if not every day, at least three times a week to be defined as regular (WHO, 2007). Some years later, WHO drew up the document "Global recommendations on Physical activity for Health" (2010), which defines the levels of physical activity recommended for the health of people. From that moment, the promotion of physical activity became a priority of public health action, often included in the health planning of various nations.

3.2 Theoretical Framework

The concept of QL is very controversial (Scott and Marshall, 2005, p. 539). It has been especially used in an economic sense; in the recent years, the concept has assumed a more polymorphic and global use. Since 1968, the Swedish Government has conducted a series of surveys on "Level of Living" and QL, using a complex range of indicators: health and access to healthcare; employment and working conditions; education and skills; housing; security of life and property; recreation and culture (Ibidem). The first research and studies on the QL from a sociological point of view date back to the 1960 and 1970 of the last century, but it was not until 1979 that the term became an index entry in "Sociological Abstracts" (Borgatta and Montgomery, 2000, p. 2300). Primary indicators were linked to subjective indicators, such as individual wellbeing and happiness; in this sense, "I have come to the conclusion that the only defensible definition of quality of life is a general feeling of happiness" (Milbrath, 1978, p. 36).

According to O'Boyle (1997), definition of QL has to take account of health fields and studies, starting from the definition of health by WHO as the presence of social, mental, and physical well-being instead of only focusing on the absence of disease. In this perspective, the WHO Quality of Life Group offered the following definition: "Quality of life is defined as the individual's perception of their position in life in the context of the culture and value systems in which they live and in relation to their goals, expectations, standards and concerns. It is a broad ranging concept affected in a complex way by a person's physical health, psychological state, and level of independence and their relationships to salient features of their environment" (WHOQoL Group, 1993, p. 5). In this perspective, main indicators of QL from a sociological point of view are social wellbeing and lack of stress. They are indicators that concern the *Lebenswelt* of healthy living, and in a more specific way, of physical activity and sports practice too.

From a general point of view, well-being is not simply defined as the absence of psychopathologies, but rather as a constellation of positive functional attitudes that are promoted to achieve strong attachment relationships, acquisition of cognitive, interpersonal and coping skills, and by an exposure to environments that strengthen the person by making them autonomous (Cowen, 1991).

Well-being is described in scientific literature according to two macro-perspectives: the "hedonistic" approach, whose focus is happiness meant in terms of achieving pleasure and avoiding pain; and the "eudemonistic" approach, the core of which is that of personal self-fulfilment, according to the perspective of "Self-determination Theory" (Ryan and Deci, 2001, p. 151). Stress is defined by scientific literature as any environmental, social or inner hindrance that requires the individual to reconstruct his behavioural patterns (Holmes and Rahe, 1967).

As Cummins (2018, p. 275) states, there is a huge literature on physical activity and individual well-being. Over the years, two interesting theories emerged one after the other to explain the link between physical activity and life quality. The first one "was proposed almost 70 years ago by the sociologist Ruth Cavan and colleagues. They had noted great heterogeneity in life quality of elderly people. They also observed that those who were 'aging well' were also the most active. Therefore 'Activity Theory' was proposed to account for the link. About a decade later, the Disengagement Theory (Cumming and Henry, 1961) provided an alternative and more elaborate explanation, centred around progressive, age-dependent, social withdrawal" (Cummins, 2018, p. 279). The links of this second theory with social and relational spheres are fundamental to understand the data that we will describe later, and a critical analysis of them.

This chapter focuses on the analysis of Eurobarometer data. At the introductory level, according to the WHO, less than a third of children and adolescents practice levels of physical-motor activity sufficient for health. Such is the case, despite the fact that the benefits of this activity on individual health are now recognized, and numerous official recommendations and information campaigns have been disseminated, both nationally and internationally. In 2004, WHO promoted an information campaign called "Global Strategy on Diet, Physical Activity and Health" (WHO, 2004), to draw attention to this phenomenon and to sensitize local governments, so that they develop policies in favour of programs that encourage physical-motor activity, especially among the youngest.

On a more specific level, a survey carried out in Italy on the profile of sports activity on young people shows very interesting results: the research investigated the physical/sports activity of children and young people aged between 3 and 17 years, describing their morphology and highlighting the individual, family and social factors that favour or discourage its activity. The data confirm a high percentage (about half of the sample) of total or occasional sedentary Italian minors. Among the younger ones, the survey shows a lower propensity to activity by girls, residents in the southern regions and inhabitants of the urban contexts poorer of parks, green areas and spaces suitable for open-air activities. The predictable and significant relationship between overweight, poor physical-motor activity and sedentary pastimes is strongly confirmed (Bologna, 2013).

3.3 Data and Methods

The aim of this study is to explore the relationship between sports and physical activity, and quality of life. Our data is from the Special Eurobarometer 88.4, conducted by the European Commission (European Commission, 2019). It was co-ordinated by the Directorate-General for Communication (DG COMM 'Media monitoring, Media Analysis and Eurobarometer' Unit).

This survey comprised a special topic on "Fairness, inequality and inter-generational mobility" from which we extracted data about life satisfaction, and a special topic on "Sport and physical activity" from which we extracted data about sport and physical activity.

Life satisfaction was measured through a four-step scale question asking whether the respondent is generally satisfied with their life. Respondents chose one of the following four answers: "very satisfied", "fairly satisfied", "not very satisfied", or "not at all satisfied".

Sport and physical activity was assessed in terms of frequencies, covering four options: "almost daily", "a few times a week", "occasionally" and "never".

Data was obtained from people aged 15 years and over. A total of 28,031 Europeans were surveyed, ranging from 500 in the Republic of Cyprus and Luxembourg to about 1600 in Germany.

In the first stage, descriptive statistics were used to illustrate the level of sport participation in the European Union. In the second stage, a regression model was employed in order to investigate whether sport and physical activity, and engagement influence the level of life satisfaction.

3.4 Sport Participation in the European Union's Countries

Data-based evidence demonstrates that sport is an important social and cultural phenomenon, as many Europeans say that they prefer it because it is a source of fun, relaxation and possibility to be with friends, see Fig. 3.1.

However, the main reason for doing sport remains the desire to improve health and physical conditions, as it can be seen in Fig. 3.2.

When it comes to frequency of doing exercises or playing sport, about 40 percent of Europeans states that they do this regularly or with some regularity but in some countries, such as Romania or Bulgaria this percent is extremely low, only 18.8 percent, respectively 16.4 percent, see Fig. 3.3.

Some differences should be noted from the socio-demographic point of view. People from the age group 15–24 are much more active than other age groups, see Fig. 3.4.

Men exercise or play sport, regularly or with some regularity, more than women (Fig. 3.5). There are not important differences and only in three countries, the

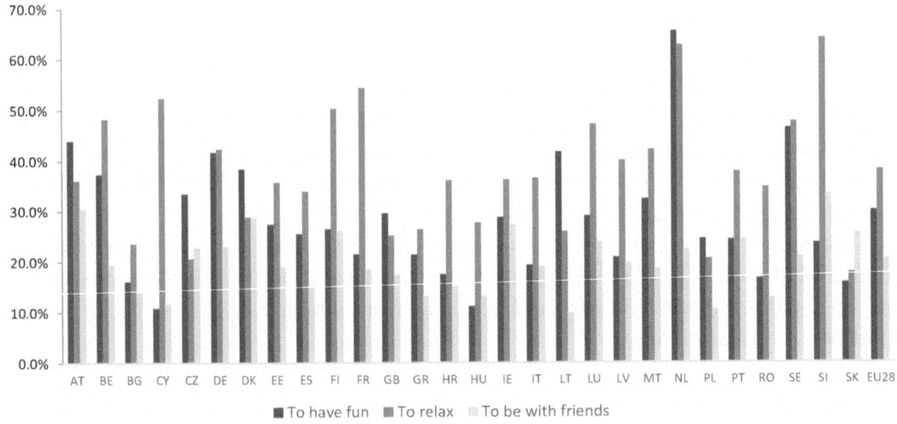

Fig. 3.1 Reasons for exercising or playing sport

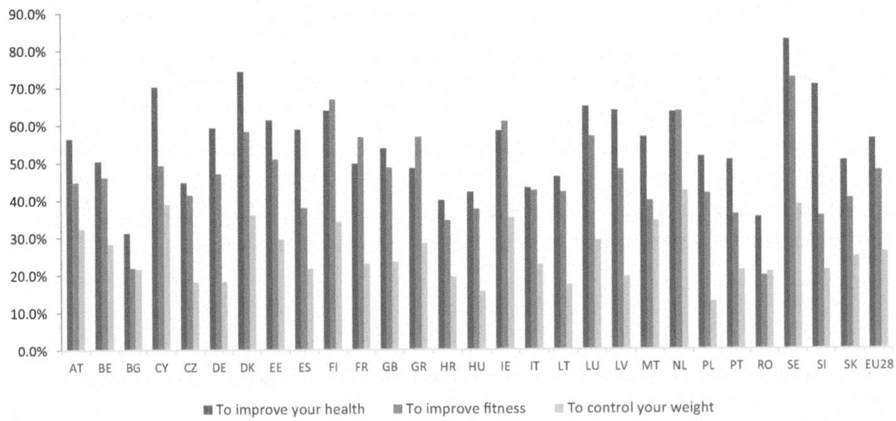

Fig. 3.2 Main reasons for exercising or playing sport

percentage of women who do exercise or play sport is higher than that of men. These are Denmark, Latvia and Sweden.

This descriptive snapshot demonstrates the importance of sport for European culture.

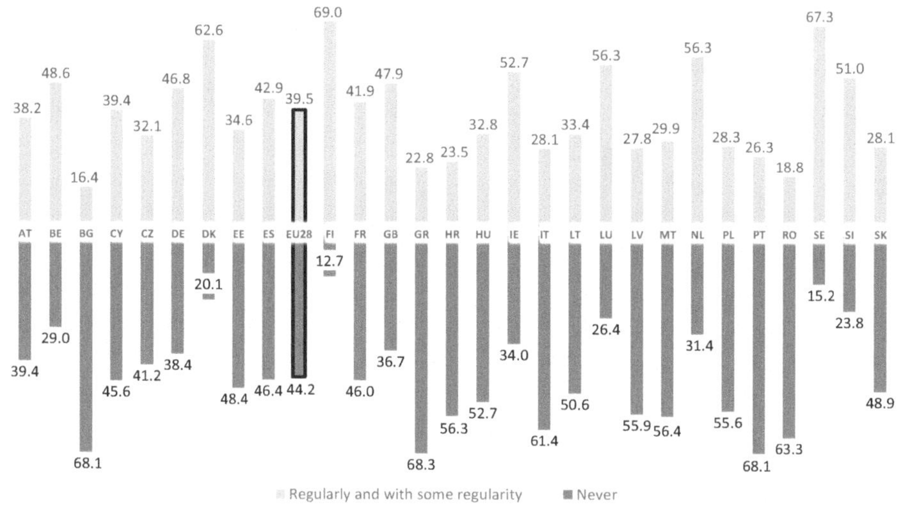

Fig. 3.3 Frequency of Europeans exercising or playing sport (%)

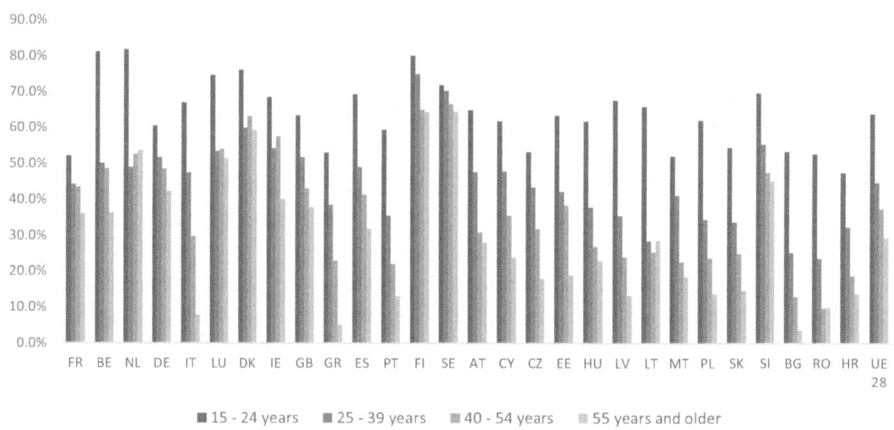

Fig. 3.4 Sport participation by age

3.5 Relationship Between Sport Participation and Life Satisfaction

In order to explore the relationship between sport and life satisfaction, further investigations were carried out guided by other relevant previous empirical studies on this matter (Varca et al., 1984; Huang and Humphreys, 2012; Diaz, et al. 2019).

A set of three independent variables was selected to capture the influence of sport and physical activity, and also the engagement in sport, on life satisfaction (LS). Therefore, our dependent variables were frequency of sport and physical activity

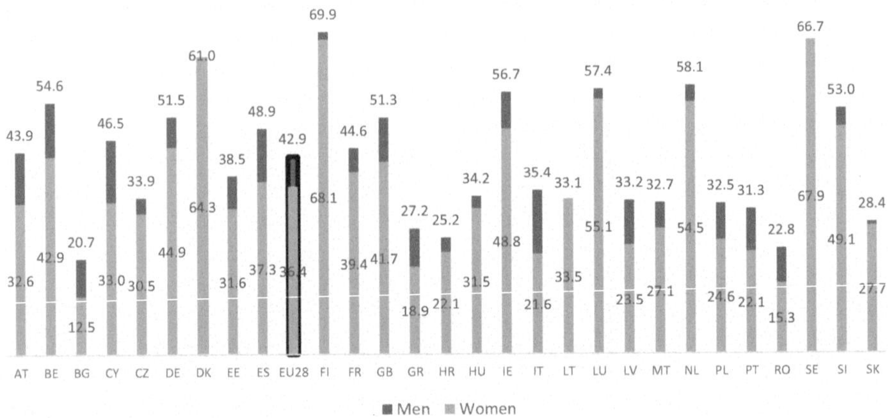

Fig. 3.5 Sport participation by sex (%)

(SPORT—four categories: 1—"almost daily", 2—"a few times a week", 3—"occasionally" and 4—"never") membership of a sport club (MEMB—two categories: 1—"yes" and 2—"no") and voluntary work in sport (VOLUNT—two categories: 1—"yes" and 2—"no"). The membership of a sport and doing voluntary work in sport were considered a proxy for intensity of sport involvement and social engagement. The variable SPORT was inserted in the model as covariate and variables MEMB and VOLUNT were inserted as factors, with "no", being the reference category.

As a dependent variable, we have considered life satisfaction, coded as follows: 1—"very satisfied", 2—"fairly satisfied", 3—"not very satisfied" and 4—"not at all satisfied."

We chose five countries as examples to illustrate the influence of the above independent variables on life satisfaction. The countries—Germany, Italy, United Kingdom, Finland, and Romania—were chosen as they represent different social and economic models, and very different welfare systems.

Descriptive statistic details of the variables used in our model, for each country, are given in Table 3.1.

Since auto-perceived life satisfaction is measured by an ordinal variable, we opted for an ordered logit regression model. Ordered logit regression, also called ordinal logistic regression or just ordinal regression, is used to predict an ordinal dependent variable based on one or more independent variables. It can be considered as either a generalisation of multiple linear regression or as a generalisation of binomial logistic regression. Five separate ordinal regressions were employed, one for every country considered.

As it can be seen in the Table 3.2, the model was statistically significant for all countries considered with χ^2 (3, n = 1592) = 65.084, $p < 0.001$ (Germany); χ^2 (3, n =1029) = 14.454, $p < 0.001$ (Italy); χ^2 (3, n = 1338) = 80.469, $p < 0.001$ (United Kingdom); χ^2 (3, n = 1024) = 29.883, $p < 0.001$ (Finland); χ^2 (3, n = 1005) = 32.403, $p < 0.001$ (Romania).

Table 3.1 Descriptive statistics

		LS	SPORT	MEMB	VOLUNT
Germany ($N = 1585$)	Mean	1.88	2.31	1.8046	1.9402
	Median	2.00	2.00	2.0000	2.0000
	Std. deviation	0.663	1.010	0.39660	0.23716
	Minimum	1	1	1.00	1.00
	Maximum	5	4	2.00	2.00
Italy ($N = 1010$)	Mean	2.24	3.05	1.9456	1.9854
	Median	2.00	3.00	2.0000	2.0000
	Std. deviation	0.719	1.000	0.22696	0.11997
	Minimum	1	1	1.00	1.00
	Maximum	5	4	2.00	2.00
United Kingdom ($N = 1336$)	Mean	1.69	2.48	1.8976	1.9401
	Median	2.00	2.00	2.0000	2.0000
	Std. deviation	0.658	1.077	0.30328	0.23744
	Minimum	1	1	1.00	1.00
	Maximum	5	4	2.00	2.00
Finland ($N = 1020$)	Mean	1.74	1.99	1.8828	1.8972
	Median	2.00	2.00	2.0000	2.0000
	Std. deviation	0.622	.858	0.32180	0.30390
	Minimum	1	1	1.00	1.00
	Maximum	5	4	2.00	2.00
Romania ($N = 1002$)	Mean	2.29	3.01	1.9771	1.9821
	Median	2.00	3.00	2.0000	2.0000
	Std. deviation	0.687	1.062	0.14961	0.13276
	Minimum	1	1	1.00	1.00
	Maximum	5	4	2.00	2.00

Table 3.2 Model Fitting Information

	Log likelihood	Chi-square	Sig.
Germany	142.555	65.084	0.000
Italy	118.447	14.454	0.002
United Kingdom	132.012	56.866	0.000
Finland	120.789	29.883	0.000
Romania	114.348	9.390	0.025

Link function: Logit

Table 3.3 reports parameters estimates and significances. In an ordinal regression, coefficients are changes in the predicted logit, and odds-ratio (OR) is the exponentiated logit coefficient. The odds ratio represents the change in odds (i.e. the odds of being above o certain category versus being at or below that category) for a unit increase in the predictor (i.e. from any value of x to any value of $x + 1$). In contrast, the odds ratio of being at or below a certain category is the inverse of the odds of being above that category.

Table 3.3 Results of ordinal regression

		Estimate	OR	95% CI Lower	95% CI Upper
Germany	SPORT	0.31 (0.05)***	1.362	0.205	0.413
	MEMB	−0.37 (0.14)***	0.689	−0.642	−0.102
	VOLUNT	−0.43 (0.22)*	0.651	−0.866	0.006
Italy	SPORT	0.21 (0.07)***	1.239	0.077	0.351
	MEMB	−0.40 (0.32)	0.673	−1.026	0.234
	VOLUNT	−0.21 (0.59)	0.808	−1.363	0.938
United Kingdom	SPORT	0.31 (0.05)***	1.367	0.211	0.415
	MEMB	−0.59 (0.19)***	0.552	−0.963	−0.225
	VOLUNT	0.02 (0.24)	1.020	−0.443	0.482
Finland	SPORT	0.36 (0.08)***	1.436	0.210	0.513
	MEMB	−0.22 (0.21)	0.806	−0.618	0.188
	VOLUNT	−0.34 (0.22)	0.709	−0.769	0.081
Romania	SPORT	0.16 (0.06)***	1.169	0.038	0.275
	MEMB	−0.35 (0.44)	0.703	−1.212	0.506
	VOLUNT	−0.42 (0.50)	0.655	−1.396	0.550

Link function: Logit
Note: $*p < 0.10$, $**p < 0.05$, $***p < 0.01$, Standard errors in parentheses, CI is confidence interval, OR is odds ratio

First observation is that, in all countries covered by our analysis, sport and physical activity has a significant influence on the life satisfaction. For instance, an increase in sport and physical activity was associated with an increase in the odds of having a higher level of life satisfaction, with an odds ratio of 1.362 for Germany, 1.239 for Italy, 1.367 for United Kingdom, 1.437 for Finland and 1.169 for Romania, holding constant all other variables.

On the other hand, it seems that intensity of sport involvement (e.g. as a member of a sport club) or engagement in sport activities (e.g. as a voluntary work in sport) do not significantly influence the level of life satisfaction, of course holding constant all other variables. For instance, being a member of sports club do not have any effects in case of Italy, Finland and Romania. However, an influence was noticed in Germany, but not in the way we expected. Thus, for Germany, we found a lower odds ratio of being more satisfied with life for those who declared that they are member of a sports club (0.689) than who mention that are not. A similar effect we found in case of United Kingdom, where for those who are member of a sports club, the odds of being more satisfied with life is 0.552 less than for those who are not members of a sports club. Moreover, in case of Germany, we also found a lower odds ratio of being more satisfied with life for those who declared that do voluntary work in sport (0.651) than who mention that they do not do.

3.6 Conclusions

Sport is a symbolic fact, a social construction, a cultural representation; ultimately, a "total social fact", in the sense used by Marcel Mauss. It gives rise to a unique process of physical, psychological and cultural training, which influences the personality and behaviour of a person, moulds character and develops in her a sense of responsibility. Among the most useful points of strengths that physical activity can instil, it is possible to include:

- The acquisition of ~~a~~ personal discipline and learning the value of rules: in this case, the rules should not be understood just as a set of prescriptions, but as a series of behaviours that lead to the achievement of a psycho-physical balance. The attitudes that necessarily characterize the performance of any physical activity improve endurance and temper emotional excesses. Discipline also leads one who practices sport to listen to himself, and to realize his own limits. Discipline also leads those who practice sport to listen to themselves and to realise their own limits. In this way, it is possible to achieve a good degree of self-control, useful for the growth of the person.
- Pain tolerance, and the acquisition of greater self-confidence: to achieve good results in sport, the person must be able to handle the hard times, to endure fatigue. In sports, people often do not get the desired results in a short time and, therefore, they must not be discouraged at the first hurdle. In a word, tenacity, determination and pain tolerance go hand in hand in training activities. Once these three qualities have been internalized, people can also transfer them outside the sporting context, as, for example, in relationships or in study activities, i.e. in those areas where it is likely to encounter disappointments or frustrations that we must learn to manage and control.
- Learning the ethics of win and defeat: sports competitions involve necessarily a winner and a loser. Athletes must come to understand that, more than the result itself, an important factor is the way they arrive to the performance: the preparation and improvement of their skills, before the defeat of the adversary, become the elements which those who practice sports should focus their attention to. Under this view, the defeat turns out to be an event of great utility, as it provides an incentive to analyse objectively the feats accomplished and to improve the weaknesses.
- The feeling of community and the sense of social participation: this is of particular relevance to team sports but can also be extended to individual sports.
- The effects of sport on aggression control: several researcher argue that the practice of physical activities allows, on the one hand, to express aggressive impulses in a socially tolerated way and, on the other hand, to develop mechanisms giving/which give the possibility to overcome them (Esposito, 2014).

However, sport participation and physical activity are not a *panacea* at all; they are not a "magic bullet". The assumptions "Sport good" (in Orwellian remembrance of "four legs good") or "*Mens sana in corpore sano*" are often taken for granted;

indeed, an effort must be made to understand that this is not always true and that everything depends on the level, quality, quantity, structure, relationship and other variables inherent in sport.

This chapter presents a general view of the relationship between sports and physical activity, implication and life satisfaction. The results clearly show a significant relationship between life satisfaction and sport and physical activity. On the other hand, it seems that the supplemental engagement (e.g. as a member of a sports club or doing voluntary work in sport) do not necessarily lead to an increase in life satisfaction.

In conclusion, to face the problem of sedentary lifestyle and low QL in neighbourhoods and cities with major social and economic problems, it is not possible to remain immobile within a *micro* perspective. The issue of quality of life, in fact, takes pollution, infrastructure and mobility equipment, public transport, outdoor facilities and spaces and other social and macro variables as empirical indicators. It is therefore not possible to ignore working hypotheses that neglect the presence of a link between environmental policies, urban planning related to mobility, and the development of infrastructural opportunities, which in turn facilitate physical activity and outdoor sports, and definitively, our quality of life (Rutten and Gelius, 2011).

References

Bauman, Z. (1997). *Postmodernity and its discontents*. Polity Press.

Bologna, E. (2013). Fattori determinanti nella pratica di attività fisico-motoria tra la popolazione giovanile. In A. M. Pioletti & N. Porro (Eds.), *Lo sport degli europei. Cittadinanza, attività, motivazioni*. FrancoAngeli.

Borgatta, E. F., & Montgomery, R. J. V. (2000). *Encyclopedia of sociology*. Macmillan.

Cowen, E. L. (1991). In pursuit of wellness. *American Psychologist, 46*, 404–408.

Cumming, E., & Henry, W. E. (1961). *Growing old*. Basic Books.

Cummins, R. A. (2018). Physical activity and subjective wellbeing. In L. Rodriguez de la Vega & W. N. Toscano (Eds.), *International handbooks of quality-of-life. Handbook of leisure, physical activity sports, recreation and quality of life*. Springer.

Diaz, R., Miller, E. K., Kraus, E., & Fredericson, M. (2019). Impact of adaptive sports participation on quality of life. *Sports Medicine and Arthroscopy Review, 27*(2), 73–82.

Esposito, M. (2014). Sport in prison. Theoretical framework and social meanings in the Italian context. *Cnopt & Hajka (Sport & Science), 4, 142–148.*

European Commission. (2019). *Eurobarometer 88.4 (2017). TNS opinion, Brussels [producer]*. GESIS Data Archive, Cologne. ZA6939 Data file Version 2.0.0. https://doi.org/10.4232/1.13288

Holmes, T., & Rahe, R. (1967). The social readjustment rating scale. *Journal of Psychosomatic Research, 11*, 213–218.

Huang, H., & Humphreys, B. R. (2012). Sports participation and happiness: Evidence from US microdata. *Journal of Economic Psychology, 33*(4), 776–793.

Martelli, S., & Porro, N. (2013). *Nuovo Manuale di Sociologia dello sport e dell'attività fisica*. FrancoAngeli.

Milbrath, L. W. (1978). Indicators of environmental quality. In *Indicators of environmental quality and quality of life*. UNESCO Reports and Papers in the Social Sciences, No. 38. UNESCO.

O'Boyle, C. A. (1997). Measuring the quality of later life. *Philosophical transactions of the Royal Society of London. Series B, Biological sciences, 352*(1363), 1871–1879. https://doi.org/10.1098/rstb.1997.0173

Rifkin, J. (2000). *The age of access. The new culture of hipercapitalism where all of life is a paid for experience*. Penguin Putnam.

Rütten, A., & Gelius, P. (2011). The interplay of structure and agency in health promotion: Integrating a concept of structural change and the policy dimension into a multi-level model and applying it to health promotion principles and practice. *Social Sciences & Medicine, 73*(7), 953–959.

Ryan, R. M., & Deci, E. L. (2001). On happiness and human potentials: A review of research on hedonic and eudaimonic well-being. *Annual Review of Psychology, 52*, 141–166.

Scott, J., & Marshall, G. (2005). *Oxford dictionary of sociology*. Oxford University Press.

Secondulfo D. (2011). *Sociologia del benessere*. FrancoAngeli.

Varca, P. E., Shaffer, G. S., & Saunders, V. (1984). A longitudinal investigation of sport participation and life satisfaction. *Journal of Sport Psychology, 6*(4), 440–447.

World Health Organization. (2004). *Resolution WHA57.17. Global strategy on diet, physical activity and health*. Geneva.

World Health Organization. (2007). *A guide for population-based approaches to increasing levels of physical activity. Implementation of the WHO Global Strategy on diet, physical activity and health*. https://apps.who.int/iris/handle/10665/43612.

World Health Organization. (2010). *Global recommendations on physical activity for health*. https://apps.who.int/iris/bitstream/handle/10665/44399/9789241599979_eng.pdf;jsessionid=DAC045D460C8F874B628485A2D90FF4F?sequence=1.

World Health Organization Qol Group. (1993). *Measuring quality of life: The development of the World Health Organization quality of life instrument*. World Health Organization.

Chapter 4
Conceptual and Operational Problems in Monitoring Participation in Sports

Antonio Mussino

4.1 Introduction

Measuring sport participation is one of the most prominent targets for evaluating sport trends and policies. Many researches have already individualised the historical, social, economic, and cultural determinants that account for the different levels of this phenomenon, both in time and space. Therefore, we know that men participate more than women, young people more than adults and elderly people, and that high educational levels positively influence participation. There are geographical clusters with respect to the attitudes towards sport activities and more general physical activities.

Regardless, a problem remains: Which policies can improve the levels of participation? Maybe a different communication strategy? The driving force of mega events (Olympic Games, World Championships, etc.)? The availability of more sports facilities? Or perhaps more economic and fiscal opportunities? Our goal as statisticians is to evaluate the results of such policies in national or local areas. Thus, we need a methodological strategy to monitor levels and trends in participation.

The most interesting and continual attempts to perform such analysis, and to coordinate them among the various countries, have been done in Europe. Europe was the cradle of modern (and postmodern[1]) sport and is one of its leading areas: out of 28 Olympic Games, 16 were organised in European countries, which is also true for most of the top sports' World Championships. In other countries (Japan, Australia, and Brazil) this type of research was performed only occasionally, coinciding with main sports events in their countries, such as the Olympic Games.

[1] This attribute will be clarified below.

A. Mussino (✉)
Department of Statistical Sciences, Sapienza University of Rome, Rome, Italy
e-mail: antonio.mussino@uniroma1.it

P. Corvo, F. M. Lo Verde (eds.), *Sport and Quality of Life*, Social Indicators Research Series 84, https://doi.org/10.1007/978-3-030-93092-9_4

In this paper, a historical review of such attempts to analyse trends of sport participation is proposed, focusing attention on the most important research strategies and their strengths and weaknesses. We will propose the main challenges for the researchers who want to face these problems.

In the second part of this paper, data from Eurobarometer 472 (December 2017) are processed in an original way to present trends of participation in sports and in physical activities in the European Union countries, along with some of their main determinants. Special attention is paid to objective and subjective indicators of the quality of life.

4.2 Some Historical Remarks

As stated above, Europe has always played a leading role in this field. In the 1970s, the problem of defining and monitoring sports was tackled. Up until those years, the historical approach to modern sport considered élite activities characterised by competition, organisation, and measurement of results. In 1975 the Council of Europe changed this paradigm with the "Sport for All Charter" (Council of Europe 1992, revised in 2001) that enounced two principles: "every individual has the right to participate in sport" and "sport shall be encouraged as an important factor of human development." The role of sport in the welfare policies was recognised and a new definition of sport ("postmodern" sport) was accepted.

In the meantime, under the aegis of the Council of Europe, the first comparative studies were performed: Castejon Paz et al. (1973), Rodgers (1977–1978), and Claeys (1982) performed important cross-national surveys, whose results became the milestone of analysing sport participation.

The new European political organization, the European Union, for many years did not consider "sport" as a theme of lawgiving, except for the so-called Bosman's ruling.[2] Now, the EU's role in terms of steering sport policies has widened and is likely to increase further. The goal is to suggest effective policies and to set realistic targets at national levels.

In the 1990s, accompanying this new attitude, there was a push to a coordinated monitoring of participation in sports in EU member states to collect data through surveys. A project called COMPASS[3] was emblematic of this new attitude and of the European Commission involvement in sport matters.

Some documents confirm that the role of sport for the EU bodies is mainly social, educational, and cultural: the Helsinki Report on Sport (European Commission, 1999) stated, "safeguarding the current sport structures and maintaining the social function of sport"; the Nice Declaration on Sport (European Council, 2000) claimed

[2]The Bosman judgment (15th December 1995) was a measure adopted by the European Court of Justice to regulate the transfer of players within EU sports federations.

[3]Coordinated Monitoring of Participation in Sports, see below.

that "sport is finally on the European political Agenda stressing the social, educational, and cultural function of sport in a new European Constitution"; and the White Paper on Sport (European Commission, 2007) discussed the "attention to societal role, economic dimension and organisation of sport."

Finally, in the Lisbon Treaty and Preparatory Actions (European Union, 2007) only a soft competence on sport (guidelines and recommendations) was given to the European Union countries; whilst, for the principle of subsidiarity, the main responsibility for sports policies was directed to the national level. In this context, the European Commission uses a periodic survey as a monitoring tool: A Special Eurobarometer on Sport and Physical Activity.

4.3 The Definition of Sport

It is important to define what we are trying to measure. When we speak about sport, we have to consider that the historical approach to modern sport regarded activities characterised by organisation, competition, and measurement of results. This definition derives from the tradition of the Olympic movement, since the end of nineteenth century, and from its structural organisation (the National Olympic Committees and the National Sport Federations).

Modern sport may be well represented by the "pyramidal" model (European Commission, 1999). In this model, the large basis of the pyramid is composed by sport clubs and their athletes; a second narrower level is composed by local (e.g. regional) sport federations, that organise games at this level, and by the athletes who participate in this games; a third narrower level is the national one, with the national Olympic committees and sport federations and the athletes who participate at this level. At the top, the narrowest level, there are the International Olympic Committee (IOC) and the international sports federations that organise the Olympic Games and international main events (World and Continental Championships).

However, sport is not only organisation and competition: it may be a spontaneous activity for wellness and fitness, for socialisation, or for enhancing the health of citizens. In other words, for improving the quality of their lives. Recreational sports (also regarded as "Sport for All") were inspired by ancient movements from Northern Europe and spread in the 1970s: they may well fit the definition of postmodern sport.

Postmodern sport may be well represented by the "church" model (Scheerder et al., 2011). In this model, the top of the bell tower is the pyramidal structure of the élite sport organisation, but the whole nave represents the new sport activities, recreational, competitive, spontaneous or grassroots-organised ones.

4.4 Two Different Approaches to Compare Participation Levels in Various Countries

We now introduce two strategies to analyse, in a comparable way, different sport participation levels and to investigate their determinants, that is to understand the strengths and weaknesses of the different sport systems and sport policies.

We start by considering that each country may have its own strategy to perform research on sport participation. In this case, the methodologies may be different. Therefore, the comparisons are difficult and reliable and comparable data lack in this field. The different definition of "sport", that we proposed above, is only one of methodological problems. In particular, the role that has been attached to simple "physical activities" is crucial.

The two strategies can be summarized as follows:

(a) To analyse the various national (or local) researches through a common framework; this approach should provide a set of guidelines in organising the researches to be followed by the boards uncharged, in particular how to consider data on physical activities. In this case, we are confronted with many different national surveys.
(b) To perform a common research in different countries with the same methodological strategy: that is the same questionnaire, sample strategy, data processing, and tabulating. In this case, we are confronted with the same survey over many nations.

In the case (a), the countries' specific cultures and traditions are taken into account in designing the research questions and the questionnaire accordingly. This condition enriches the possibility of going deeper in the analysis, but creates difficulties when comparing the results. There may be problems in reliability and validity, as the same results may measure different aspects.

As examples, we find the already mentioned Rodgers' research, but the main contribution is due to the COMPASS project (Gratton et al., 1999 and 2011): its aims were to gather comparative information in different European countries, to process them in a framework that was the operationalization of a "general model" of sport participation, and to propose a set of "core questions" that could be used in future researches to simplify such analysis (Mussino, 1999 and 2004). This project was stopped in 2004 for lack of funding, but it led the way to new approaches in terms of cross-country comparisons.

Also inspired by COMPASS is a well-structured initiative under the umbrella of European Association for Sociology of Sport (EASS). In May 2010, a group of researchers from the Mulier Institute in the Netherlands, and from the University of Leuven in Belgium, proposed in Porto, constituting an expert group called Meeting for European Sport Participation and Sport Culture Research (MEASURE) (Hoekman et al., 2011). The tool that this new group used to gather information and evaluate different national sport systems was a "fact sheets" collection compiled by experts of the different local situations. This research produced many interesting results (Scheerder et al., 2011).

We question what the advantages and disadvantages are of this strategy. The advantages are: an opportunity to use rich national survey data, the comparability of cross national time trends, the possibility of having information in a short time, etc. The disadvantages are: the information is obtained using different definitions and methodologies, the data used to insert in the sheets are chosen in a subjective way by the local experts, the possible ecological fallacy produced by aggregate data, etc.

As examples of strategy (b), we refer to the standard Eurobarometer surveys, which have been continuous in the new century (2002, 2009, 2013, and 2017). These surveys are performed in the same time, with the same questionnaire (translated in the UE countries' languages), with the same sample strategy, and the data are processed to obtain the same comparable results.

This approach should allow us comparability and validity of the data. On the other hand, we lose the specificity of the countries' different traditions and approaches to sport. The advantages are: the methodological choices are common in terms of sampling strategy, questionnaire, etc. The disadvantages are: such surveys are very expensive; the small sample size in each country allows an accurate estimation only of the global population, not of its strata; the translation of the common questionnaire in many languages leads to problems of definition (Mussino, 2014), etc.

A particular case of approach (b) is represented by the parallel surveys in Brazil and Italy (Mussino et al., 2013). The same core questions were included in the Multipurpose National Surveys, realised in the same time (October, 2015) by the Instituto Brasileiro de Geografia e Estadistica (IBGE) and Istituto Nazionale di Statistica (Istat). Therefore, the results are highly comparable. This strategy could also have allowed another comparison in Brazil between sport participation attitudes before and after Olympic Games (2016, in Rio de Janeiro), realising a new survey after this mega event.[4]

4.5 Eurobarometer 472: Some Results and Indexes

In this second part of this paper, we introduce Special Eurobarometer 472, performed (fieldwork) in December 2017 (European Commission, 2018). It is one of the periodical[5] surveys requested by the European Commission, Directorate-General for Education, Youth, Sport and Culture and co-ordinated by the Directorate-General for Communication. The Eurobarometer 472 is a public opinion survey on sport and physical activity participation and attitudes, carried out by TNS Political & Social network in the 28 (at that moment) EU Member States: 28 031 EU citizens were

[4]In this case, political evolution in Brazil stopped the experience.

[5]The others were performed in 2002, 2009, and 2013.

interviewed face-to-face at home and in their native language. The methodology, as we previously said, was the same for all countries and territories covered in the survey. In spite of the limits that we introduced above, it is the only updated research tool to study the phenomenon of sports participation in Europe.

In the official report published in March 2018, the analysis was conducted separately for sport and physical activity. Following the COMPASS framework (Mussino & Cosmai, 2019), the synthetic crosstab of the two areas (Table 4.1) is transformed in a new variable COMPASS, with six categories: (a1) regular sport activity, (a2) regular physical activity, (b) almost regular activity, (c) irregular activity, (d) occasional activity, and (e) no activity.[6] Adding (a1) and (a2) we have the percentage of citizens performing an activity that is "health enhancing" (HEPA, Health Enhancing Physical Activity) for the World Health Organisation (WHO), which means three or more times a week. This new variable COMPASS will guide for our analysis (World Health Organisation, 2007 and 2015).

The COMPASS frequencies distribution (rounded figures) is proposed in Table 4.2, compared with the previous years' Eurobarometer surveys.

The first impression is the continuing persistence of the sharp decline in regular participation (a1+a2: 49.1% in 2009 and 33.8% in 2017). This decline is due to the consequences of the economic crisis at the turn of 2008. It is less marked for sport activity, which is the most structured, and dramatic for the physical activity, highlighting the non-compliance with the WHO directive on HEPA.

The regular activity probably turns into almost regular activity (in fact this grows, albeit slightly), but from this we pass to the lack of activity (which grows from 13.2% to 25%, and now to 28.7%). Even irregular and occasional activities, while receiving flows of regular participants, decrease by increasing the ranks of sedentary people.

However, the most troubling result is that almost three out of ten EU citizens have a sedentary lifestyle. Furthermore, since the differences in participation profiles between the various countries are very high, in 2017, we find that in some countries sedentary people are more than one out of two. We compare the different countries' profiles in Table 4.3.

Regarding the HEPA regular activity (a1+a2), the countries with the highest levels (absolute majority) are The Netherlands (69.4%), Sweden (63.8%), Denmark (60.0%), and Finland (57.6%). Finland leads the ranking for regular sport activity (41.4%) and The Netherlands for regular physical activity (44.3%). There are countries with anomalous results in one of the two categories, due to the organizational profile of their sports system. On the other hand, there are countries with an absolute majority of sedentary people, such as Portugal (56.1%), and Malta (51.3%), or very close to this result, such as Italy (49.0%), Romania (44.6%), and Bulgaria (41.8%).

Comparing results in Table 4.3 with a similar table drawn up for 2013 results (Mussino e Cosmai, op.cit.), we discover that only Cyprus (+3.6%), Poland (+1.4%),

[6]The percentages for the categories are computed adding the cells as coded in Table 4.1.

Table 4.1 Sport vs. physical activity

		Physical activity—frequency							
		Five times a week or more	3–4 times a week	1–2 times a week	1–3 times a month	Less often	Never	Missing answer	Total
Sport activity—Frequency	Five times a week or more	3.3% (a1)	0.9% (a1)	1.0% (a1)	0.3% (a1)	0.5% (a1)	1.2% (a1)	0.0% (a1)	7.1%
	3–4 times a week	1.7% (a1)	3.4% (a1)	3.1% (a1)	0.9% (a1)	1.2% (a1)	1.5% (a1)	0.0% (a1)	11.9%
	1–2 times a week	2.6% (a2)	2.3% (a2)	8.6% (b)	2.1% (b)	2.1% (b)	2.8% (b)	0.1% (b)	20.7%
	1–3 times a month	0.5% (a2)	0.6% (a2)	1.1% (b)	1.6% (c)	0.6% (c)	0.4% (c)	0.0% (c)	4.8%
	Less often	1.0% (a2)	0.5% (a2)	1.5% (b)	1.5% (c)	3.9% (d)	0.9% (d)	0.0% (d)	9.3%
	Never	4.6% (a2)	2.7% (a2)	4.1% (b)	2.4% (c)	3.7% (d)	28.4% (e)	0.1% (e)	46.0%
	Missing answer	0.0% (a2)	0.0% (a2)	0.0% (b)	0.0% (c)	0.0% (d)	0.0% (e)	0.1% (e)	0.3%
Total		13.7%	10.5%	19.4%	8.7%	11.9%	35.4%	0.4%	100%

Table 4.2 Trend of COMPASS variable in three Eurobarometer surveys

COMPASS indicator	Code	2009	2013	2017
Regular sport activity	(a1)	21.2%	20.7%	19.0%
Regular physical activity	(a2)	27.9%	16.3%	14.8%
Almost regular activity	(b)	21.2%	22.0%	22.5%
Irregular activity	(c)	7.2%	6.6%	6.5%
Occasional activity	(d)	9.3%	9.4%	8.5%
No activity	(e)	13.2%	25.0%	28.7%
Total	–	100%	100%	100%

Table 4.3 COMPASS variable in the 28 EU countries (% in the country)

	COMPASS categories							
Country	a1	a2	b	c	d	e	Total	Index
SE–Sweden	37.7%	26.1%	23.7%	4.9%	4.2%	3.3%	100.0%	135.6
NL–The Netherlands	25.1%	44.3%	16.3%	5.5%	3.3%	5.5%	100.0%	135.3
DK–Denmark	31.4%	28.6%	23.1%	4.3%	5.9%	6.7%	100.0%	119.5
FI–Finland	41.4%	16.2%	25.0%	4.7%	5.9%	6.7%	100.0%	116.2
LU–Luxembourg	30.1%	14.4%	28.9%	7.5%	5.7%	13.5%	100.0%	77.7
DE–Germany	18.3%	23.8%	29.5%	5.6%	6.6%	16.2%	100.0%	69.1
SI–Slovenia	30.7%	11.4%	22.2%	5.9%	16.1%	13.6%	100.0%	57.2
LV–Latvia	15.4%	28.9%	20.5%	7.9%	10.2%	17.2%	100.0%	56.6
BE–Belgium	19.6%	18.7%	26.6%	8.3%	13.3%	13.4%	100.0%	54.8
EE–Estonia	16.0%	24.0%	25.5%	6.8%	8.0%	19.7%	100.0%	51.3
UK–United Kingdom	30.6%	10.3%	18.7%	7.7%	8.6%	23.9%	100.0%	36.4
IE–Ireland	33.4%	6.4%	20.5%	4.8%	10.3%	24.5%	100.0%	36.0
FR–France	15.1%	19.1%	29.0%	7.1%	4.8%	24.9%	100.0%	35.7
LT–Lithuania	19.4%	14.8%	21.8%	7.7%	9.0%	27.4%	100.0%	18.7
SK–Slovakia	12.8%	18.9%	23.2%	7.5%	12.2%	25.4%	100.0%	16.1
HU–Hungary	17.9%	17.4%	17.8%	5.5%	10.0%	31.4%	100.0%	10.7
AT–Austria	16.3%	11.2%	23.3%	12.2%	12.7%	24.4%	100.0%	4.6
CY–Cyprus (republic)	26.0%	5.8%	18.6%	5.2%	11.1%	33.3%	100.0%	−0.7
ES–Spain	28.1%	5.1%	18.1%	3.0%	8.3%	37.4%	100.0%	−1.6
CZ–Czech Republic	12.4%	9.4%	24.1%	11.2%	18.3%	24.6%	100.0%	−11.0
PL–Poland	14.1%	11.9%	19.8%	7.3%	10.5%	36.4%	100.0%	−18.8
HR–Croatia	11.1%	12.1%	19.3%	7.6%	17.3%	32.6%	100.0%	−24.4
GR–Greece	10.9%	12.0%	22.5%	6.0%	10.5%	38.2%	100.0%	−24.6
BG–Bulgaria	6.8%	11.5%	17.0%	7.9%	14.9%	41.8%	100.0%	−52.8
MT–Malta	21.1%	3.1%	10.2%	4.4%	9.9%	51.3%	100.0%	−58.3
IT–Italy	9.2%	6.3%	20.7%	6.0%	8.9%	49.0%	100.0%	−61.2
RO–Romania	9.8%	8.0%	14.3%	9.2%	14.0%	44.8%	100.0%	−62.9
PT–Portugal	11.3%	5.7%	17.4%	2.9%	6.5%	56.1%	100.0%	−70.2
EU–Total	19.0%	14.8%	22.5%	6.5%	8.5%	28.7%	100.0%	17.7

United Kingdom (+0.6%), and Estonia (+0.1%) obtain better results with respect to HEPA activity. All the others have worse results, with a sharp decline for Croatia (−13.9%) and Romania (−13.2%). As to the number of sedentary people, it increases everywhere, except in Cyprus (−11.3%), Bulgaria (−7.4%), Belgium (−2.0%), and Greece (−1.2%). There are troubling balances in Croatia (+19.5%), Romania (+12.3%), Austria (+10.6%), Slovakia (+8.6%), Czech Republic (+7.6%), and United Kingdom (+6.4%).

A synthesis of the rankings proposed in Table 4.3 can be a weighted additive "index,"[7] calculated with the following formula:

$$index = \{2 * (a1 + a2) + b - c - d - 2 * e\}.$$

Countries with positive scores have a prevalence of active lifestyles, those with negative scores have a prevalence of sedentary lifestyles.

The ranking in this index individualises positive scores for the top countries in the North Europe (Sweden 136, The Netherlands 135, Denmark 120, and Finland 116), virtuous countries in Central Europe (Luxembourg 78, Germany 69, Slovenia 57, Latvia 57, Belgium 55, and Estonia 51), and other countries with a positive score (United Kingdom 36, Ireland 36, France 36, Lithuania 19, Slovakia 16, Hungary 10, and Austria 5). The negative scores are individualised as follows: countries with critical levels of sedentary lifestyle in Mediterranean and East areas (Portugal −70, Romania −63, Italy −61, Malta −58, and Bulgaria −53), and other countries with negative scores (Greece −25, Croatia −24, Poland −19, Czech Republic −11, Spain −2, and Cyprus −1).[8]

4.6 Eurobarometer 472: The Determinants

Traditionally the main variables that discriminate levels of participation in sports and physical activities are geographical position, gender, age, and education. In the previous paragraph, we already analysed some geographical clusters and their influence that can be extended to the gender differences.

At the EU level, the gender gap still persists. In Table 4.4, the figure shows a male prevalence, except for the "no activity" category. The male advantage is stronger in Regular sport activity, and the disadvantage in sedentary life style is about ten percentage points.

In reality, differentiating by geographic cluster, the situation is different. Indeed, where participation is higher, the contribution of women is greater. We use the "index" variable to simplify the analysis. In Table 4.5, this variable is computed for men and women in the various countries.

[7] The "index" is proposed in the last column of Table 4.3.

[8] The figures are rounded.

Table 4.4 COMPASS results by gender

Gender		Men	Women	Total
COMPASS categories	Regular sport activity	21.8%	16.3%	19.0%
	Regular physical activity	14.9%	14.8%	14.8%
	Almost regular activity	23.7%	21.4%	22.5%
	Irregular activity	6.6%	6.2%	6.4%
	Occasional activity	9.3%	7.8%	8.5%
	No activity	23.6%	33.5%	28.7%
Total		100.0%	100.0%	100.0%

Table 4.5 Index by gender in the EU countries

Country	Men	Women	Country	Men	Women
SE–Sweden	131.1	140.3	SK–Slovakia	12.8	19.5
NL–The Netherlands	128.6	142.1	HU–Hungary	18.2	3.4
DK–Denmark	113.7	125.4	AT–Austria	17.9	−7.7
FI–Finland	112.4	119.8	CY–Cyprus (Republic)	27.8	−27.1
LU–Luxembourg	84.9	70.8	ES–Spain	27.4	−29.3
DE–Germany	76.9	61.9	CZ–Czech Republic	−5.1	−16.6
SI–Slovenia	65.5	49.1	PL–Poland	−2.9	−33.0
LV–Latvia	77.7	39.7	HR–Croatia	−24.1	−24.5
BE–Belgium	66.1	44.3	GR–Greece	−7.9	−40.7
EE–Estonia	64.0	41.0	BG–Bulgaria	−49.6	−56.1
UK–United Kingdom	53.5	19.8	MT–Malta	−44.6	−71.6
IE–Ireland	52.4	19.9	IT–Italy	−33.6	−86.2
FR–France	59.2	14.3	RO–Romania	−46.8	−78.2
LT–Lithuania	23.3	14.5	PT–Portugal	−43.3	−94.1
EU–European Union; men 34.0; women 2.6					

In all countries the female index has worse results than the male one: both the values are positive, both they are negative. There is an exception in the results of some Northern countries, where the index for the females is higher than the one for the men: The Netherlands (up to 142.1), Sweden (140.3), Denmark (125.4), and Finland (119.8). This feature is also seen in Slovakia, albeit at a much lower level (19.5 vs. 12.8). In Spain and Cyprus, without the contribution of women, the index turns out to be positive.

In Table 4.6, we find the confirmation of the discriminating power of age. The differences are substantial, both between the categories of "young", "adults" and "elderly", and within them.

In the "15–24 years" category, almost one in three young people is classified among active sportsmen: 11 percentage points more than young people aged 25–34. Among the over 74 years, sport activity is obviously reduced, but physical activity persists, even though one in two old people is sedentary (Table 4.6).

The last discriminant variable we consider is the educational level. To standardize analysis, only records of people aged 25 and over were processed. Increasing levels

Table 4.6 Age (in classes) by COMPASS categories

	Regular sport activity	Regular physical activity	Almost regular activity	Irregular activity	Occasional activity	No activity	Total
Young 15–24	32.4%	13.5%	27.3%	5.6%	6.5%	14.6%	100.0%
Young 25–34	21.4%	13.2%	28.1%	8.3%	9.1%	19.9%	100.0%
Adult 35–50	17.5%	13.8%	24.5%	7.7%	10.7%	25.8%	100.0%
Adult 51–64	16.5%	16.2%	21.2%	6.8%	8.5%	30.7%	100.0%
Elderly 65–74	15.9%	17.9%	15.8%	4.7%	8.0%	37.7%	100.0%
Elderly 75 e +	11.1%	14.3%	14.8%	2.9%	5.1%	51.8%	100.0%
Total	19.0%	14.8%	22.5%	6.4%	8.5%	28.7%	100.0%

Table 4.7 Educational levels by COMPASS categories

	Regular sport activity	Regular physical activity	Almost regular activity	Irregular activity	Occasional activity	No activity	Total
Completed primary or lower	10.6%	13.1%	12.6%	4.2%	8.4%	51.2%	100.0%
Completed secondary	13.8%	14.1%	20.3%	6.8%	10.9%	34.0%	100.0%
Completed post-secondary	21.2%	16.5%	26.1%	7.6%	7.2%	21.3%	100.0%
Completed upper level	25.5%	17.2%	29.4%	6.8%	6.9%	14.2%	100.0%
Total	17.0%	15.0%	21.8%	6.5%	8.8%	30.8%	100.0%

of education correspond to a growing involvement in sports and physical activity and to a very strong decrease in sedentary lifestyle (Table 4.7).

4.7 Eurobarometer 472: More Subjective Indicators

To better characterize the role of an active lifestyle in a citizen's quality of life, it is useful to consider subjective indicators too; we consider two of them: satisfaction with one's life and the motivations that lead to the practice of a sport or physical activity.

Table 4.8 shows the greater share of people satisfied with their lives among those who practice an activity and how this share increases when the practice is regular and even more if it is in sports.

Table 4.8 Life satisfaction by COMPASS categories

	Regular sport activity	Regular physical activity	Almost regular activity	Irregular activity	Occasional activity	No activity	Total
Very satisfied	34.4%	28.3%	25.8%	17.8%	15.3%	12.1%	22.0%
Satisfied	57.4%	58.9%	63.6%	66.7%	66.5%	59.9%	61.1%
Unsatisfied	8.2%	12.8%	10.6%	15.5%	18.2%	28.1%	16.9%
Total	100.0%	100.0%	100.0%	100.0%	100.0%	100.0%	100.0%

On the contrary, the percentage of being dissatisfied is much higher among sedentary people. This confirms how important an active lifestyle is for citizens' quality of life.

The last but not least indicative variable is the motivation for practicing a sport or physical activity. In the Eurobarometer questionnaire, the question allowed multiple answers on a battery of 15 items, plus the generic "other" answer.

Table 4.9 shows the percentages of answers according to the COMPASS indicator's categories (excluding "no activity", of course). The average number of items respondents chose as classified in that category is placed in the last row. The global mean percentage is in the last column.

The answers "Health improvement", "Fitness", and "Relax" have the first three places in all the rankings. Aggregating the answers, five clusters of items can be identified[9]:

- the most suitable (36.3% of overall indications) cluster can be labelled as *wellbeing*; it includes "Have fun", "Relax", and "Fitness");
- the *health protection* cluster (21.4%) includes "Health improvement" and "Counteract aging";
- the *sport-related items* cluster (16.3%) is in third place; it includes "Physical performance", "Self-esteem", "New skills", and "Spirit of competition";
- the *physical improvement* cluster (13.6%) includes "Physical appearance" and "Control weight";
- last is the *socialization* cluster (9.7%); it includes "Be with friends", "Make acquaintances", "Meet other cultures", and "Social integration".

Therefore, the sport-related items are only in the third position and this confirms the soundness of the choice to use the COMPASS indicator, instead of processing the various activities separately, as they used to do in the official Report.

The first two positions are related to the United Nations Sustainable Development Goals 2030 (SDG) n.3 "Ensure healthy lives and promote wellbeing for all at all ages" (World Health Organization).

[9]The answer "Other" reaches 2.7%.

Table 4.9 Motivation item to participation by COMPASS categories

	Regular sport activity	Regular physical activity	Almost regular activity	Irregular Activity	Occasional activity	Global
Health improvement	69.6%	54.1%	55.0%	45.2%	33.6%	55.5%
Physical appearance	31.5%	14.8%	21.6%	13.1%	10.3%	20.9%
Counteract aging	19.0%	17.8%	13.1%	9.1%	8.9%	14.8%
Have fun	40.4%	29.9%	32.0%	24.3%	16.3%	31.4%
Relax	41.9%	39.8%	42.1%	34.5%	27.0%	39.2%
Be with friends	25.7%	15.8%	22.0%	13.5%	10.4%	19.7%
Make acquaintances	8.3%	5.5%	6.0%	3.9%	2.5%	6.0%
Meet other cultures	3.3%	2.1%	2.6%	1.1%	1.1%	2.4%
Physical performance	41.7%	25.6%	29.0%	16.4%	12.6%	28.8%
Fitness	62.4%	45.2%	51.6%	37.9%	23.0%	48.8%
Control weight	32.9%	18.7%	24.9%	18.5%	11.8%	23.8%
Self-esteem	19.5%	9.9%	11.8%	7.9%	6.4%	12.5%
New skills	11.5%	6.3%	6.1%	2.4%	2.1%	6.8%
Spirit of competition	10.5%	2.7%	5.2%	2.3%	2.0%	5.5%
Social integration	5.6%	3.5%	3.7%	1.6%	1.2%	3.7%
Other	2.9%	13.4%	5.7%	11.4%	20.1%	8.7%
Average item indicated	4.3	3.1	3.3	2.4	1.9	3.3

4.8 Some Final Considerations

Retracing the logical thread of the contribution, some concluding considerations can be formulated.

Participation in sports and physical activities is one of the constituent elements of citizens' wellbeing and, consequently, of their quality of life. Such participation can be stimulated by appropriate sports policies by national and/or local governments. It is important that the results of these policies are monitored with adequate methodological tools.

Since the 1970s, social researchers have carried out research to monitor in a comparative way, in time and space (between the various countries), the trends and the determinants of this participation.

Two different approaches to compare levels of participation in various countries have been proposed along the years, since 1970 up to now: (a) to compare many different national surveys that follow common guidelines, or (b) to perform a common research in different countries with the same methodological strategy. Approach (a) would seem preferable, as it takes into account the specific cultures and traditions of countries in the various researches' designs. Approach (b) is rougher, but simpler and it is what we used in this contribution.

Our analysis has been improved using typical indicators of approach (a), valid for monitoring the active lifestyles of European citizens. Thus, we introduced and calculated an ordinal qualitative indicator (COMPASS), which takes into account equally the sporting and physical activities, while also differentiating them. For a better synthesis of some relationships, a quantitative indicator ("index") was also calculated.

The elaborations carried out have confirmed the trends that have already emerged in the past years, with results that we can consider as a valid tool for monitoring the situation in the European Union's various countries.

A final consideration must be made on the consequences of the pandemic caused by the COVID-19 virus and of the lockdowns in various countries. They probably have caused a polarization of behaviours: the regular active ones should have been stable; on the contrary, we can expect a significant increase in the number of sedentary people, involving in this category the almost regular, irregular, and occasional participants. As we wait for the next surveys, we hope that the strategy proposed in our work will be adopted[10]: we have proved it is valid to evaluate the new trends.

References

Castejon Paz, B., de Dios Garcia Martinez, J., & Carbalada, R. (1973). *Rationalising sports policies. Outline of a methodology*. Council of Europe.

Claeys, U. (1982). *Rationalising sports policies. Sport in European society: A transnational survey into participation and motivation*. Council of Europe.

Commission of the European Communities. (2007). *White paper on sport*.

Council of Europe. (1992). *European sport charter* (revised 2001).

European Commission. (1999). The Helsinki Report on Sport COM/99/0644 final.

European Commission. (2018). *Sport and physical activity. Special Eurobarometer 72.3*. European Commission DG Education and Culture.

European Council. (2000). *Nice declaration, declaration on the specific characteristics of sport and its social function in Europe*. Nice.

European Union. (2007). Lisbon treaty: Amending the treaty on European Union and the treaty establishing the European Community. *Official Journal of the European Union (2007/C 306/01)*.

[10]In Italy, Istat (Istat, 2020) measured the sport and physical activities practiced during the lockdown, but without a clear definition of these activities or a correct measure of their frequencies.

Gratton, C. , Mussino A., Rossi Mori B., Rowe N., (1999). *COMPASS 1999. A project seeking the co-ordinated monitoring of participation in sports in Europe.*

Gratton, C., Rowe, N., & Veal, A. J. (2011). International comparisons of sports participation in European countries. An update of the COMPASS project. *European Journal of Sport & Society, 8*(1–2), 99–116.

Hoekman, R., Breedveld, K., & Scheerder, J. (2011). Introduction to the special issue on sports participation in Europe. *European Journal of Sport & Society, 8*(1–2), 7–14.

Istat. (2020). *Le giornate in casa durante il lockdown.* Roma Istat Report 5 giugno 2020.

Mussino, A. (1999). Conceptual and operational problems in measuring participation in sports. *Bulletin of the International Statistical Institute, 52nd ISI Session, LVIII*(2), 345–346.

Mussino, A. (2004). L'armonizzazione delle statistiche sulla partecipazione sportiva: una sfida europea. *Rivista Italiana di Economia, Demografia e Statistica, LVIII*(1–2), 149–176.

Mussino, A. (2014). Levels and typologies of participation in sports in Europe: Methodological and operational challenges. *Journal of Sports Science, 2*, 32–46.

Mussino, A., & Cosmai, R. (2019). Sport and physical activity in Europe: How to measure active lifestyles. In A. Bianco, P. Conigliano, & M. Gnaldi (Eds.), *Italian studies on quality of life* (pp. 373–386). Springer Nature.

Mussino, A., de Oliveira, A. F. S., & Taffarel, C. N. Z. (2013). Il Diagnostico Nacional de Esporte e Lazer: conoscere per governare un Sistema sportivo. In *Rivista trimestrale di Scienza dell'Amministrazione,* n.1 Anno LVII, Milano, F. Angeli.

Rodgers, B. (1977). *Rationalising sports policies. Sport in its social context: International comparisons.* Council of Europe.

Scheerder, J. et al. (2011). *Understanding the game. Sport participation in Europe.* J.H. Mulier Institute.

World Health Organisation. (2007). *HEPA Europe*. WHO Regional Office for Europe.

World Health Organisation. (2015). *Physical activity strategy for the WHO European region 2016–2025.* WHO Regional Office for Europe.

Chapter 5
Football: No, Nothing Will Be As Before

Bruno Barba

5.1 The Darkest Days

The months of Spring 2020 have been tormented months. Months that we won't be given back any more, months we have we have spent discussing vital topics: health, economy, psychology—and in which we thought it was possible, perhaps desirable, to put aside the world of sport, as it is: conditioning, participated and personally experienced.

"There is something more important to worry about" many a person said such things, "how can sport matter when hundreds of people die every day?" We can understand such a point of view, in those days of dramatic emergency, but that did not consider a natural fact: life, not only shows, must go on. But sport is life.

Of course, there were moments when everybody's mind—not only of the many involved personally—was directed elsewhere; but the idea that sport is simply "people's opium" or "panem et circenses", besides being old-fashioned and ideologically connotated, does not consider the cultural role played, in the different contexts, by football, basketball, volleyball and baseball. Football has lost its central role, and has suffered from this, it has become precarious and marginal like all that was not hospitals, data about deaths, medical appliances, patients in intensive care units.

The aim of my modest contribution is "to put again" sport, or better football, in the centre of the debate, giving it the role it deserves; and it will deserve in a different world.

Here are then some considerations about football, that is to say the most relevant sport in the Italian context.

B. Barba (✉)
Dipartimento di Scienze Politiche, Università degli Studi di Genova, Genoa, GE, Italy
e-mail: salvatore.bruno.barba@unige.it

P. Corvo, F. M. Lo Verde (eds.), *Sport and Quality of Life*, Social Indicators Research Series 84, https://doi.org/10.1007/978-3-030-93092-9_5

The tragedy, the fears, the sad everyday data do not make us forget that man is the result of many identities, many desires, many passions. The idea that, when overwhelmed by circumstances, we have to lose something of our own self is misleading, besides being ethically and philosophically wrong. It is in the stimulus—like in the moment of performance (Turner, 1986)—that man finds his own self.

Nevertheless, between these two perceptions—is football useless or essential?—political and sports authorities and the related institutions responsible for deciding the beginning of activities have continued to disagree.

Football has demonstrated, once more, how clear is its function as "a total social fact" Mauss, 1923); how, as a cultural event, it perfectly represents the way a people represent themselves: to what extent it corresponds to a "model" (Benedict, 1934), and therefore it can accompany visions, perceptions and tensions of the society it refers to.

The end of football has been prophesied for a long time, giving reasons linked to structural limits, to excessive expenses, to the unsustainability of the system, to the transformation of a sport into a show. It was believed, then, that "internal phenomena would be responsible, but nobody imagined that it could be stopped by external phenomena. There was a moment when the football industry was on the point of collapsing. The loss of income deriving from television rights and the box offices have been a serious problem for the clubs' budgets, while the team members' salaries, above all for the big European teams, have become an item of expenditure difficult to sustain.

Apart from easy stereotypes, and "excesses of culture" (Aime, 2004) even during the emergency the Italian behaved like an... Italian. Disputing, taking sides, rekindling the old myth of "campanile".

There have been delays and contrasting opinions on the stopping of the competitions and trainings. We have seen the emerging of a structural characteristic of society—individualism, that is anarchy, the lack of power, the protection of personal interests, always diverging and competitive—and an equally congenital feeling: the fear of economic effects that cancelled games or games played without spectators may cause.

Everything considered, our pre-covid 19 society, perfectly expressed, even in the peculiar way of considering football, its own strong structural individualism, its own polemic vein, its own passion for finding a scapegoat, for "hate speech" and even for racism. "The interests of a faction prevail over the ones of the movement" said the ex-player Marco Tardelli "not even the pandemic was able to reunite the intentions of the various components. The players have not been consulted" (La Repubblica 30/05/2020). Then, it is true that closing down, in the darkest days of the pandemic, has obliged everyone to agree—it has taken weeks, but also the world of football, in mid-March, accepted the fact that the suspension of every activity was the best solution; but the debate is now on the way to reopen.

A certain positive signal, still talking of the economy, might be the one concerning the "reduction of salaries" and "of revenues". However it is, and contentions are certainly not over—starting to talk of "reduction" in a world such as the one of professional football, accustomed to "plus", to the exponential increasing of earnings, to multimillionaire contracts, to the pay of agents, is a very important step. Moreover, players benefit only if the system resists and if they get to a congruous and equal solution. A message to launch to people, to the supporters but not only them: "we, the people of football, we too are here".

To quote Umberto Eco (1964), the public opinion has divided as follows: the "apocalyptic" dreamers of a pure sport and so impossible to recreate, at least for a certain time, and the "integrated", convinced that, like the whole economy, also football should have started again. The latter, however, are aware that the "trade-off" between health and economy has not had and still has not an easy solution, not anywhere, nor in any context. While among the former, the apocalyptics, we must insert those groups of ultras who opposed the recovery of the championship without spectators: "behind closed doors is not football". As if life was not touching, walking in the streets with masks, avoiding the social contacts we used to have. "Put a good face on it" is an expression that sportsmen should know very well.

It is obvious that "unlocking", even though gradually, means also considering a sector so important, vital and meaningful. And this not only for the economy—in Italy football has a revenue of 4.8 billion euros, constituting 1% of GDP, every year it pays 1 billion 250 000 euros in taxes (70% of the revenue from the whole of Italian sport), four million people practise it, and thanks to its economic activity it has created employment for 300.000 people)—but also for what it represents for society. Many a person, in the boring if not dramatic and painful days of lockdown, would have liked the consolation of the victory of their beloved team, of a formidable enterprise of their champions, of a strong emotion, making them feel alive, or at least more alive...

If it is true that viruses have redesigned so many times the course of history, as Jared Diamond (1997) demonstrated, the future world will have to take into account some firm features that have accompanied mankind in the past. We are facing a "new experience of crisis" (Ostronoff & Bonato, 2020); a lot of our behaviour, a lot of attitudes, a lot of perceptions will change. We will have to "recreate the world", as Tim Ingold (2018) says. Also, our relationship with sport is going to change—we do not know to what extent but it will certainly do so. An epochal revolution is taking place both in the social field and in the sports field.

5.2 A Matter of Identity and Globalisation

Globalisation, which so many intellectuals from—to Khann (2020) to Zizek (2020)—have brought about, as hope, panacea or potential danger for the political and social transformations we are going to experience, accomplishes its obscure action in that perpetual laboratory we call football. Suggesting new and unusual behaviours, preparing global society for new scenarios. For example, as the economist Jeremy Rifkin states studying "new ways of behaving, education, work, social life, in order to continually maintain a safety distance one from the other" (2020,

p. 18). Is not football assuming such a posture, when we talk of distancing the referee, in the changing rooms, in everyday life, during the training.

The global stream itself has prepared us for a flexibility of behaviour, a quickness of change which in the pre-Covid era (do you remember when we used to plan everything?) was impossible to foresee.

And furthermore, considering the example of the German model, a "perfect machine" and the Bundesliga, the first European championship of a certain rank to start again after 15th May, could not we understand that "only cooperation, solidarity and a common effort can solve the problem. . . .?" (Harari, 2020, p. 67).

Anyway, in such an interconnected world, in which data move so quickly that we created the expression "in real time", another contradiction became evident. Even though we must recognize "that it is impossible to stop the rapid international spreading of new diseases, and the human networks for the potential infection are wide open"; every state, every sport association, even different teams of the same championship, chose to take different decisions.

These premises are useful to introduce a reflection, rather than (rhetorical) questions: could Italian football have "reacted" to the emergency as German football did, decisive and united? And above all how could Italian football—considered as a system, that is the whole of its components: teams, Associations, players, sports doctors—separate from the cultural milieu in which it is plunged, to which it belongs? The anthropologist Roberto DaMatta, referring to the function football has in Brazil, tells how this sport "allows a series of national matters to be expressed, alternating perceptions and intellectual elaborations with emotions and feelings really felt and experienced" (DaMatta, 1982, p. 40). Football is seen as a vehicle for the dramatization, ritualization and staging of Brazilian society. Just the same can be said of Italian football, vector of passions and emotions, amongst the most meaningful of immaterial heritages, always able to highlight peculiar interests. Are we or not the heirs of Guicciardini and Machiavelli?

Continuing with the theme "football and globalisation", once we referred to ideas, tactics, contributions of players and technicians from everywhere, of knowledge; today also of strategies to face the dangers of Covid. Every proposal, code of behaviour, protocol is the result of observation and exchange, that is of the reinterpretation each government and association have realized starting from the one elaborated by someone else. This is a perfect metaphor for the general cultural process: an "interpretative copy", phenomenon of transculturalization, a creative dynamic.

And the process of osmosis between football and culture works in another direction as well: it is not always easy to perceive in which direction we are going, whether towards homologation or extreme differentiation.

5.3 We Have Missed It So Much, Why It Is Right to Start Again

Sometime terrible catastrophes produce clear changes of direction, others are useful to reinforce pre-existing balances. Others to turn upside down certainties and balances of power.

We have survived, we got used to it. The long period of reflection could have better employed, as the great moments of crisis can be used by institutions to "reform". We need in every field, also in football, responsibility and imagination.

In those all alike, empty and repetitive days of March, April and May, besides memories, historical commemorations, it has been possible to reflect on football, the way it was and the way it is changing. As Lévi-Strauss states (1988), from a great distance we can observe details which we miss when we are near.

Football is going to become a ritual with new rules. More and more repetitive, able to suspend every day routines, so getting more and more a holiday time, notwithstanding difficulties.

Like in a tragic Carnival, today we witness a reversing of roles, of references. Doctors, trainers, cleaners, sanitization workers, even drivers, become if not more important than the players, that is those we have reputed to be the protagonists on the scene, at least as central and essential as them.

The abstinence was long and unusual, and we missed all of it: controversies, violent passions (not violence); tales (mythologies) and the heroes of that world. Even those who used to snob the sacred rituality of the weeks marked by the championship and Champions League missed it; in the same way we learned to give up other "profane rituals": no school trips, no journeys, graduations forbidden, interruption of sport events, the disappearing of "nightlife", and any other social habit which we were used to practising, "More time for ourselves", it was said: to read, to tidy up, to meditate. We even missed those essential factors of our national sport such as overexposure, the lack of balance. This year also the European Championships have been cancelled, we have lost one of those opportunities in which football presents itself in its most complete form: a factor of identity and inclusion, an expression of schools—that is to say football cultures—opportunities to teach or learn History, Politics and Geography. We all need this football: superfluous, futile, but so impassioning to make us love it and to push many people to consider it necessary. Like Theatre, Cinema, Literature and Art: a nourishment of our spirit.

Perhaps the emergency opened the eyes of many politicians, communicators, "insiders". Perhaps the various components in the world of football have realized that saying that the speed, frenzy, obtuseness we all use in our foolish race to towards self-destruction—of the planet, of environmental resources, of forms of sociality—was irremediably destroying also a world, that of sport, that many state to love, but few really respect. Football is recommencing for economic reasons—to get television rights- and for existential reasons: the return to normality, the restoration of a more "human" and solid football.

For sure the most cynical underline that for a long time a sort of diffuse and gigantic Daspo (the prohibition for supporters to go to the stadium) will last; that chairmen will obtain more money from selling rights to televisions, that nowadays the income from the sale of tickets are a marginal item in the society budgets. Many still mock the Germans, and the promoters of that solution proposed by the leadership of Borussia Monchengladbach, with the opportunity for their subscribers to see themselves reproduced on cardboards lined on the stadium stands. Others -the British, organised broadcastings, through an application, of choirs to incite the team.

Some think like Davide Ravan, young author of the most authoritative text on popular football (Ravan, 2019), that "ideally, the "tricolore" could be dedicated to the memory of the many, too many, victims of Covid-19. It would be a noble gesture, which would give football an aura of nobility it lost decades ago and that would help the whole world of football to gain credibility in the eyes of society, which does not follow football or has stopped following it. As a passionate fan, for such a decision, I would be willing to accept a whole year of closed stadiums and championships behind closed doors, because I would know that, in the end, I would subsidize again with my presence at the stadium a world made of Men. And not of unscrupulous schemers ready for any action to make money" (Ravan, 2020).

It might seem a matter of respect: here is another keyword of this future we are already living. Respect for one's profession, one's thinking, one's being. Yet, on the contrary, what other way do we know of "respecting" the dead, the memory, the extreme hardships we are facing if not being aware of one's role? Workers have done their duty going back to their factories, teachers engaging in remote teaching; football players can but go back to the football ground.

If it is true that in existential terms we will save ourselves if we can think we are a species, only one race, mankind as a whole; avoiding reasoning in terms of superiority, exclusion, prejudice; if we can put arrogance aside, and hatred, indifference for others and an irrepressible desire to consume; if we evaluate life's priorities and which gestures, which duties, which awareness to elicit; well, if all this is true also football must give its contribution.

5.4 And Now, Reflections On ….. "The Field"

Cold, not very exciting, disquieting: so many adjectives have been wasted to describe the reality we are cohabiting with. Then, what kind of entertainment is this "behind closed doors"? A remote exaltation, lifting elbows, a muffled atmosphere, ridiculously coloured with the supporters' cardboard shapes, those disinfected benches, those athletes sitting on the sidelines with masks on. . .images that only a few months ago we could have fancied reading a novel by Stephen King, or watching, paralysed by fear, a horror film. We could not save football from this surrealistic atmosphere with which we had to live in our street, in our cities, even in our homes, and for months.

No, "privilege" a word that has insistently returned in the storytelling, to underline how some milieu, like football, are an immoral and rare world, if anything it has had the opportunity of revealing itself through other factors: the frequent throat swabs, the continuous medical care, dramatically lacking for many "normal" people and with fatal results. Moreover the opportunity of training in perfectly endowed houses for so long a quarantine: gardens to train for shooting at the goal, true gymnasiums with advanced equipment. So, this is the umpteenth confirmation that many lucky players live in a sort of gilded word, not a cage. Even though the "democratic" pandemic has not saved players, leaders, and presidents.

During these months of discussions another important datum has emerged. Apart from some discordant voices, like Inter's ex-president Moratti, it was highlighted that it would have been really wrong to cancel great exploits, disappointments, eliminations, hopes, goals, in name of the rhetoric of let's cancel everything. In any field of our lives—work, affections, study, that is all our experiences—we could adopt this rule. Other sports, it is true, cancelled their season completely, in this case absolutely opposing the thesis of sports as an expression, a mirror, a lens and a model of society. But is football a metaphor for life or not?

This will be an anomalous season, exceptional in response to the emergency, but not "falsified": it would be so if we had changed the rules along the way. "The seasons—Russo confirms—must be completed whatever it takes, even if they should end in December" (Russo, 2020). Maybe we could discuss a lighter formula (with the introduction of Play-off and Play-out, for example) for the next championship "2020–2021", keeping in mind that the Quatar championship will take place in winter 2022 and that the European Championships have been planned for 2021 after this year's postponement. Obviously the rules must be clear and fixed before the competitions begin.

We also have to accept the idea that we could never eliminate our fears and anxiety about this virus or others. The so called "zero risk" does not exist when we get on a train or a plane, when we go around the suburbs of the metropolis, when we drive for long distances on motorways, when we live in one of the most polluted, developed and industrialized areas on the planet.

From this point of view, the restauration of normality occurred in May, trainings started again, first individually later collectively. These trainings were not aimed at reaching a result, a victory, but rather had an existential aim, if possible even higher: resurrection, the return to everyday life.

5.5 And Then. . . . A Renaissance

Football might become, with its blander and thus human rhythms, with its "dense" meanings (Geertz, 1973), that popular festival, which it had not been for many years: a hymn to the joy of renaissance to a newly found sportiness. The primary purpose of competitions will not only be "victory" but again amusement, making us feel alive and even solid. Telling us of a festival we need.

We have to change a lot of things, to eliminate superfluous and harmful ones (hatred, rancour); to renew something (passion), to make reforms, as someone put it.

As it has always happened in history, moments of renaissance alternate with violent crises. We ought to hope for not only a reduction of elite sport, but a radical reform including amateur football and above all the basic, juvenile one, which should also improve sport grounds. Once for all bureaucracy should be lessened, aiming at equal opportunities, taking up a way leading to professional female football, which has recently become appreciated. A virtuous circle will be activated so that the strongest will protect the weakest and even finance them. A utopia? Maybe, but only discovering again the value of cooperation which has helped man to survive any adversity, pestilence or conflict, could we really say we have won the battle. To sum up, a decisive step enabling us to overcome individualism and leaving room for noble thoughts, inside which the welfare of all, the social aspect of problems can be recognized. We wish that sense of community (Aime, 2019) we seemed to have lost could be restored and that also football needs. No one saves himself alone, never and nowhere.

Of course, football will remain a privileged observatory of reality; it could also become, after this terrible collective tragedy, a purified if not healed place; a new place, ennobled by the previous hardships. We cannot believe in a total reverse of our paradigm: but if it can improve society at least a little, it can do so even more for the world of sport. We must be visionary on this matter, in contrast with so much pessimism about man's destiny. Many ask, referring to our system of values: "and if normality was disease?"

No doubt a more "normal" football, on a human scale, less individualistic, that is to say more caring for the needs of all the members of the "caravan", and not protecting the corporate interests, a football system based on univocal strategies, shared decisions, of harmony among all the parts: little and big associations, associations and players, associations and supporters, too often considered "of little value" also during the pandemic. All this could really mark a rebirth of the whole movement.

For sure, under many aspects the world before had to be changed and this crisis can be seen (also) as an opportunity. But there is also the other side of the coin. There is the desire of many to return, 1 day, as soon as possible, to feel again those lost sensations, those tactile, visual even olfactory perceptions, those caresses and those exchanges we practised and later suspended. We must remember that our body is culture: social distancing is and always well be a "diminutive". Among the difficulties to face there is, in fact, the one of new bodily postures, also in football.

A sport of contact, football has always "related" cultures, identities and historical periods.

Today, restrained exultance, the physical block on the emotions relate a different reality; the "changing room"- summarising image which does not explain its importance and density—becomes an anonymous and sterilized place, permeated as it used to be, on the contrary, by the presence, by the almost tangible charisma, by the protagonists' smell; we must verify that football players are responsibly, consciously, obliged to maintain a different psychological approach, in an emergency situation. "I wish a return to where show and the sporting spirit can win at last over the aggressive use of an extreme sense of membership, over the territorial identification of the team almost as a tribal expression, and, even worse over the political and personalised exploitation. A sport in which, again, shaking hands at the beginning and at the end of the competitions, not only among athletes, but also among spectators can be the rule not the exception. In which sport is again a show and a symbol of progress of man towards himself, his own feeling, overcoming limitations, and not something to show, to wave and use "against" someone in the ephemeral illusion of a victory "forever" (Sbetti, 2020).

To conclude, we can say that we have at least, learned one thing: that technology offers opportunities and does not "oblige" us to behave in a predetermined way. If it is true that we have had to cope with live transmissions via Skype, remote teaching, interviews, or better, self-promotion of sportsmen through social media, it is also true we have missed "analogic communication" as well, that is necessary communication (Turkle, 2015).

Also, for the football storyteller new scenarios open. Jean-Charles Sabattier, a television commentator of BeIN Sports, Qatar colossus of television broadcasting based in France, referring to matches commentated "behind closed doors" has spoken of "an aquarium-like atmosphere, a dissonant one" (L'Equipe, 16/05/2020). According to him, it would be necessary considering these exceptional circumstances, to speak with a more sober tone.

When our national team won the European Championship in 1968, the World Championship in 1982 and in 2006, overcoming great moments of technical and moral crisis, and, after the death of a young player of the Fiorentina team, Astori, the football world seemed to find unity, solidarity, and in the media we could read the expression "a golden seed". It is the Renaissance. Going back in time, we remember Batali's and Grande Torino's enterprises: unforgettable sports enterprises, for the rebirth of a nation can but pass through sport, a sign of vitality, of joy of a new desire.

Unhappily, these proposals and intentions were unheeded, sometimes in a resounding way. I wonder whether this time from this tragedy, the strength to improve things will be found.

We return to play not to fail; against fears, to save minor football—among the various proposals—the idea of creating a "wages guarantee fund" for players with a salary of 50 000 euros before tax was successful: a solution favouring the second, and above all, third division, in very serious difficulties due to the lack of incomes; and, even more, for the sports press and for that whole world known as "insiders". They will play for Bergamo and all the cities which suffered so much. They will return to play for love.

There is an expression attributed to many—it is the destiny of the profoundest maxims—which says: "you either win or learn, you never lose". It echoes Kipling's equally famous one—"If you can meet with Triumph and Disaster and treat those two impostors just the same" (1895).

Let's hope everyone will learn something from this tragedy, so that this crisis has not been useless.

References

Aime, M. (2004). *Eccessi di culture*. Einaudi.

Aime, M. (2019). *Comunità*. il Mulino.

Benedict, R. (1934). *Patterns of culture*. Houghton Mifflin.

DaMatta, R. (1982). *Universo do futebol: esporte e sociedade brasileira*. Pinakotheke.

Diamond, J. (1997). *Guns, germs and steel. A short history of everybody for the last 13,000 years*. Jonathan Cape.

Eco, U. (1964). *Apocalittici e integrati: comunicazioni di massa e teorie della cultura di massa*. Bompiani.

Geertz, C. (1973). *The interpretation of cultures: Selected essays*. Basic Books.

Harari, Y. N. (2020). *Chiudersi è sbagliato, serve una solidarietà globale*. In AA.VV. Il mondo che sarà. *Il futuro dopo il virus* (pp. 63–71). Gedi.

Ingold, T. (2018). *Anthropology. Why it matters*. Polity Press.

Khann, P. (2020). *Dopo il virus nascerà una globalizzazione regionale*. In AA.VV. Il mondo che sarà. *Il futuro dopo il virus* (pp. 31–37). Gedi.

Kipling, R. (1895/1910). *Rewards and fairies*. Macmillan and Co.

Lévi-Strauss, C. (1988). *De près et de loin*. Odile Jacob.

Mauss, M. (1923). *The Gift*. Cohen e West.

Ostronoff, L. J., & Bonato, M. (2020). *Brasil-Italia: Reflexões sociologicas da quarantena*. Le Monde Diplomatic ed.

Ravan, D. (2019). *Il calcio è del popolo. Geografia del calcio popolare in Italia*, Bepress.

Ravan, D. (2020). *Il ballo della ripartenza. Ovvero partire o stare fermi un giro*, La notiziasportiva.com. Retrieved from DIALOG. https://www.lanotiziasportiva.com/il-ballo-della-ripartenza-ovvero-partire-o-stare-fermi-un-giro/

Russo, P. (2020). *Il coronavirus sta facendo implodere il calcio*, rivista Contrasti. Retrieved from DIALOG. www.rivistacontrasti.it/coronavirus-calcio-pippo-russo-campionato-serie-a/

Sbetti, N. (2020). *Il pallone di fronte al Coronavirus*, rivista il Mulino, Retrieved from DIALOG. https://www.rivistailmulino.it/news/newsitem/index/Item/News:NEWS_ITEM:5108

Turkle, S. (2015). *Reclaiming conversation. The power of talk in a digital age*. Penguin Press.

Turner, V. (1986). *The anthropology of performance*. Paj Publications.

Zizek, S. (2020). *Vedo un nuovo comunismo germogliare dal virus*. In AA.VV. Il mondo che sarà. *Il futuro dopo il virus* (pp. 73–79). Gedi.

Part II
Italian Cases

Chapter 6
Urban Sport Population: How the Sporting Habits Have Changed

Fabio Massimo Lo Verde and Vincenzo Pepe

The theory of urban populations (D'Ovidio & Nuvolati, 2011; Martinotti, 1993) and their classification are a consolidated theme of sociology that has contributed to deepening the sociology of lifestyle studies. More generally, the study of the sport in the city constitutes an essential area of knowledge of the change in urban lifestyles, whether you are talking about sports or talking about enjoying the sports show (Gratton & Henry, 2001; Wilcox et al., 2003)

More recently, studies have focused not on the relationship between cities and sporting events as on urban planning in relation to the demand for space for sports practices (Sam & Hughson, 2013). However, no studies analyze the relationship between the city and the new configurations of urban populations who play sports. Many urban people of sportspeople we meet in all towns not only in the western world. In these chapters, we analyze three of these: runners, cyclists, and skateboarders.

How do they live the urban space recoded as a space for their physical and spiritual well-being? How do they relate to the different functions with which the urban spaces they use were born? How do they intervene in the planning processes of space aimed at psychophysical well-being? How do they organize their "demand for sport functionality"? And how they relate to urban space technologies?

F. M. Lo Verde (✉)
University of Palermo, Palermo, Italy
e-mail: fabio.loverde@unipa.it

V. Pepe
Department of Economics, Business and Statistics, University of Palermo, Palermo, Italy
e-mail: vincenzo.pepe@unipa.it

P. Corvo, F. M. Lo Verde (eds.), *Sport and Quality of Life*, Social Indicators Research Series 84, https://doi.org/10.1007/978-3-030-93092-9_6

6.1 Urban Sports Population: The Rise of a New Citizen?

A structural difference highlights the distance between the urban and social aesthetics that characterize cities in advanced economies and cities in developing countries. It is not a question of signs of development or underdevelopment commonly recognized as 'perceptible' (orderly traffic versus disorderly traffic, well-paved roads versus bad roads, spaces characterized by order and cleanliness, to quote Freud, versus spaces characterized by disorder and dirt, silent spaces versus noisy spaces and, above all, spaces with breathable air versus spaces with unbreathable air, and much more). Instead, it is the presence or absence of spaces and paths that show how the protection and health and the psychophysical well-being of the people living in that city are considered an object of public interest. This is one of the four pillars that characterize urban life's space according to the functionalist approach that Le Corbusier wanted to give, for example. At the end of the 30s, in the well-known Athens Charter: living, working, recreation and circulation were the pillars that characterized cities' lives and the main functions that it had to perform at its best. The separation of house and street, the visible distinction between residential and office buildings, the separation of spaces for private and public transport and pedestrian traffic, the presence of greenery spaces, cultural enjoyment, etc., were to be the tangible signs of this citizen-oriented functionality.

Since the city became a place of mass production and consumption, within these pillars of urban life, the different figures of the metropolitan population emerge. But while in the modern city, the nineteenth and above all twentieth century city, centred around the Fordist production system, the dimension of production tends to override that of consumption and, therefore, of recreation, generating metropolitan lifestyles and profiles around production itself (office workers, workers, service workers, etc.) who occupy spaces mainly as places of transit to reach the city. In the city of consumption, the postmodern city is centered on the post-Fordist system of production. The dimension of consumption (Saunders, 1981), understood above all as aesthetic enjoyment and recreation, overrides display. Urban spaces no longer become places of transit between home and work, but places of happiness according to an aesthetics of space that gives places the meaning of 'spaces of enjoyment, recreation, fruition, and pleasure. Multi-functionality then becomes the connotation of spaces: from places of transit to places of recreation, in a continuous circle of functions whose regulating system is time. In other words, how the effects of the organization of the 'city timetable' are articulated.

Within the modern city spaces, the flows of different metropolitan populations cross (Martinotti, 1993; Nuvolati, 2006)—residents, commuters, city users, businessmen. And each of these types uses the city more or less in the function of production or consumption. The former reside there and create flows of movement 'within' the city, from home to work. Quantitatively they remain the majority in many cities of the world. As a United Nations report (2019) points out,

Table 6.1 Tourism destination cities (2019)

Rank	City	Total international visitors	Rank	City	Total international visitors
01	Bangkok	22.78MM	11	Seoul	11.25MM
02	Paris	19.10MM	12	Osaka	10.14MM
03	London	19.09MM	13	Makkah	10.00HM
04	Dubai	15.93MM	14	Phuket	9.89MM
05	Singapore	14.67MM	15	Pattaya	9.44MM
06	Kuala Lumpur	13.79MM	16	Milan	9.10MM
07	New York	13.60MM	17	Barcelona	9.09MM
08	Istanbul	13.40MM	18	Palma de Mallorca	8.96HM
09	Tokyo	12.93MM	19	Bali	8.26HM
10	Antalya	12.41MM	20	Hong Kong SAR	8.23MM

Source, *Global Destination Cities Index 2019*, https://newsroom.mastercard.com/wp-content/uploads/2019/09/GDCI-Global-Report-FINAL1.pdf

> In 2018, 1.7 billion people—23% of the world's population—lived in a city with at least one million inhabitants. In 2030, a projected 28% of people worldwide will be concentrated in cities with at least one million inhabitants

The quality of life and subjective well-being are, for this category, a function of individual conditions and the supply of services for recreation and leisure appropriate to articulating the needs they feel as "citizens."

Commuters, the second group, are those who travel daily from 'outside the city' because they live in metropolitan areas or the nearest hinterland, or in another city close enough to allow commuting. Eurostat tells us that in Europe

> 8.1% commuted to work in a different region. Outbound commuter flows in the EU-28 can be divided into two separate groups: national commuters accounted for 7.2% of the total number of persons employed, while less than 1 in 100 people (0.9% of the EU-28 workforce) commuted across borders (Eurostat, 2018).

Well-being and evaluation of the quality of life are linked to the travel conditions they undertake daily, their duration, the state of the vehicles they use, and the quality of other interconnecting services between their places (Chatterjee et al., 2020). Above all by the city's capacity to which they travel to adequately 'welcome' them daily.

The third consists of leisure travelers, tourists, guests, and those who enjoy the city as a place of relaxation aesthetics typical of "visitors."

According to the Global Destination Cities Index 2019, the report compiled by Mastercard, the 20 most visited cities by travelers from all over the world are, for the most part, in Asia, although in second and third place are two European cities (Table 6.1).

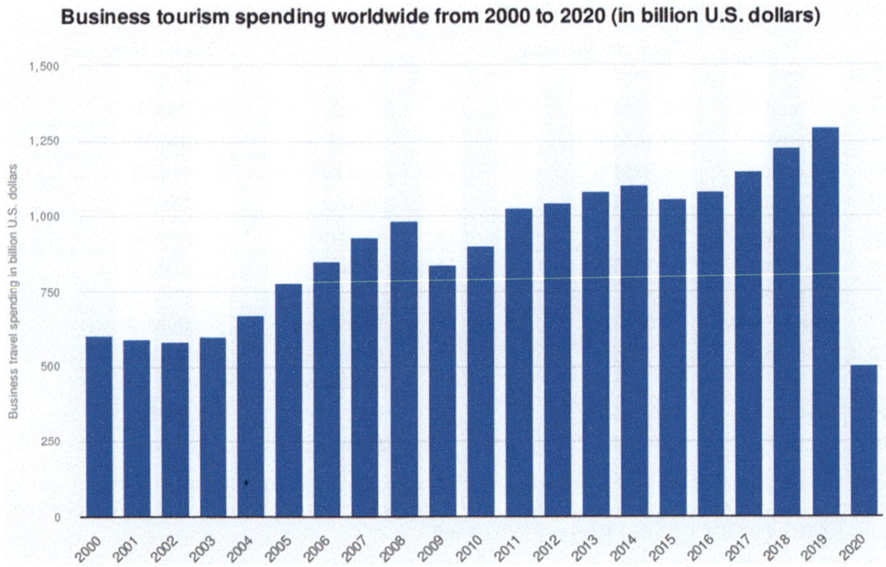

Graph 6.1 Business Worldwide Tourism. Source, Statista, 2020, https://www.statista.com/statistics/1093295/business-travel-spending-worldwide/

City users are the population that seeks amenities, territorial and cultural attractions in cities, and services for tourists and, overall, a city offer oriented towards consumption and fruition. Subjective well-being and quality of life take on a different connotation, more centered on the 'exceptionality' of the travel experience than on the security provided by everyday life's ordinariness.

And, finally, the businessmen, those who see and use little of the city except during work breaks. They are the temporary colonizers of the places of production and the transit spaces towards production places. Increasingly present in the world's major cities, they are represented by global managers who have a detached but attentive relationship with the aesthetic and usable spaces of the city.

The demand for city service of Business travelers is different because of the additional requirements. It includes convenience, value for money, high-speed internet, loyalty schemes, complimentary breakfasts, and more. Activities often included in business travel are meetings, exhibitions and/or business events. In 2019, global business tourism spending reached 1283 billion U.S. dollars (Graph 6.1).

In many cases now, and especially for Millennials, business travel is mixed with leisure time, giving rise to the so-called "bleisure" or "bizcations" trip. The growing percentage of trips that take on this characteristic, especially among Millennials, would highlight the "life satisfaction curve" (peaking at 46 years of age) (Graph 6.2).

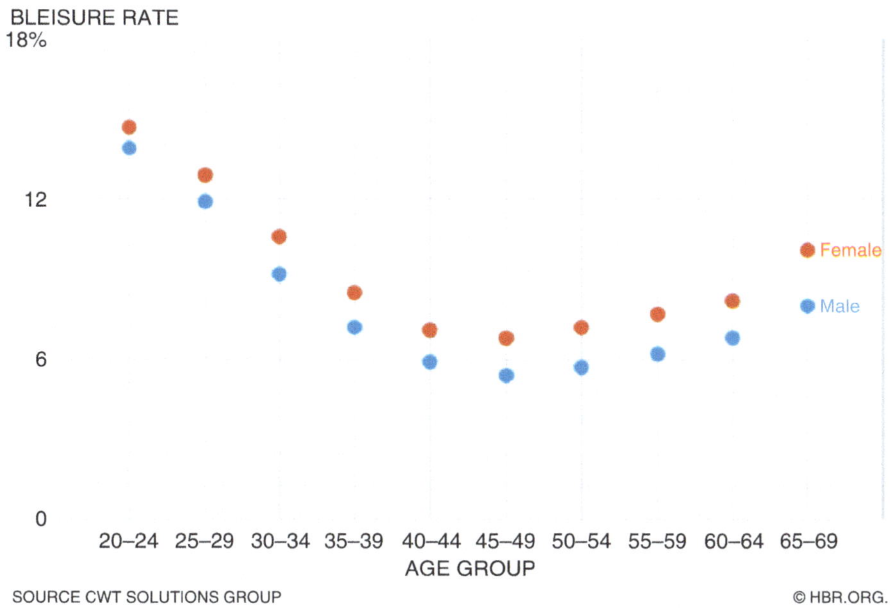

Graph 6.2 Work and Vacation (Age). Source, Harvard Business Review, https://hbr.org/2016/09/how-many-people-really-combine-work-trips-with-vacation

And the farther they go, the more they'll bleisure and, of course, in the cities of the world overall (Graph 6.3).

To these, Nuvolati (2006) adds the population of flâneurs, the "loiterers" in transit.

[They live] with significant interests of direct knowledge and integration with the urban territory and its inhabitants (Nuvolati, 2006, p. 153).

They are artists, intellectuals, researchers who, unlike businessmen. They have interests that lead them to "integrate" into the local context. And they get to know it with a tendency to move according to serendipity in the choice of places and relations, with a marked desire to "lose themselves" in the city, slowly scouring the territory, far from the rhythms of efficiency, production, or consumption. And they are certainly growing in numbers among the populations of the world's cities.

But new metropolitan populations have emerged since the 1980s, indicating the change in daily life in postmodern consumer cities. They are the result of a cultural trend that combines several macro-trends in action that are declined in the lifestyles of the urban middle class: the growth of the demand for psychophysical well-being, health protection, the defense of an ecologically compatible urban lifestyle, safety, and individual control of one's own life and the space in which one lives, participation and protection of common goods and public space. But also of healthy leisure, playful, environmentally friendly, and rewarding, 'functional' to the efficient rationality of urban life and fun.

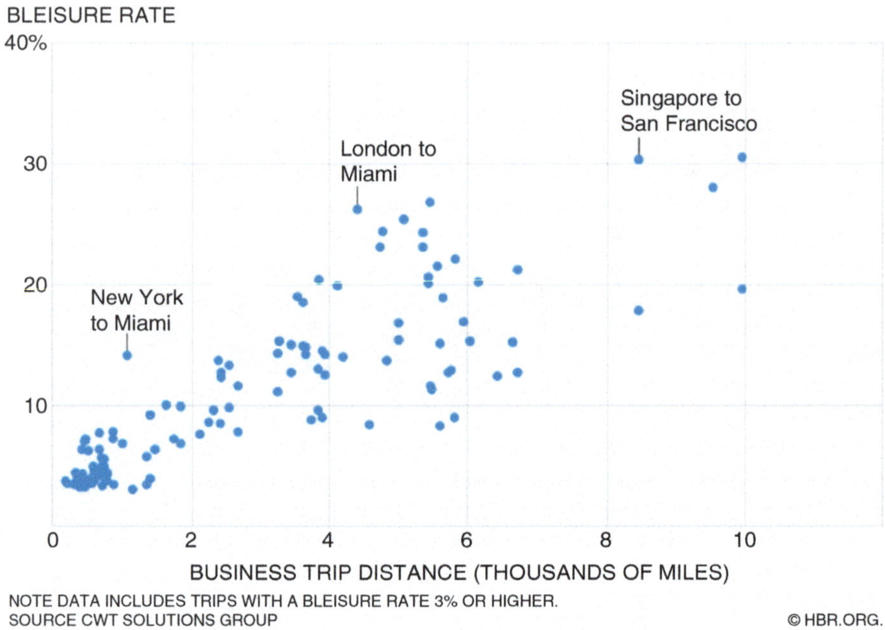

Graph 6.3 Work and vacation (trip distance). Source, Harvard Business Review, https://hbr.org/2016/09/how-many-people-really-combine-work-trips-with-vacation

To use free time, not to waste it, to invest it in recreational activities that generate well-being for the mind and body and that, at the same time, can allow a light sociality (amicability) and, sometimes, ephemeral, but fun, occasional or situational, but that can also be cemented through the activities of serious leisure (Stebbins, 2002), such as amateur sports practice.

Cultivating public space as a place for recreation understood as aimed at subjective growth and the search for meaning, as a sophisticated articulation of the principle of accumulation and efficient productivism that connotes neoliberalism but declined as a practice that increases subjective experiential capital. The accumulation of amateur sporting success also constitutes this. And so, urban public space becomes the arena of performance competition with oneself, rather than competition with others, except occasionally. But, most of the time, without competition.

At the same time, space becomes an object of continuous attention and rediscovery in the everyday life of the urban middle class, which has learned to protect it through its de-standardized form of individual production: the practice of sport as a compensatory anti-stress activity, as an activity to prolong the acquisition of success, as an activity to cultivate sociability, as an activity to make political participation or peaceful public resistance.

The new metropolitan sporting population looks at urban space by measuring distances in terms of the number of steps and walking times, the difficulty or ease of routes, the walkability of floors and the percentage of the slope of inclined planes, the height and availability of walls to climb or obstacles to climb over. And it is this measurement that translates the concept of subjective well-being and quality of urban life. Although, based on the sporting activity they practice, they differ in gender, age, educational qualification, profession, and position in work. They are all sportsmen and women who are keen on measurement—of distances, travel times, etc.—or attracted by the numbers linked to the sporting activity they practice. In other words, they are attracted by the numbers related to the measurable response that comes from their body and mind (quantitative self), which gives rise to their measurable "subjective well-being."

They are male and female, very young, young people and adults. They have the most diverse professional profiles. They belong to social circles whose social stratification is just as varied, and they are differently educated. But they are all 'sporty,' fit, environmentally friendly, healthy, nature-loving. And sometimes they are transgressive, no-logo, anti-system, and borderline from a law-abiding point of view. However, they all love the city's spaces at certain times of the day and/or night, according to a chronotopia that depends on the type of sport they practice. And they are now present in all western cities. They are *runners*, *cyclers*, *skaters*, and *traceurs*.

6.2 Urban Spaces, Sport, Well-Being

From a sociological perspective, we can analyze the sports population as social actors who interact with space. But, as Satta and Scandurra claim (2015, p. 231), more generally Social actors do not move in a space-time vacuum but are in a *constant dialectical relationship* with space (*ibidem*, italics ours).

In our opinion, in some cases, as in that of skaters or tracers, this "dialectical relation" with space is the result of a continuous mediation between body, space and techniques for controlling body in the space. And this "mediation" contributes not only to build different ways of interacting with urban space, but also to build different forms of appropriation of space. This different "appropriation" can assume both the "predatory" characteristics, typical of those who exclusively *use* the space, and the characteristics of "care," distinctive of those who *cultivate* and *protect* the space. In this second case, we can speak of a new form of recognition of urban space, which translates into a different awareness of the right to belong as a citizen actor. This actor *produces* urban space and its collective sense, making it more suitable for one's own and collective well-being.

In their seminal paper, Satta and Scandurra argue that urban sports activities are not reducible to simple physical activities because, through sports activities, canons of corporeality/subjectivity are built and rebuilt to define which bodies may legitimately occupy public space and which are to be excluded or marginalized.

Sociological reflections about this topic have had a significant contribution thanks to Henry Lefebvre's works in 1974.

Lefebvre reconstructed a sort of "social history" of space linked to the idea that every type of space, including urban space, reflects the lifestyle of the society that insists on it, especially by observing its system of production (Lefebvre, 1974, IX). Indeed, in its reconstruction, space itself, like time, becomes a mode through which the mode of production is declined. And so we can say that there is a history of space understood as a product of the different systems of production (ibidem, XXII). Following Lefebvre's reasoning, we can say that space becomes an element of appropriation and domination, a factor of conflict, mediation, rights claimed or denied, of "control", and escape from the control of bodies in space. No more and no less than other containers in which social actors' daily lives are articulated, space "produces" and "reproduces" social distance and proximity, social inequality and equality, cohesion, and conflict. All of these conflict areas appear in a "spatialized" form precisely because of the articulation of daily social life in space. And in a particular way in urban space. It is in this space that social differences are articulated. In this space, certain practices are "allowed" and "forbidden" to use Lefebvre's image. And, we would add, the "control" of space, as well as its domination, is what constitutes the articulation of the power of reproduction of a social order that becomes the legitimate order.

As argued many years ago by Lepetit et al. (1993)

> Reconstructing the practiced spaces (space is to be understood sometimes in a topographical sense, sometimes metaphorically, sometimes in both senses) that are at the origin of the spatial categories made their own by the actors or mobilize them is a methodological imperative.

Lefebvre distinguishes, as we know, between perceived space, conceived space, and experienced space. There are therefore the "representations of space", the result of relations of production, which impose an "order", what, in the terminology coined by Bourdieu, we might call a "field"—which is a cognitive, sign-like, codifying order, which Lefebvre calls "of frontal relations" (ibid., p. 53). It is the space conceived by technicians and space scientists, town planners, engineers, architects. The strategically "conceived," "cut" space is what he calls the "dominant" space in a society, which is what we are interested in analyzing here concerning the space produced, on the other hand, by those who inhabit it daily, those who act in it.

In our hypothesis, this aspect generates a shared «semanticisation» of space; what intervenes in the attribution of meaning to that space, in terms of shared semanticisation, is the practice that is carried out in it, as in the case of sports practice.

To analyze how the dynamics of the decision-making process concerning the granting and prohibition of spaces, for example, becomes a sociologically relevant element for observing the relationship with the space of metropolitan sports populations. In particular, it is necessary to observe the relationship between the space "cut" according to the logics that provide for certain uses and the representation that these populations have of that space as a "place for practice".

Alongside this tripartition, as is well known, Lefebvre posits the concept of "spatial practice", that is, how a society produces and presupposes its space. In this key of interpretation, it is in our opinion that we have to imagine space as an environment that can be despoiled; that is, that can be taken care of with the practices of urban life, especially with that carried out in the time away from work. The cared-for space—that is, a space that is cared for because one feels it to be the space in which one lives intensely, with the attention of those who want to protect its health—is representative, again in the sense in which Lefebvre says. It is a space in which the "symbolisms in space" take on importance, the signs that constitute that part of space that is constituted in the imagination of those who, for example, live the city following a vision that is not the "official" one—that of "conceived" space.

The "representative spaces" that we intend to analyze due to the relationship between sporting practice—which is the practice in space—and constitutes a bodily way of occupying space and the spatial representations that metropolitan sporting populations have.

Alongside the spaces "cut" according to the logic of production, the spaces that we can define as "norm-constituted", which echo their connotation in functionalist terms, constructed according to a logical think oriented towards what can be ordered and controlled, there are, however, "counter-spaces", again to quote Lefebvre, whose construction is the result of the entire social construction of meaning. It is the result of practices implemented by social actors that produce different meanings.

These are the spaces constructed by the different subcultures formed precisely concerning that space (an example is the 'space' of nightlife). These are "counter-spaces", again to use Lefebvre's terminology, in which expressive, "creative" practices can be articulated, which use that space as an environment with which to interact for the realization of a creative project in which, for example, the body intervenes as a means of artistic poiesis itself; or, on the contrary, in which practices of use of that space are articulated from an oppositional point of view with respect to that established by the times and modes of production and organization aimed at efficient functionality. The process of legitimizing the meanings that spaces take on is always the result of collective action. Instead of legitimization through the uses, a community of individuals/bodies makes of space that this becomes a place. Suppose it is true, in fact, that a place can take on subjective meanings (think of what the places of one's childhood, one's youth, or the places of one's daily life, etc. take on when one is far from home, etc.), on the other hand. In that case, when these spaces become places of collective memory, their meaning changes, taking on a characteristic that can be assimilated, for example, to that of the 'commons', which are such insofar as they are "places of collective memory". And the presence of regulations governing access to the 'commons', i.e., the presence of places accessible to the community for public recreation, was one of the revolutions that gave rise to the democratization of leisure, which improved the quality of life and increased individual and collective well-being in cities.

At the end of the nineteenth and the beginning of the twentieth century, for example, the industrialization of culture, and therefore also of sport and leisure practices, completely changed part of the economy of the city, increasing the demand and supply of leisure services during the phase of industrial expansion in many countries. Again with Lefebvre, we could say that how the economy has been

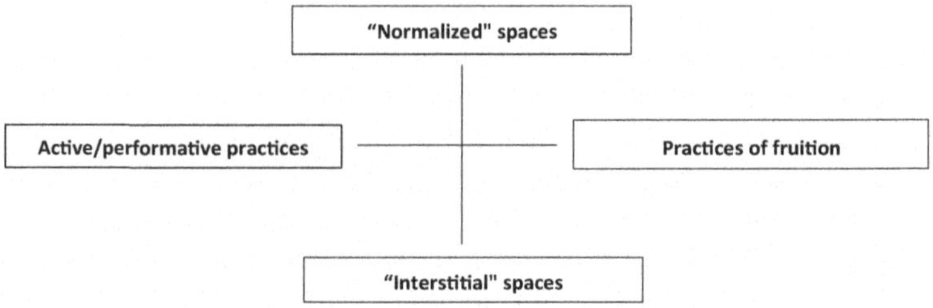

Fig. 6.1 Schematization of spaces (by Authors)

'spatialized' has changed since then. And the spatialization of the work-leisure relationship has changed, repositioning the social functions and symbolic value of some of the leisure activities whose demand was charged with meanings, including political ones, to becoming a demand for social rights.

Similarly, the absence of regulations governing access to the commons, i.e., the lack of such places to practice sport, significantly reduces the perception of well-being concerning the assessment of the quality of life, as has been amply demonstrated.

If we want to schematize, we could imagine a space that can take on connotations that are polarised concerning strategically or socially constructed dimensions (Fig. 6.1).

We can then identify a space that is the "norm-constituted" space, which is functional to the city's need for spatial and temporal order, corresponding to the Lefebvre's conceived space. The places in this space live out the productive, recreational, and mobile geometries and synchronize the city. Opposed to this, however, is the space that De Certeau would define as "interstitial". It is the space obtained from use, the space experienced outside the functional order for which it was conceived, both in a "physical" sense—as in the use of a space that had another function, now unused—and in a symbolic meaning—a new use superimposed (Tumminelli, 2010) on the normal one. From our point of view, the production and reproduction of space—in the triple description of which Lefebvre says—concerns both the mutation of meaning that bodies assume in their relationship with urban space through processes of legitimation offered by the different possibilities of use of spaces; and, conversely, the mutation of meaning that places assume through the uses that are made of the body in those places. In the same dimension, but in an opposite symbolic field, we find the interstitial spaces, those "counter-spaces" or spaces far from the norm-constitution of official planning. These include all those spaces that take on a symbolic value reconstituted based on spontaneous cultural codifications, often forgotten, abandoned, or simply differently used or not used, and "oppose" the very idea of a norm-constituted order.

Therefore, this polarisation is contrasted by the other, inherent in the practices implemented by the different urban populations, but specifically by sportsmen and women. Practices can be articulated in the use of spaces, enjoying, for example, the amenities in which a place is located. It is a way of using space that we might consider active but not transformative in symbolic terms; on the other hand, we find practices in the form of performative activity, a dynamic and transformative form of spaces in symbolic terms. The bodily dimension and the interaction between body, space, and social identity change considerably if we analytically imagine the four quadrants of the different sports populations.

The theory of practices was introduced in sociology by Pierre Bourdieu's work and subsequently taken up and deepened in the works of other authors [Reckwitz, 2002; Schatzki et al., 2001, Warde, 2005]. As it is known, to overcome the dilemmas existing in sociological theory between structuralism /constructivism, structure/ agency, macro/micro, holism/individualism, Bourdieu introduces the concept of "practice" considering it as the articulation of routine actions incorporated into those that he defines "social fields". With "social field" he means universes or microcosms in which actors and institutions are integrated and interact with each other on the basis of specific rules that apply to that specific field. In Reckwitz's words, which distinguishes between *praxis* and practices, meaning with the first human action opposed to thought

> a 'practice' (Praktik) is a routinized type of behavior which consists of several elements, interconnected to one another: forms of bodily activities, forms of mental activities, 'things' and their use, a background knowledge in the form of understanding, know-how, states of emotion and motivational knowledge [Reckwitz cit., 249]

The field constitutes, in Bourdesian theory, the space of "structure". But even in the field, rules are not formalized: they are implicit rules, which need to be "internalized" by social actors to demonstrate the implementation of *modalities of actions* that, as such, take on the connotation of *appropriate* strategies for the actors who interact in that specific field. With the theory of practices, we then introduce a new concept of the consumer seen no longer as "sovereign" concerning "discrete" choices regarding consumption—purchasing decisions—but as an individual who uses a cultural repertoire that reproduces itself in the daily routine, continuously regenerating its social meaning. However, the *flow* and the *sequence* of actions are more important than the discrete act as the effect of a decision. Therefore, the *disposition* more than the *decision*, the awareness and the practical conscience rather than the final deliberation, ends with the choice of space and the "strategy of sportive action". It is, therefore, the action that predominates over thought, the material dimension over the symbolic one, the "bodily" practical competence rather than the "theoretical" competence [Warde cit., 286].

In short, the sporting activity analyzed as practice, which is what metropolitan sporting populations have in common, legitimizes, through the use of the body, the meaning assumed by places, reconfiguring action and places into a new object of identity reflection. More specifically, the practice of sport legitimizes the change in the meaning of places, constructing a narrative that is often different from the one given by the official urban reading. The space in which the practice takes place becomes a space that evokes, above all, well-being, health, creativity, performance, but also self-realization, authenticity, and freedom as values.

This narrative has spread further through the practice of sharing different moments of use of space via social media. The other space, social media space, welcomes and reproduces narration to share.

Runners and joggers, as well as cyclists, can be placed among those who implement active practices of space use but not transformative: they use ordinary spaces because, for example, they were designed for them or because they are easily accessible for those who do that type of sport—tree-lined streets with limited traffic or low urban traffic intensity, city paths in green areas, etc. On the other hand, skaters and tracers, as well as children playing football in a square or a street, or clandestine tango dancers in night-time squares, can be placed among those who carry out active practices with a robust transformative content of the space on a symbolic level: they act in the space by modifying its meaning of use as well as the use itself, the original destination, declining their performative activities that make that space a space of practices, but also of spectacular fruition of a performance. None of us linger to watch runners or cyclists doing their sporting activities: but we do stay to watch skaters or tracers, tango dancers, or kids playing football. And their use of space is counter-intuitive, counter-spatial even, to quote Lefebvre. The former tend to use mainly "normalized spaces". The latter tend to use primarily "interstitial spaces".

We ask ourselves the cognitive questions: how does this process of attribution and change of meaning of spaces occur? How does the process of "appropriation" take place? How do the spaces practiced by sporting populations become places whose access and use take on the connotation of a right, both in the form of a demand for space for articulating a right of citizenship and a demand for the restoration of an inhibited space? And finally, can we say that it is a citizenship right whose presence improves—or whose absence worsens—the quality of life? And so can the demand for these spaces be read as a demand for sports services to improve the quality of life?

6.3 Runners: Running for Oneself, Running with Oneself

In a book published 5 years ago (Scheerder, Breedveld, Borgers, eds., Scheerder et al., 2015), the President of European Athletics reminds us that researchers speak of "first and second running waves" and even a running 'tsunami'. Observing the last 25 years, people who practice jogging not only for enjoying but also to participate in more or challenging "races" increased considerably.

Every day, from dawn until the early hours of the morning, or during the lunch break, or even at the end of the day, and especially at weekends, in all the cities of the world, we can see groups of people or individuals jogging through the city in shorts and running shoes, at a fast pace, often with music playing through their headphones, another essential accessory. Thirty or forty years ago, not only very few people jogged. Those who did jogging were considered 'oddballs', perhaps victims of some obsession or some personality trait that was sometimes perceived as worrying. Or

Fig. 6.2 Runners participate in a marathon. Source https://www.istockphoto.com

professional sports champions forced to train in all conditions. In any case, people who had time to waste.

Today, we are accustomed to regularly seeing—not only in parks and gardens, but also among cars, busy roads, and crowded pavements—droves of joggers running around us to keep up the pace. They jump over obstacles and dodging between people, sometimes meeting our not-so-astonished gaze as we observe in their faces an expression somewhere between tired and ascetic.

And indeed, initially, running originated as an activity aimed at the athletic preparation of professional athletes (Bale, 2004) and extracurricular school activity (Scheerder et al., 2015, p. 1). No one was 'rushing' unless they were in a hurry. It would be the cultural revolution of the 1960s—and especially the 1970s—that would change the whole dynamic of recreation in public space precisely because of the decreasing formality of social action in the public sphere that would enable this spread (ibid.).

The de-institutionalization of sporting practice, coinciding with a slow process of spreading the centrality of sport in the everyday life of contemporary societies, has led to an increase in both joggers and runners. That is, both of sportsmen and women who like to run to 'keep fit', to distract themselves, to get rid of stress and, in short, to have fun; and of those who instead run because they want to take part in the city running competitions organized by the various sports federations. But always in their spare time.

Some authors identify two different phases of the spread of running as a leisure activity in urban areas (Scheerder et al., cit.) (Fig. 6.2):

> First, no longer was running only practiced on a private track and field court, but also along the public road. Afterward, road running—but also running in other public spaces, such as a park or wood—became more popular among less competitive runners, meaning that track and field running lost its monopoly (*ibidem*, p. 2).

It was the beginning of the spread of what was to become a fitness culture, involving runners who wanted to become professional athletes and joggers who had no intention of competing but just wanted to cultivate their hobby. And they would do this by keeping fit and doing their activity 'when they wanted and where they wanted', the first example of how leisure sport would be de-institutionalized (Lo Verde, 2014).

The 1960s–1970s were thus the period of the first wave of running.[1] Some athletes, authors of jogging books—Jim Fixx, Bob Anderson, Bill Rodgers—became gurus for amateur runners. In 1970, running was declared sport of the year by a well-known Chicago newspaper (Scheerder et al., cit., p. 3). As happens with every practice that spreads in free time as a mass practice, this too was intercepted by the market, which immediately saw it as an important business area. This area consisted of the various segments of the production chain, starting with the production of the necessary equipment, first and foremost footwear.

In the 1980s, running became the sport best suited to the 'urban rhythms' of the Yuppies (ibid.), the up-and-coming young people who populated American cities. And it also began to spread, albeit more slowly, in European cities where fitness culture was beginning to spread, emancipating young people from the *maximalist ideologies* that reproduced an idea of the body as a 'prison of the soul'. In this prison, one had to take little interest either because it was unimportant for realizing an authentic life oriented towards the cultivation of the spirit, as in the religious vision; or because it was trivial for a life whose objective had to be the acquisition of class consciousness. However, in the European capitals, as in the U.S. capitals, city marathons began to be organized to attract many runners. And, above all, many joggers (Fig. 6.3).

The first wave ended in the early 1990s (ibid.), while the second wave began in the late 1990s when jogging

> can no longer be defined from a cultural or health perspective only. As a dominant part of our daily lifestyles, the running phenomenon is a multifaceted picture, including cultural, social, health-oriented as well as economic dimensions (*ibidem*, p. 6).

The features of this second wave are fascinating for our work. While the first wave was characterized by male and young runners' presence, women were excluded from marathons until the early 1970s. It was not until the 1984 Los Angeles Olympics that the women's marathon was introduced—the second wave of joggers also included young women.

[1] Robert Zemeckis' amusing stunt well illustrated that the 1960s–1970s was the period of popularity of running in the film Forrest Gump (1994), which seems to underline this with subtle irony. The protagonist runs from one part of the United States to another for about a year and a half. And during his run, he gathers several affiliates who follow him without knowing why he is doing so. And the exciting thing is that he does not know the reason either. Somehow, without meaning to, Forrest Gump, and especially running, represented the counterculture that was spreading in those years and that saw in "breaking the rhythms of production" but introducing rhythms that were just as tiring and demanding for other purposes the definition of a new social destiny for humankind

Fig. 6.3 Joggers during a workout. Source https://www.istockphoto.com

For the identification of the number of participants in this activity, it is complicated to know its size for various reasons: many runners or joggers are not registered in any platform or club, many have a low constancy in the activity, many do not participate in competitions that require the registration of participants, etc. In any case, to bring an example that highlights the number of practitioners, we can recall some data regarding participation in a running activity in the USA provided by the Outdoor Participation Report[2] of 2018[3] and 2019.

The trend shows a significant increase from 2006 to 2017 but indicates a more general interest in outdoor exercise, both among runners (Graph 6.4) and walkers (Graph 6.5).

6.3.1 Running Business

The business-related to running has increased considerably since those years and steadily. In particular. Running equipment, shoes, t-shirts, shorts, etc., determine the

[2]https://cdn.ymaws.com/www.americancanoe.org/resource/resmgr/general documents/2018_outdoor_recreation_part.pdf

[3]The survey was conducted by IPSOS and a weighting technique was used to balance the data to reflect the total U.S. population ages six and above. They define a participant as *an individual who took part in the activity at least once in the given year*

Graph 6.4 Running/jogging and trail participants (USA). Source Statista, September 2020

Graph 6.5 Walking for fitness (UK). Source Statista September 2020

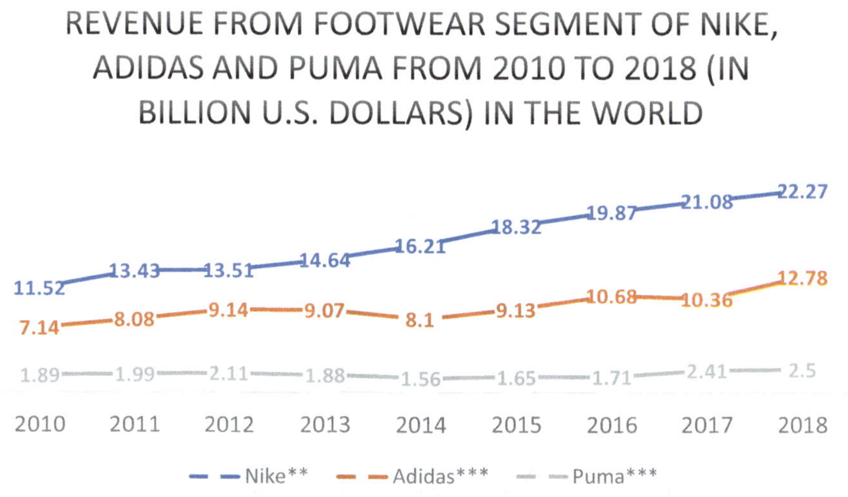

Graph 6.6 Footwear segment. Source Statista September 2020. *PUMA figures come from the company's yearly group management report. 2018's. Adidas figures come from the company's annual report. 2018's. ** Fiscal year end of May 31 of the respective year. *** Fiscal year end of December 31 of the respective year; figures were converted from euros on that day of each respective year using the OANDA Currency Converter

significant increase. In the case of shoes in 2018, it will reach more than 30 billion dollars (Graph 6.6).

The statistic represents the global revenue of the three major manufacturers of jogging/running shoes, Nike, Adidas, and Puma, from their respective footwear segments from 2010 to 2018. In the annual report, we can read that

> [. . .] of Nike's footwear revenue in 2018, almost six billion dollars was generated in the Europe, Middle East & Africa region and a further 3.6 billion U.S. dollars came from the emerging markets of the Asia Pacific and Latin America. However, North America remained the biggest regional market for Nike as footwear sales there reached 9.3 billion U.S. dollars in 2018. In comparison, sales of Nike apparel in North America generated revenue of just under 5 billion U.S. dollars and sales of equipment was 595 million U.S. dollars
>
> Although it is still behind Nike in the global market, Adidas' footwear segment is growing steadily, with 403 million pairs of shoes produced in 2017, the highest figure to date. Western Europe continues to be the market in which Adidas generates the largest share of its revenues. In 2017, 29% of the company's net sales came from Western Europe. North America is the company's second-largest market, with a 21% share of Adidas' net sales.

Owing to the market dominance of Nike and Adidas, Puma's footwear sales have remained relatively constant in the last few years. However, there has been a spike in the company's footwear sales since 2017, where sales broke the two billion U.-S. dollar mark for the first time since 2012. The footwear segment nevertheless remains the company's biggest earner as sales in its apparel segment stood at around 1.7 billion euros in 2018 and sales of its accessories generated close to 777 million euros in revenue."

The most significant number of joggers/runners spend around $120 on shoes but the distribution is concentrated among those spending between $60 and $160 (Graph 6.7).

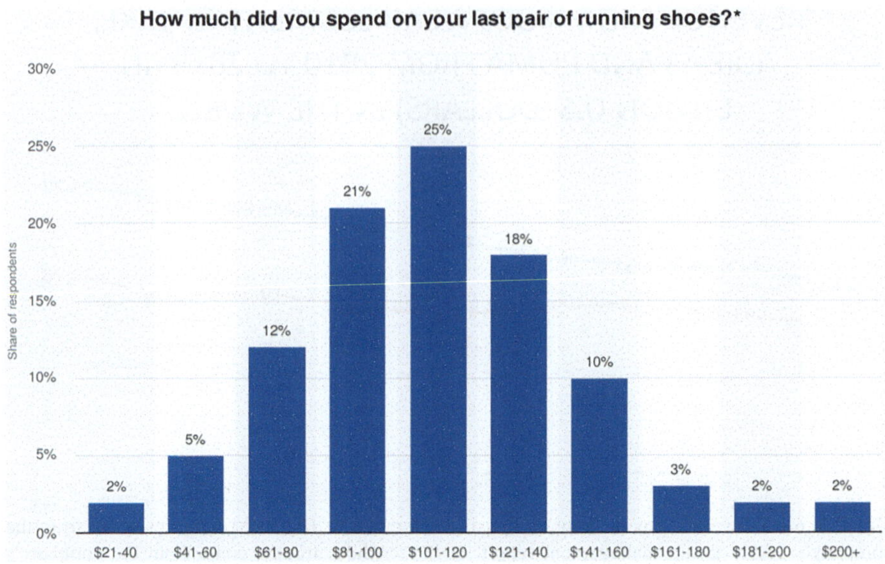

Graph 6.7 Running shoes spending. Source Statista September 2020

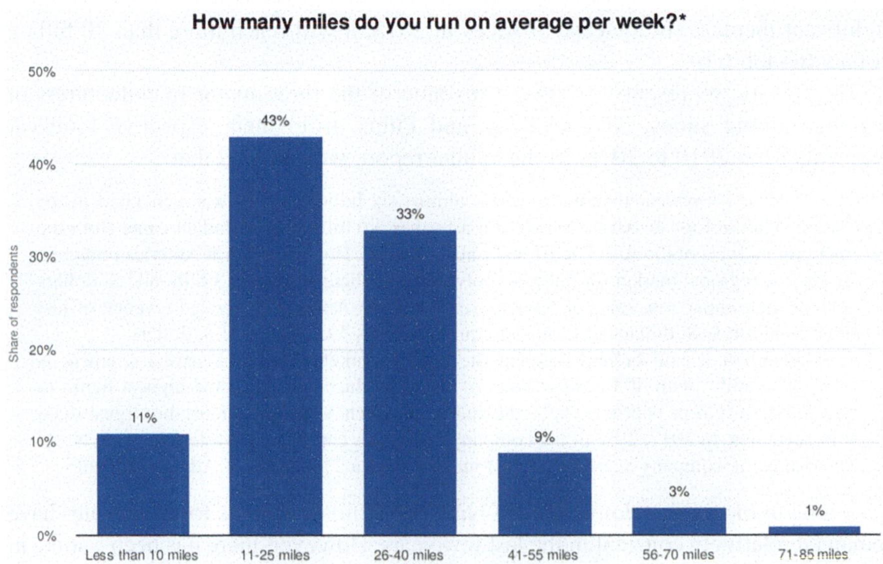

Graph 6.8 Miles per week. Source Statista September 2020

The shoes used by runners and joggers are of considerable importance, if only because their wear is a function of the number of kilometers covered. On average, that's a lot (Graph 6.8).

6.4 Runners' Reasons

Considering that the reasons why people choose to jog are varied—people start running to get fit, to lose weight, to have fun, to relieve stress, to socialize, to improve and overcome their 'limits'—and jogging/running is cheap, flexible and simply sporty, several 'profiles' have been isolated in the most recent research on runners (Janssen et al., 2020):

(a) *Casual Individual Runners*, a cluster composed of relatively more women, runners <35 years of age, higher education, and students than the other types. It comprised relatively more 5 km and 10 km runners. Moreover, data show that for those in this cluster, running is not the main sport and that the central part has not experienced running, participated in fewer events than others, and runs more individually;
(b) *Social Competitive Runners* prefer to run with friends, colleagues, small groups, and clubs and run for more than 5 km and 10 km.
(c) *Individual Competitive Runners* look, above all, to the advantages of running, and run is a part of their "identity". Cluster is composed more of males than females, and most participants are with lower or middle education and the lowest number of students. Moreover, for them running is the primary sport, and they prefer long training distances, frequent training sessions, and participating sports events;
(d) *Devoted Runners* are similar to those who belong to cluster 3 but less competitive than other groups and most experienced and, with social, competitive runners, had the most club runners.

Some scholars (Scheerder et al., 2011, 2015) also divide runners into four groups according to the level of competition and professionalization that characterizes them. They distinguish between *performance running* and *participation running* and arriving at an exciting classification that sees a broad base of participants and only a small number of runners who constitute an elite:

(a) elite running;
(b) high-level competitive running;
(c) performance running;
(d) participation running

Other scholars (Borgers et al., 2015, p. 48), although referring to a specific geographical area, construct a classification that in our opinion can be exported to all urban areas and according to which a distinction is made between:

(i) *the individual runner*, who has the essential value in the possibility of organizing the sport efficiently and flexibly, without being dependent on a fixed schedule, location, or other people, moderate about running behavior and run once or twice a week and for less than 1 h per running. They cover about 6–15 km per session.

(ii) *the social-competitive runner*, who put less importance on the health motives. For them, running is a "real" sport. It is strongly correlated to an identity domain, perceiving themselves as athletes and other runners; they run from three to five times a week. For them, sociability and competition are two important motivations.
(iii) *the social-community runner* prioritizes health and fitness as reasons for running and are relatively low frequent runners (once in a week generally). They prefer to run in organized and group settings because of their needs for social contact and sociability.
(iv) *the health-and-fitness runner*, a health-and-fitness runner, because these are main motivations; they run once or twice a week, up to 10 km per training session, and prefer to run in a group or sporting club environment.
(v) *the performance runner*, who see themselves as the only 'real' sports participants. For these groups, accessible, flexible, and individual characteristics of running and maintaining health and fitness are the main motivations to run. They like to set goals and challenges, overcome limits, and persist in hard work, with a minimum distance run per session of 10 km.

Joggers are, therefore, part of the broader part of participatory running. This would also be how the second wave has declined, while the first would be characterised above all as *performance running*.

According to some scholars, this is the moment of a third wave involving mainly young people interested in other types of racing, first and foremost urban trails (Scheerder, Breedveld, Borgers, cit., 11). In our opinion, often they combine the two dimensions, even if manifesting a more "playful" and less performative competitiveness.

Without considering the motivations that move them, Smith [1998, p. 179 et seq.], one of the first scholars of the sport mentioned above, produced a classification of the types of runners. Amongst joggers, he identifies athletes, i.e., those who compete in official competitions and can win them; runners, i.e., constant practitioners who participate in competitions but whose objective is not necessarily to win but to complete the race; and joggers, i.e., those who run from time to time. More recently, other scholars [Hallmann & Wicker, 2012] have classified runners into serious runners and fan runners based on their motivation to run, more professionally in the former case; and stay fit and healthy in the latter case.

6.5 Runners and Digital Technologies

The de-institutionalization of sport is part of the broader trend towards the de-institutionalization of leisure practices. And it is declined, firstly, as a possibility of choice concerning "when" and/or "where" to practice it; but, secondly, also because of "how" one wants to practice it and "with what method". From this point of view, therefore, given its low cost and the almost absence of entry barriers, running is a practice that is absolutely in line with this process.

Besides, the use of increasingly sophisticated digital performance control technologies, which exploit knowledge not only from sports science and technology but also from health and nutritional sciences, would appear to be slowly replacing the skills and knowledge of sportspeople in general, and runners in particular, acquired through the intervention of the instructor, personal trainer, dietician and sometimes even the doctor.

This would be a substitution/supplantation determined, on the one hand, by reasons that see, in the release from the relationship with a figure with a function of "guide", the will of absolute autonomy in the process of acquiring technical sports competence. On the other hand, by the diffusion of the self-perception of acquired knowledge of one's own body, an awareness that gives security and above all "self-confidence". It has changed the very framework in which the 'management' and 'self-control' of the body and, at the same time, the management of that part of the self that takes on importance precisely about its 'corporeality' are inserted.

The case of runners can be considered emblematic of this use of technologies that replace, even in the initial phase of learning to practice, the guidance of a trainer. Among runners, the figure of the guide usually made up of athletes "old in the role" with extensive experience, is now flanked by the use of apps that take on the meaning of "tools of governmentality" [Zenger, 2013, iii], i.e., tools to manage and, at the same time, learn, acquiring more information about one's body and one's ability to perform—moreover often through the "game" constituted by the same mode of use and design of the app.

According to Millington, we can argue that there is a high social risk in this kind of trend.

Millington, quoting Deleuze, argues that

> "[...] With the products described above, the individual effectively becomes a "dividual" (Deleuze's, 1995): she or he is deconstructed and quantified through measures such as speed of movement, caloric expenditure, and heart rate" [Millington, 2014, p. 486].

Millington also claims that

> [...] this habitus enables the surveillance of the self that means, the surveillance of the measure how (on) what is measurable: everything is measurable with technology. Health and fitness apps "[...] privilege not just individualized self-care but networked individualism" [487].

So, according to Lupton, we consider the use of fitness, jogging, and health apps as a result of a long process of "digitizing health and medical information" [Lupton, 2014, p. 607]. This trend started in the mid-1990s (in the "web 1.0" era), when people talked about health and health services offered when there was a surge in sites where people spoke about fitness and health services. These sites also allowed each individual to contribute and display the information regarding their "state of health". This opportunity was expanded in the 2000s (the "social web"- or "web 2.0—era"), when it was possible to access and share information relating to health and fitness. As claimed by Lupton [*ibidem*],

> In this age of digital "prosumption" (combining production and consumption of Internet content), the ideal of the "digitally engaged patient" (otherwise referred to as the "e-patient") has become dominant.

The same can be said for amateur athletes who become "e-and-social runners".

The offer of services such as the constant online control of one's sporting performance—intercepted above all by the maximalists of recreational sport who do not renounce performance measurement—is thus flanked by services that instead have the function of monitoring the state of well-being and health for those who practice sport for purely health-related purposes.

This process, which can be interpreted as one of how the de-institutionalization of sporting practice is declined in one of its phases, that of the initial learning of the basic techniques of movement, is flanked by a further process of rationalization and standardization of practices in their execution precisely because of the need for self-control that replaces the hetero-control managed by trainers, coaches, athletic trainers, etc.

In short, while de-institutionalize, sports practice tends to spread widely—especially among different age groups, but also among different social and income groups—especially as an 'active' declination of a lifestyle, as an epiphenomenon of participation in public well-being that begins with respect for one's own and other people's bodies and is typical of a truly 'sporting' mindset, i.e. one that has made a 'healthy' lifestyle a way of being in the world that often goes hand in hand with respect for the environment and nature [Hitchings & Latham, 2016].

Along the same interpretative line, but in an extreme form with this health tendency, the process of de-institutionalization is also declining in the diffusion of certain sporting practices in which emotion is accompanied by that perception of the flow of which Csikszentmihalyi [1990] speaks. Apart from sometimes being extreme, these are activities that offer an emotional involvement in those who practice them that is totalizing and, for this very reason, satisfying. This connotation typically assumed by extreme sports, however, has also involved the world of fitness. The new fitness practices are sometimes presented as sports that oppose the market and its rules, fighting commercial sport and intercepting, on a global level, that part of 'resistance to public order' which, in reality, translates into resistance in the private dimension. These are characterized by choices that take on the connotation of refusing the rules of commercial sport. In particular, these would seem to be the choices of runners, cyclers, skaters, and tracers.

Runners were among the first to use apps for sporting activity. Even among runners, it is possible to meet extreme enthusiasts who, along with the intention of "taking care of the body", in the double meaning mentioned above, have also developed a passion for overcoming performance limits and for sharing information about their successes with virtual communities [Bridel et al., 2016].

What would characterize the experience of runners, for example, is the fact that this is perceived above all as an activity aimed at "escaping the stress and seeking well-being" [Shipway & Holloway, 2013].

6.6 From Trainer to the App: The Domain of Sport Tracking Technologies

The use of fitness apps has become more widespread among practitioners of certain sports than among others. Usually more so among those who practice sports considered to be among the healthiest, even in medical circles, as they are aerobic (running being one of them, but also gymnastics) and, at the same time, among fans of physical activities that can be pushed 'to the extreme'. It seems to be an indirect effect of the ongoing process of digitization of everyday life and the pervasiveness of the increasing relevance of the game dimension in the process of acquisition and development of digital skills [Frissen et al., 2015; Ritterfeld et al., 2009; Zichermann & Cunningham, 2011].

And, It seems an effect of the spread of socialization to self-diagnosis brought about by a wider diffusion of the new 'digital culture' of health [Lupton & Jutel, 2015]. Or, again, as a form of extreme of the process of individualization of sports practice by practitioners who, as pointed out before, want to choose not only "where" and "when" to play the sports activity, but also "how" and "with what method" to play it, without any guidance other than that coming from the skills they have acquired through previous experiences or through self-training [Zenger, 2013; Fotopoulou & O'Riordan, 2017]. This would be most often the case among runners during the preparation for a race, a period during which motivational incentives become much more necessary.

Among runners and joggers—using Smith's classification—using the app, for example, the use becomes an indirect way to acquire more incentives to increase the distance covered daily. But the same would not happen among non-app users [Dallinga et al., 2015]. The use of data would have a positive effect on the so-called "intrinsic motivation", as well as on the "extrinsic" one constituted by "social approval", namely the enjoyment and satisfaction with the level of performance achieved [Asimakopoulos et al., 2017]. Furthermore, app users would set up a preparation schedule even for the weeks dedicated to training [ibid., 4]. Moreover, they perceive themselves as healthier and more energetic, maintain a healthy diet, and believe they are more likely to pursue goals—and thus performance—"almost like an athlete". At the same time, they report changing their lifestyle, losing weight, and persuading others to go jogging.

In general, several studies have reached the same conclusions that have monitored the use of different portable technologies for sports practice [Fujiki et al., 2008] and mobile as a personal coach [Kass, 2007]. Amongst these, it can be seen that when, more generally, someone wants to 'modify' their behavior about certain daily habits that have to do with lifestyle, the tendency is now to adopt Activity Tracking Technology although, after some time, they tend to abandon it [Gouveia et al., 2015; Kuru & Forlizzi, 2015].

According to some scholars, in some cases, two different experiential needs are mixed, namely, on the one hand, a measured sense of performance, i.e. a more "instrumental" objective of the use of the app; and, on the other hand, a lived-sense of performance, i.e. the experiential experience of using the app during the sporting performance which increases motivation [Tholander & Nylander, 2015, p. 2920; Van Horen et al., Van Hooren et al., 2019].

In this sense, technology, in general, would become a tool that, together with memory and emotional memories, allows one to "look inside" more effectively, as would be the case during the performance of exercises that, effectively monitored, allow one to record a bodily experience of the effort expended that is "more conscious" and "governable". It is for this reason that runners are said to be among the first—and most frequent—users of Activity Tracking Technology, i.e.

> [. . .] all kinds of technologies that people can utilize to learn about their physical activity data and make better decisions about their activity levels [Kuru, 2016, p. 848].

It is also because technologies for runners have been on the digital market for a long time [Jensen & Mueller, 2014], especially watches with accelerometers, pedometers, heart rate monitors, etc. Sport Tracking Technology (STT) is therefore particularly relevant. Sport Tracking Technology (STT), therefore, takes on particular relevance and, it would seem, precisely because app-users intend, through their use, both to measure the performance goals achieved and to "record" the results [Kuru, cit., 850]. Apps thus become the driving force behind their emotional experience during running. As with many other everyday objects that take on a symbolic value that goes far beyond their use and economic value [Norman, 2003], interaction with apps thus acquires a specific connotation. The use of the smartphone itself—which constitutes the "protective" hardware of a tool of emotional mediation such as the app ends up being for many runners—becomes a mode through which the practitioners of running, more generally, recompose and share their social identity: the identity of "winning athletes", an identity that is characterized by performative capacity, "winning" will, ability to overcome limits, risk-bearing, etc. And this 'sporting identity' can be profiled because the practices implemented are scientifically governable through the perfect control of the 'measures' that guarantee the well-being of body and mind.

The fact that digital technologies could have a reactive motivating function concerning inactivity had already been pointed out by other studies in recent years [Stephens, Allen, Sthephens & Allen, 2013; IJsselsteijn et al., 2004]. Other studies show that the particular "user experience"—the type of interaction with the object, i.e., ease of use, its "aesthetics", etc.—positively influences the continuation of the activity one decides to carry out. Kuru's research [cit.] shows, however, that this happens, especially with smartphone apps. Users, therefore, evaluate these as being more appropriate for greater control—at the same time—of health, diet, the sporting activity itself, and, consequently, of psychophysical well-being, confirming that they are tools for activating self-esteem and psychological well-being. Exploration, incorporation, identification, and mastery are the phases of using the apps identified by Kuru—and that also allows us to interpret how runners use the apps. Running, in itself, becomes.

"a way of getting rid of daily turmoil, feeling free, and relaxing".

But it also becomes the framework within which one accepts challenges and observes one's level of competitiveness with others as a function of one's performance [ibid].

The different phases "socialize" the same use of technologies. In the first phase, exploration, also known as the transition phase, the runner investigates which technologies he can use concerning how he perceives his own identity as an athlete.

In the second phase, incorporation, the app "enters" into the runner's daily life, especially about the possibilities of tracking; in the third phase, identification, the runner develops an emotional bond with both the practice of running and with the app that allows him to track his results. In the last phase, mastery, the one in which, according to Kuru, the runner becomes addicted to running but dominates both the practice and the technology.

In general, and especially since introducing new tracking and measurement technologies, what is the relationship of runners/joggers with urban space? And how does well-being relate to the use of space experienced by the runner?

6.7 Runners and Urban Space

Recently, public authorities affirm that the built environment can be an essential factor that may make participation in physical activity and sports more attractive and contribute to more engagement in these activities. And, if we analyze leisure activities in "everyday life" in each town, we can find a correlation between the increase of public space for de-institutionalized sports activities and the increase of participation in sports practices. Some studies on walking (Saelens & Handy, 2008), have pointed that conditions related to the built environment (such as density and mixed land use) and infrastructure (connectivity, presence of dedicated infrastructure, perceived safety) lead to higher levels of walking. Other studies (Ettema, 2016), have pointed on characteristics of the running environment showing that they are associated with both the perceived attractiveness and therapeutic capacity of these environments and the frequency of running.

Other studies show how the characteristics of the environment influence the same evaluation of well-being and health (MacBride Stewart, 2019) and, therefore, how the direct activity carried out in the environments favors a positive evaluation of the space as it is perceived as an object of intervention and individual action. This intervention and action contribute to modifying its characteristics. In short, the evaluation of personal well-being, the evaluation of the surrounding space, and the perception of the intervention on the space through one's activity—such as through participation in running—would be strongly correlated. Therefore, the practice of sport would seem to activate in runners/joggers a sense of "participation" in maintaining the good conditions of space, a sort of "protection through practice". This relationship can be highlighted using indicators such as the number of participants in city running activities who are residents, the number of city races, but also the number of tracks that can be used by runners or the number of members of runners' sports federations. The latter is an "indirect" figure since we have seen that most joggers tend to do this activity without joining any club. Still, the number of members can be considered as a proxy for the number of participants.

S. Francisco, for example, ranks first in a list of the top 50 running cities. It has 16 running clubs and 246 races in 2016. And per data from Strava alone, San Franciscans logged 12 554 runs per week for a total of 64 037 miles in 2015. Other rankings include Boston, Washington, New York, Chicago, etc. In each case cities, metropolises that "welcome" and offer services to runners and joggers.

It is an example of how the normal space remains a privileged space along with running routes, by runners and joggers. Running is placing the body in space by interacting through a bodily activity linked to intentional and inintentional movements. For the more experienced runner, knowing where he or she is running means knowing how to measure the space that contains it, distances, geometries and angles.

And measuring space means measuring the interaction of the body in that space, the number of steps, the number of heartbeats, gait time, walking time. The 'body and space' relationship modifies the perception of identity through measurement, through the use of the space itself, of its amenities, of the things and people one encounters and avoids. The social identity of runners and joggers is stabilized through this experience; it' lives' on the well-being generated by the body-space relationship understood as a 'specialized mode of use'. It is, however, a way of staying outside of production, remaining within the logic of efficient rationality that sees in repeated practice the imposition of a 'rhythm' to safeguard the same productive rationality. But those who run actually "slow down" their progress. He runs to stop in the pleasure of the interaction between body and space. He cares for his health by safeguarding the body-space relationship with the practice that has fewer barriers to enjoy.

If we look at what Lefebvre wrote, we can say that running is the form that draws the most lymph from the *normal* space. And the runner is often "the guardian" of this space.

6.8 Cyclists. The Road Is Mine: The Bicycle as a Tool for Social Transformation

6.8.1 Introduction

The previous paragraphs describe the existence of a triadic relationship: the social agent (moving between individual and social request); the sports practice (the relational process that takes place, within social contexts, through mainstream sports, de-institutionalised sports activities and the use of specific technical means); the space-time (as a field of practices).

The definition of sports practice used here is not to be understood solely in its meaning of institutional sports. It is possible to analyse sports practice as the activity that acts against stress and promotes well-being; the activity involving competitive performance towards oneself and others; the activity that enables new areas of relationships; the activity that encourages the sharing of interests and ideas about society; the activity promoting participation in political life and/or implementing forms of public resistance (the actual declination of that depends on the sport practised and its social significance, which invests in—and depends on—the technological means used for that practice). In this perspective, the number of individuals who perceive themselves as sportsmen and sportswomen, and who are perceived by others, expands enormously [cf. Lo Verde in this chapter].

6.8.2 The Origins of a Social Item

The bicycle has often been revolutionary. 'Before becoming the king of the road, the bicycle was the prince of the parks. Young English aristocrats showed off their skills in controlling their bicycles in front of their friends as they rode through Hyde Park. However, this curious high-wheeled machine was not intended as a regular means of road transport, nor was it a means for families to get around the countryside. Use for transportation and tourism would be achieved by the safety bicycle—a low-wheeled vehicle with a diamond frame and chain drive on the rear wheel—in the 1880s and 1890s' [Bijker, 1995, p. 19]. Soon around 1890, the bicycle was the must-have object par excellence. A fast and reliable means of transport that could take you anywhere, anytime, for free [Smith, 2020].

The bicycle was immediately able to shake up certain social beliefs. Especially in gender and class relations. The 'poor man's nag', as it was soon dubbed, transformed some social aspects. Women were particularly enthusiastic, abandoning their bulky Victorian-style skirts for trousers and more 'rational' clothes and taking to the streets. 'I think riding a bicycle has played the most significant role in women's emancipation of anything in the world. Whenever I see a woman riding on two wheels, I stop and look at her and rejoice. . .the image of authentic, unbridled femininity New York Sunday World in 1896 [New York Sunday World in 1896, in Smith, 2020] (Fig. 6.4).

In the 1890s, the bicycle became the symbol of the 'New Woman', independent, progressive and interested in having a say in politics. As reported by Godey's, a women's monthly magazine of the time: 'In possession of her bicycle the nineteenth-century daughter makes her declaration of independence' [Smith, 2020].

'In 1898, a cyclist was riding through the English countryside. She was wearing a pair of knickerbockers, which seemed the most practical and comfortable garment for a woman on a bicycle. After a while, she saw a tavern and decided to stop there to quench her thirst and have a little rest. But to her surprise, the owner did not let her sit in the coffee room for women, telling her that she had to make do with the public bar if she wanted to be served. The owner objected to the cyclist's clothing [. . .]. The cyclist protested, of course, and sued the innkeeper, but the judge recognised the right to refuse table service in the coffee room in those circumstances. The story did

Fig. 6.4 Women and bicycles in the late nineteenth century. Photo from universal history archive, universal images group/getty

not end with this judgement but had a considerable resonance as an episode in the struggle for women's rights' [Bijker, 1995, p. XI]. By 1898 bicycling had become such a popular activity in the United States that the New York Journal of Commerce claimed commercial losses to restaurants and cinemas of over $100 million a year. Bicycle manufacturing became one of the largest and most innovative industries in America. One-third of all patent applications concerned bicycles, a number so high that the US patent office had to build a new building to handle them all [Smith, 2020]. In the first decades of the twentieth century, France became Europe's leading producer of bicycles.

'The effect of bicycles on the development of cities will undoubtedly be revolutionary,' said a writer in an American sociological journal in 1892. In an article entitled *Economic and Social Influences of the Bicycle*, the author predicted cleaner, greener, quieter cities with happier, healthier and more open inhabitants. Thanks to cycling, he wrote, young people 'see a wider slice of the world and broaden their horizons. While they might otherwise seldom be able to go further than the distances they can walk from home, by cycling, they are constantly moving from town to town, learning about all the counties and, on holidays, not infrequently exploring different states. These experiences help develop a more energetic, autonomous and independent character...' [Smith, 2020].

During the first decades of the bicycle, bear witness that the use of this new technology has become one of how 'the right to the city', to use Lefebvre's words

Fig. 6.5 Marshall Walter Major Taylor: Photo from Gl archive, Alamy

again, is articulated, and social identities are re-structured for entire categories of people (Fig. 6.5).

But cycling also became a sport. After the first race in 1869, the Paris-Rouen, a new 'cycling' sports culture became dominant. In 1903, the Tour de France was born, followed and gradually imitated by hundreds of thousands of fans. In Italy, the Touring Club was founded in 1890 [Cavazza, 2009, p. 111]. And it was precisely this that constituted the fruitful interweaving of holidays, the mobility revolution and the organised demand for sporting activities.

The first cycling superstar was an American, a black man, Marshall Walter' Major' Taylor. A professional in 1896 (barely a teenager) set seven world records during his cycling career. His performance on the standing mile (1.41) lasted for 28 years [Smith, 2020].

In Italy, the emergence of the 'travelling cyclist', the 'tourist cycling'—preceding the 'sportive cyclist' (the Giro d'Italia was born in 1909)—helped give rise to a particular form of holiday, the *sports holiday*. It would spread, along with other types of holidays. Its style would take on the connotations of interest healthy movement and the enrichment of the spirit through knowledge of pleasant places, as had already happened in Great Britain with the Cyclist's Touring and France with the Touring Club.

In Italy, the bicycle had from the beginning populated the northern cities and especially Milan, soon becoming the most popular means of transport. From the first decade of the twentieth century, and thanks to reducing the cost of purchase, the bicycle became the means of transportation for workers, the petty bourgeoisie, artisans, etc. Between 1890 and 1910, the number of bikes circulating in Italy increased threefold, from the initial 200 000–605 000 [Elia, 2009, p. 137] and about 1 300 000 in 1919.

6.9 Cyclists and Cycle's Agency

From different points of view and with different emphases, the *agency* of the objects has been thematised in the last decades so much that it now seems legitimate to imagine moving from the question of whether it exists to the question of what it is [Volontè, 2017, p. 33].

Actor-network theory (Ant) [Latour, 2005, 2006] is mainly devoted to the 'hybrids', machines, rules, artefacts, all factors typically neglected by much sociology. For Ant's approach is necessary to redefine a complete theory of agency through a reconstruction of the actual functioning of frames as the "place" of interactions (defined as inter-objective to underline the role played in frames by "non-human" factors). Within these frames, humans define representations of the world and their actions [Martin, 2005].

According to Miller's ethnographic approach, artefacts are therefore not mere consequences of human action. They exert their agency on the human in a circular movement that is not necessarily repetitive: the social is extrinsic in the material, which, as external and material, affects the social by determining its transformation. In their role as external shores of social change, objects exercise an agency that cannot necessarily be traced back to the original intentions of social subjects [Volontè, 2017, p. 40]. When placed in a social context, the artefact's effect is not predictable (the output does not reflect the input). It depends on that same social context in which it is placed, on the constitution of meaning that those humans operate, and which for reasons I cannot go into here is hardly replicable by other humans [Volontè, 2017, p. 41]. Human subjects cannot be treated as pre-social and pre-cultural beings who, simply, enter into relationships with objects. The importance of material culture lies in the relations, which are ineliminable, with which subjects and objects constitute each other [Meloni, 2013].

The *social agency* of objects, as Gell defines it, belongs neither to the subject nor to the object in the social situation, but to the relationship they establish and would be lost both if the subject and the object were missing [Volontè, 2017, p. 43]. The social agency can be exercised relative to "things", and social agency can be exercised by "things" (and also animals) [Gell, 1998].

For Gell, objects are carriers of the agency of those who create and use them [Pucci, 2008]. They participate from within the relationships between social agents and the general environment. In the perception of the social agent, objects become part of a relationship. In the relational dynamic, the tool becomes a mediator in Latour's sense. The 'intermediary' represents that which carries meaning or force without transformation. Between the input and the output, there is little room for transformation. The outcome is largely predictable, knowing the input. Otherwise, the mediator transforms what it 'carries' (meaning, force or otherwise). Our ability to predict output cannot be based solely on knowledge of the input. Still, it must take into account the role played by the mediator as an element in the relationship the social agent has with the social and its environment [Latour, 2005, p. 39].

According to the *Social Construction of Technology* (Scot) approach, technologies are undoubtedly shaped by social structures and power relations, but also by the imagination and emotional participation of individuals. Values, skills and goals are formed in local cultures and allow us to understand technological creativity. The starting assumption of the Scot theoretical approach promotes the idea that modern society should be analysed as a unique fabric [Bijker, 1995, p. 4]. The analyst must not assume *a priori* the existence of clearly distinct scientific, technical, social, cultural and economic factors. Thus, legitimate questions arise: how can social processes be linked to interactions between individual subjects such as technicians and users? And how can the microanalysis of individual cases lead to a general theory of social and technological change processes? [Bijker, 1995]. Linking micro-stories with macro-structures involves questions about the internal structure of technologies: about the nature of the work of inventors, about the interaction between knowledge, technical skills and machines, about the epistemology of technology. But it also involves highlighting the crucial role played by the politics of technology.

Technological products are endowed with certain flexibility of interpretation. This flexibility leaves room for both producers and users to redefine the uses and meanings of technological products. In this sense, the process of technological development does not appear linear but the result of continuous dynamics that de-structure and re-structure social structures of meaning. A specific practice of a technological artefact may be innovative both in terms of the use to which it is put and the social and political significance. A new narrative may arise and decline a new social practice that may depart from institutionalised usages. The latter, on the contrary, promote a more orthodox relationship with technology in line with pre-existing social dynamics that contribute to reinforcing already established systems of meaning. It is worth pointing out, however, that like walking for De Certau, cycling allows urban spaces to be "personalised" by "creating unexpected itineraries and connections between places de-connected to other practices of displacement [Favole, 2015, p. 45].

6.10 Cyclists. Practice and Space

"The bicycle is mythical, epic and utopian" [Augè, 2008, p. 69]. Certainly, cycling in many countries is part of social history, especially in the twentieth century: for example, in Italy, France, Belgium, Spain and so on. The Giro d'Italia, especially after the Second World War, has nourished the collective imagination with challenges and dreams. The Giro d'Italia has marked eras, representing the social changes taking place over the years through its passage through the streets and lanes of Italy. It has marked the stages of economic and technological progress and changes in social customs [Pepe, 2014]. And it has 'marked' space, giving it the relevance that the memory of places transfers.

The study of sporting practices enhances the analyses conducted on lifestyles [Gratton & Henry, 2001; Wilcox et al., 2003]. The sporting population is increasingly central to the demands for a continuous redefinition of the relationship with space as a field of sporting practice. Requests metaphorically addressed to the city (as the privileged space of sports practice in contemporary society). And indeed, the population that practices sport, in the sense indicated in this work, assumes a role in the dynamics that see the public decision-maker invested with intervention inputs through public policies aimed at redefining spaces in terms of "sports consumption" [Sam & Hughson, 2013]. Each sporting practice becomes a tool in itself, whose purposes can overlap (individual well-being, improvement of the environmental conditions of places, targeted use of spaces, etc.).

In this dynamic between sporting practice (action) and space (field), an essential role is played, in different ways depending on the sport practised, by the technical means (or means) that enable sporting activity, at times profoundly modifying it when an 'epochal' innovation occurs. Therefore, every sporting practice creates a particular relationship with the technical means and the space and the restricted community of sportsmen and sportswomen and the broader social community.

In this sense, space and medium are not to be understood objectively. The subjective and social meaning that space takes on depends on the relationship between the (embedded) individual and space (as a multiform place) and the precondition of the relationship between the (embedded) individual and the medium. The relationship (individual-medium) that is realised in its actual unfolding (movement, rhythm, effort, sounds, etc.) and on which the lived experience and therefore the social and individual narrative interpreted by the social agent will depend.

Within this relationship, the technical medium takes on a particular significance. It becomes a recognised and recognisable symbol and is undoubtedly widely shared by the sporting community. Not only does it have an objective meaning linked to the type of sport practised, but it is also a representation of a lifestyle that is also characterised by value and evaluation aspects. In some cases, the medium transcends its technical boundaries to become a recognisable social 'entity' whose emotional connotation and broad social significance is identifiable. The "technological" aid mediates between physicality, space, emotionality and signification. Within this enlarged universe of sports practices, the technical means take on a solid symbolism that refers to precise social meanings and social emotions that are shared and to be shared. In this sense, the practice of sport takes on the form of a daily ritual *a la* Collins [Collins, 2004]. And if this assumption of meaning belongs, albeit to varying degrees, to all sporting practices and their technical means, at first glance, no sporting technology seems to possess, in modern and contemporary times, the social history of the bicycle. Within the broad meaning of sporting practice used here, no technical means have 'been elevated' to a shared symbol of a particular approach to space (whose boundaries between urban and non-urban become liquid and permeable); to a symbol of the will to create a precise trajectory of identity (individual, socially connected and shareable); no other medium has, more than once in history, acquired this transgressive and political dimension, marking and accompanying profound social and urban transformations; finally, no other technical medium has 'granted' its sporting protagonists the dimension of social myths [Barsella, 1999; Barthes, 1957 trad. It 1974; Augè, 2008].

Today, various types of cyclists contribute to defining and redefining this relationship: the *sports cyclist* (especially the numerically more significant amateur cyclist, about the use of urban and non-urban spaces, than the more committed sportsmen and women—amateurs and professionals); the *city cyclist* (the cyclist who uses the bicycle not occasionally as a means of transport—*frequent cyclist*), the individual who uses the bicycle for an individual activity for his or her well-being or as a means of transport or for various leisure activities; the *tourist cyclist* (the cyclist—the individual who uses the bicycle to explore, visit and learn about the places and beauties of the city and neighbouring areas, or who makes his or her own journeys by bicycle).

The bicycle transforms how individuals relate to space and, in particular, to urban space. More than other technologies, the bike 'intervenes' in the triadic relationship with a power of agency (derived from social agents) that must be taken into account in the relationship between body, space and techniques of control of the body in space to which Satta and Scamacca refer [cf. Lo Verde].

In a somewhat romantic way, but one that fully captures a particular aspect of the bicycle and of the relationship that the sportsman, above all, has with 'his' means of transport, Augè wrote that the bike 'is patient and faithful. The bike is another part of its owner; we would never want to separate ourselves from it. With due proportion, the bond that unites us with it is somewhat reminiscent of what Aristophanes evoked in Plato's Symposium: the true cyclist only fully exists when the lost half of his initial being is restored to him, he is one with it. The bond that unites the cyclist to his bicycle is, literally, a bond of love and gratitude, which time does not consume, but strengthens, if life separates them later, in the form of memory or nostalgia" [Augè, 2008, p. 56]. The bicycle has also been praised as a tool that increases human energy efficiency compared to some epoch-making inventions such as the wheel, the horse harness, and ocean-going ships [Ilich, 1973 trad. It 2006]. A bond with the bicycle, which transfers into the relationship with space a desire for active abandonment to the possibilities of travel and discovery.

These socio-historical elements, briefly presented here, show that cycling is a social and sporting activity with some special features. Let us try to highlight them.

Let us take up the diagram of the socially and strategically constructed polarisation of used space proposed in the previous paragraph. Along the first axis (vertical), the polarisation winds between *normalized* spaces and *interstitial* spaces. We find *performative* practices and *fruition* practices at the opposite poles of the second axis (horizontal).

Concerning the second axis (practices), we can note the first peculiarity of cyclists. They are in a sort of intermediate position between runners and skaters. Runners tend to represent citizens who live their practices mainly within the *normalized* spaces, those 'built' for recreational purposes (such as parks). The practices of runners are of a *fruition* type, in which the *transformative* aspect, also in symbolic terms, of urban spaces, appears to be absent. The 'revolutionary' intention, so to speak, of researching, using and redefining urban spaces (*interstitial* spaces) has, when present, less urgent and less political instances. The runner may run where he can, even in the street. His practice does not ask for the transformation of ordinary spaces; at most, the runner asks not to be seen if he runs on the pavement. His main objective is physical well-being, 'air time' against stress and worry.

There's a difference for skaters. Skaters' short story needs to recognise and be recognised as a category of alternative and emerging 'sportsmen'. And in the initial phase, skaters can be perceived as belonging to a 'sect'. Social recognition comes through the redefinition of urban spaces in which to stage their sport. Their political 'charge', the search for and the redefinition of *interstitial* spaces, 'occupied' through *performative* practices (therefore *transformative* in terms of use and symbolic representations), is more evident. This 'political charge' is often untied, so to speak, the immediate need for input and concrete instances is introduced into the political-institutional system. Instances that are waiting will be expressed when the institutionalisation phase of the practice of a sport occurs.

Cyclists practice their sport by articulating both of these two 'demands' according to the types of cyclists we have highlighted. Both sport cyclists and tourist cyclists are certainly users of ordinary spaces through *fruition* practices. The actual sporting practice, performed by amateur and professional athletes, represents a sort of necessary escape from city spaces. The need to travel long distances for good training makes it essential to get out of the city. But this necessary escape does not represent a desire to redefine spaces. Instead, it is an escape from the city using routes already finalised from a mobility point of *view* but adequate to the intended training characteristics (flat roads, climbs, undulating routes). The cyclist must spend at least a couple of hours on the bike to feel satisfied. He has to meet the pre-established agonistic objectives, often achieved in groups with other cyclists, to justify the investment made in the bike purchase. It is an object, and a symbol experienced, indeed, but also displayed. We can say the same for cycle tourists, whose primary purpose is to enjoy the space, amenities, landscape and cultural routes. For cycle tourists, the meaning of escape falls within the functionalist recreation a la Corbusier; therefore, it falls within an escape from the modern city, in a sense specified in the preceding pages. In other words, the cycling escape and its necessity indicate the continuation of the modern type of city in which the productive dimension prevails. For sportive cyclist and the cycle-tourist, the recreation is outside the city or inside the city, but always within the framework of the intended urbanistic purpose. The practice itself must respect the rules (above all traffic rules).

For Augè, cyclists[4] represent the new flaneurs who, as they pedal, realise with wonder that the city has to be looked at, to be seen (seen directly, without the intermediary of a camera), that it is beautiful right from its most modest streets, and that it is easy to navigate [Augè, 2008, p. 27].

Alongside *sport cyclists* and *cycle tourists*, who use ordinary spaces for their enjoyment, there are *city cyclers*. Their practices (*performative*) lead to *transformative* demands on *normalized* urban spaces (and are increasingly taking on the characteristics of legal input for regulatory recognition) and a particular type of sport cyclist—*mountain bikers*. Although barely sketched out here, this classification reveals the complexity of cycling as a sport.

In terms of pure sport, *city cyclers*, those who use bicycles to get around the city, are not sportsmen. They can be, and often are when they do not use the bike as a means of transport. However, *city cyclers* experience their practice as physical activity aimed at their psychophysical well-being as an intervening variable contributing to social practice's significance. In this broad sense, city cyclists are and perceive themselves as "sportsmen". Not only that. The use of the means of transport imposes a redefinition of space. The practice itself is an instance of remodulation of city spaces to be articulated between sharing (with other means of urban transport) and exclusivity (city spaces and routes dedicated to the exclusive use of bicycles) [Lazendorf & Geertsema, 2014].

6.11 Cycling. Contemporary Trends Between Technology and Ecology

The demand for exclusivity in the use of space is a sign of a revolutionary, transformative request. This request appears increasingly urgent with the phenomenon of the spread of electric bikes. The growth trend in sales of electric bikes, which are currently driving the entire production sector, shows that city cyclists, in particular, are demanding recognition and a global rethink of the productive city. And skaters, who move around the city on electric scooters, are moving in the same direction. The significance of the choice of electric and zero-impact transport provided by the bicycle is defined by the possibility of measuring the benefits produced by these forms of eco-sustainable mobility, almost provocatively using an economic-efficiency language. The European Cyclists' Federation (ECF) estimates that the benefits of cycling in Europe amount to around EUR 150 billion per year [ECF, 2018]. In contrast, the European Commission has calculated the negative externalities, i.e. the costs for the environment, health and mobility, of motorised road transport at EUR 800 billion per year.

---

[4]Compared to the classification proposed here, for Augè, talking about the Velib (bike sharing) initiative implemented in Paris, cyclists would mainly correspond to cycle tourists.

Eco-sustainable awareness is gaining momentum, especially among young people. In 2014, data recorded by Eurobarometer showed that 8% of respondents said they used a bicycle every day (for Italians 6%, an increase over the previous year); but the most relevant figure, in prospective terms, is the use of two-wheelers among young people, which reaches a percentage of 13% [EC, 2014]. In 2018, Istat recorded that the supply of shared mobility services continues to grow: bike-sharing is present in 48 cities with more than 41 000 bicycles (+37.6% on the previous year), while the car-sharing fleet, present in 35 cities, counts about 8 000 vehicles (+7% on the previous year), and the share of low-emission vehicles rises from 25.9 to 29% of the total [Istat, 2018]. According to preliminary studies by the European Commission, a positive and unexpected effect of the lockdown measures adopted in March 2020 was the sudden increase in bicycle use [European Commission, 2021].

In Italy, in particular, bike-sharing is booming. According to data provided by Isfort in 31 selected cities (capital cities with fleets of at least 80 bikes), the number of bikes available more than tripled between 2005 and 2019. The total number has reached 35 000 vehicles (15% electric); rentals have risen from 5.6 million to over 12.5 million (55% free-floating); registrations to the service have increased by 60% [Isfort, 2021].

The sports practice of city cyclists denotes a *transformative* demand for urban mobility. This demand has taken the form of legal input that more and more legislators are embracing. According to data from the European Cyclists' Federation (ECF), the total amount spent by European cities on implementing cyclist policies is around 1 billion. This is just during 2020, the first year of the coronavirus challenge. It has involved creating more than 1000 kilometres of cycle lanes, pedestrian streets and initiatives to reduce car traffic. In 2020, Barcelona provided 20 kilometres of new cycle lanes. As a result, cycling has increased by 10% compared to pre-pandemic levels. Milan launched the *Strade Aperte* programme in April 2020 and aims to increase the city's cycle lanes to just under 100 kilometres by the end of 2021: the Corso Buenos Aires cycle lane, the city's busiest, is used by 10 000 cyclists a day, an increase of 122% in just a few months [Franceschini, 2021].

The situation in Italy relating to the endowment of cycle paths records an average development in the capital cities in 2018 of 23.4 km per 100 square kilometres of land area (Graph 6.9), with a growth of +16.8% compared to 2013. There is a clear difference between North and South: in the capital cities of the North, the index is 56.3 (more than double the average), while in the capital cities of the South, it drops to 5.2, confirming a considerable gap in urban infrastructure dedicated to cycling.

The transformative practice of the cyclists represents, in an emblematic way, the already mentioned multifunctionality (cf. Lo Verde) of the post-modern city. For city cyclists, multifunctionality is articulated as a dimension of sharing the same space-time and as, and increasingly so, redefining exclusive space-time (cycle paths, pedestrianisation, sharing systems, etc.). Multifunctionality enriched with a new meaning linked to the way of practising citizenship. The effect is the reshuffling of the continuous circle of functions which have as their system of regulation of space not only time but norms responding to actual political instances. Instances directed, formally or through mere practice, to new forms of institutionalisation of city living and mobility within the city. And the phenomenon appears to be global. For

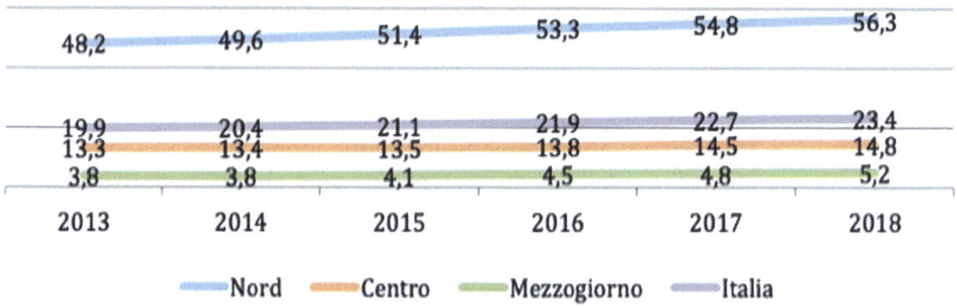

Graph 6.9 Density of bicycle lanes in provincial capitals/metropolitan cities(a), years 2013–2018 (km per 100 square km of land area) in Italy. The value refers to all municipalities for which data are available in the reference year. Source: Isfort elaborations on Istat data

example, in the United States, 'While the pandemic is limiting travel in large US cities—especially by underground and bus—hundreds of thousands of Americans are moving to a basic form of mobility: the bicycle' [New York Times, 2020].

More recently, Isfort's 17th annual report in Italy recorded an increase in the propensity (desire) to use bicycles [Isfort, 2021]. This propensity appears to be confirmed by the data on sales of electric bikes, which have been steadily increasing since 2016 (as we will see in the next paragraph). This increased propensity to cycle has also been boosted in response to changes in certain daily practices imposed by the pandemic phase. While the restrictions imposed by the authorities have certainly had an impact, the data provide indications that people are moving towards new trajectories of demand for goods and social practices. It should be emphasised that the current pandemic phase is bringing into play the need to thematise and problematise a set of variables that all appear to be affecting various sectors of social life. Economic and employment crises, the reorganisation of working methods, the dominance of online platforms for everyday activities, social distancing (and fear of contagion), the enhancement of proximity and public space, and the redefinition of practice spaces: a kaleidoscopic and never before experienced mixture of novelties and innovations, imposed 'from above' and pushed 'from below', multidimensional (social, economic, environmental, institutional…) and intersectoral (economy, transport, work…), cyclical and structural. All concentrated in the short period of this pandemic period, making it stimulating to consider the current mobility trends (both general and active) of Italians, at least on the two main fronts of demand volumes and modal repositioning [Isfort, 2021, p. 1]. In this perspective, the demand for new exclusive spaces for city cycling should be included, which take the form of the cycle paths mentioned above. Referring to the Italian situation, the number of cycle paths is continuously increasing, even if with some very significant territorial differences. The average development in capital cities in 2018 was 23.4 km per 100 sq. km of land area, with a growth of +16.8% compared to 2013. However, the gap between North and South is vast: in the capital cities of the North, the index rises to 56.3 (more than double the average), while in the capital cities of the South, it plummets to 5.2, confirming a considerable gap in dedicated urban infrastructure for cycling which, together with several other factors, heavily affects the still very low levels of cycling use in southern urban areas [Isfort, 2021, p. 10].

The propensity recorded underlines that it is particularly men and young people increasingly practising city cycling. Among the motivations, there is a substantial increase in the number of people using the bicycle for work and/or study trips [Isfort, 2021]. These tables suggest a picture that, if confirmed in the post-pandemic phase, indicates that, primarily, regular city cyclists have seen their idea of sustainable mobility consolidated due to the restrictions experienced in this period. Also, the audience of occasional city cyclists is changing its mobility choice in favour of sustainable mobility. Some studies in Italy reveal it is almost 26% of the total number who claim to use the bike [Isfort, 2021, p. 10]. It seems plausible that an audience of people who have used a bicycle during the pandemic has "discovered" individually sustainable mobility. In other words, many people may have discovered that the imagined difficulties which advised them to use public or private motorised transport (journey times, road hazards, fatigue, etc.) no longer appeared to be so. On the contrary, the practice of city cycling has led them to experiment with new ways of using space that is more environmentally friendly, less stressful, healthier and more economical. The current mobility conditions favour these trends due to the various restrictions put in place by public decision-makers (less polluted air, to give just one example). Trends will also have to be confirmed in a post-pandemic phase if and how the current conditions will be established. But it seems reasonable to imagine that the 'pandemic experience', so to speak, may leave a legacy of structural changes in the relationship with space, especially urban space.

6.12 Cycling Business

Although the bicycle has been a revolution since the early twentieth century, it has had alternating periods of popularity. If we look at the trend in bicycle production between 1950 and 2007, we see that, although there has been a steady increase, there are years when the trend reverses. After a decline between 1974 and 1977, there were further declines in the 1980s and early 2000s. However, the balance remains positive, and the increase is much more significant from the early 2000s until 2007 (Graph 6.10).

Even though we have to wait for the medium and long term consequences of the current pandemic phase, the strong revival of the bicycle sector began in 2016, therefore long before the start of the Covid19 pandemic.[5] In Italy, according to

[5]In an interview with Sole24ore (16 September 2020), Piero Nigrelli, head of the Ancma bicycle sector, said: "The last incentive to purchase bicycles dates back to 2009, when sales reached two million, but then slowed down in the following years to 1.5 million-600,000 per year and then fell again starting in 2014. For 2021, however, it is very likely that this slump will not occur because this time, along with the incentives, measures have been introduced in favour of those who use bicycles, especially in the city".

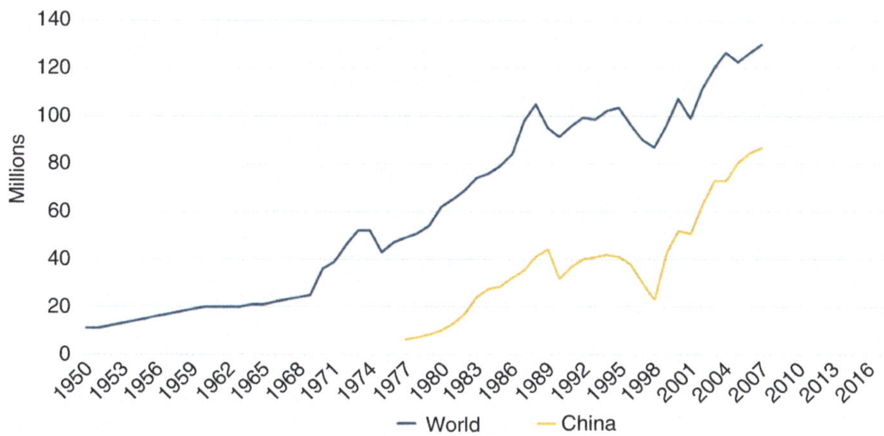

Graph 6.10 World bicycle production, 1950–2007. Source: Worldwatch Institute, Vital Signs 2008

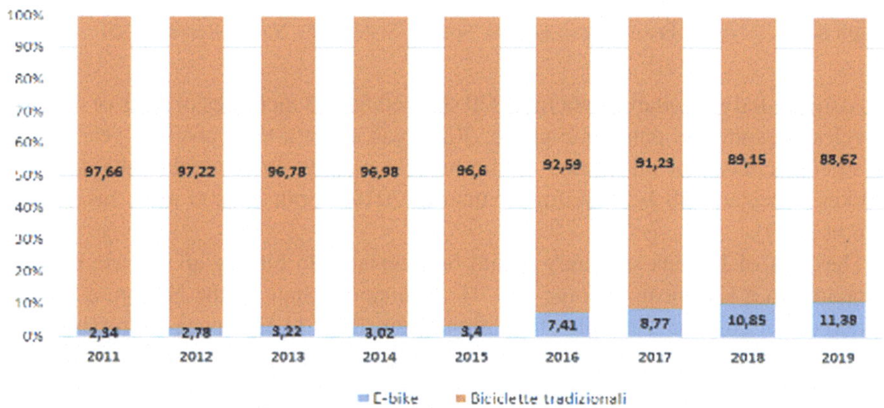

Graph 6.11 Percentage sale of bicycles by type. Italy. Source. Isfort processing of ANCMA data

Ancma's data, the bicycle market was driven by electric and pedal-assisted bicycles; before 2016, the electric bike market was around 50 000 e-bikes sold in 1 year. In 2016, 125 000 sold with an increase of more than 120%. Finally, in 2017 almost 150 000 bikes sold (+19%).

The 2019 data confirm the positive trend of the bike sector for both the traditional and e-bike markets. In Italy, the industry with the highest percentage of sales growth is e-bikes. Still, the sale of conventional bikes testifies that the bicycle continues its phase of "conquest" of the Italian public (Graph 6.11).[6]

[6]To give an example of the relevance of the bicycle market, in Italy alone, exports in 2017 amounted to 6.2 billion. The export revenues of wine, one of the Made in Italy products most appreciated abroad, are much lower. Ferrari's turnover was less than half [Lega Ambiente, 2020].

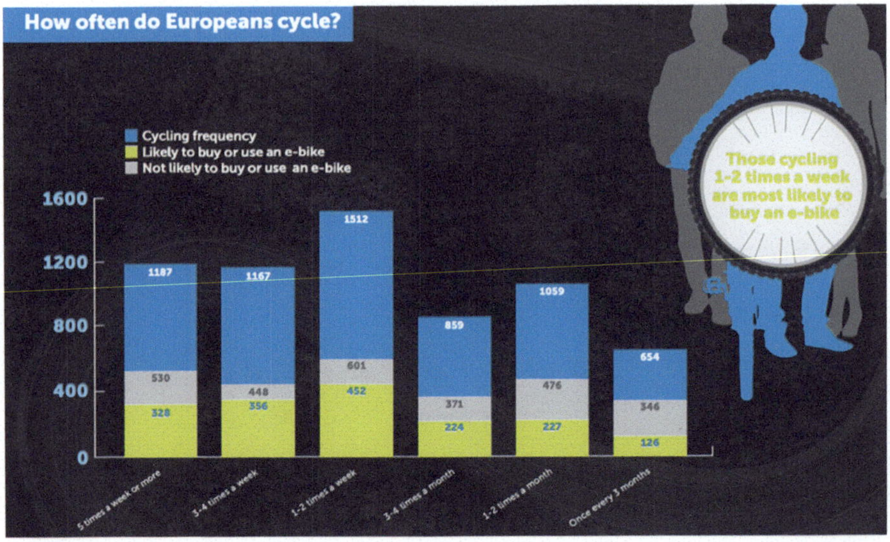

Graph 6.12 – Cycling Frequency in Europe. Source: State of the Nation Report, 2020

Also, for Italy, available data for 2020 showed record increases in sales of electric bicycles. Despite the pandemic phase, 2020 was again a very positive year. Sales recorded increases in all sectors of the bicycle market. In particular, the sales of e-Bikes expected will be 20% higher than in 2019 (about 40 000 more bikes sold than in 2019).

The 30% of Italians said they would be interested in buying an electric bicycle compared to a European average of 17% (Shimano's State of the Nation, a survey carried out in 2020 on a sample of 13 000 citizens from 11 European countries). The very high percentage recorded in Italy is essentially attributed to the availability of the bike bonus provided by the Italian government to help the sector during the economic crisis caused by the Covid19 pandemic. Potential urban cyclists are motivated to buy an e-bike by: climbs and long distances (32%); the desire to improve their physical (30%) and mental (22%) fitness; the desire to reduce the environmental impact of their means of transport (18%). In the 18–24 age group, this percentage increases to 26% [Shimano, 2020] (Graph 6.12).

Europe is, after the Asia-Pacific region, the fastest-growing market. The Old Continent accounted for 20.12% of the global market in 2018. In 2019, three million units sold in Europe out of a total bicycle market of 20 million units, a 23% increase over the previous year (Conebi, the industry partner of the European Cyclists' Federation). The forecasts of three European cycling associations (ECF, Conebi and Cycling Industries Europe) highlighted this trend in their reports: over the next 10 years, Europeans should buy a total of ten million more bicycles per year, reaching the figure of 30 million units sold in 2030, a 47% increase on 2019. This would make bike sales more than double the number of cars currently registered each year in the European Union (Graph 6.13).

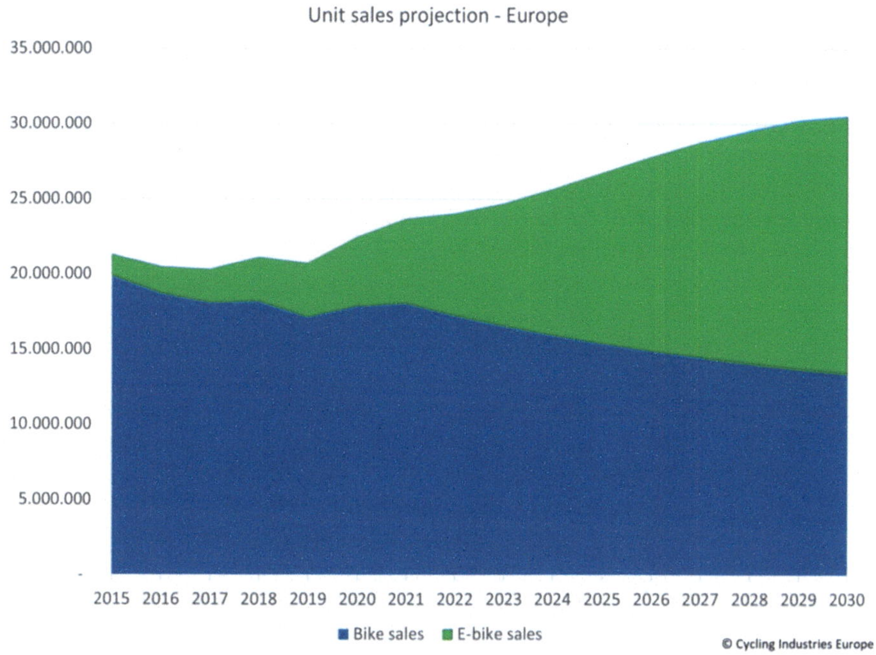

Graph 6.13 Bikes sales 2015–2030. Europe

Global e-bike sales reached $14.775 billion in 2018. A figure set to grow by 6.39% between 2019 and 2024, according to pre-covid19 estimates. The success of the e-bike in recent years is linked to the innovation factor: the focus on the interface between e-bike and cyclist, i.e. apps that improve the integration of information on speed, kilometres travelled and battery status. The apps have added new possibilities for *self-training*, in line with what is happening in many other areas of individual consumption and not only in the field of sport.

There are numerous social benefits linked to the sustainability of active mobility in general and cycling, particularly [Brand et al., 2021, The climate change mitigation effects of daily active travel in cities, in Transportation Research Part D: Transport and Environment, no. 93]. Alongside these social benefits, there are also personal benefits. Of course, individual and social benefits are partly closely linked. Cycling is good for the planet, but it is also suitable for everyone. The health dimension of sport is increasingly present. Cycling is part of the growing wellness trend seen in other sporting practices [Sassatelli, 2010]. The practice of cycling is articulated around the search for well-being that has become a social object and a consumer good [Tallarita, 2017].

The ECF has calculated in economic terms the beneficial effects on the health of people in Europe (longer life span, better health throughout life, mental well-being, etc.). The value amounts to almost €200 billion. New technologies confirm this for building bikes and the need for connected bikes to monitor training and routes. ‘Some of the bikes produced today are high-tech products. New, lightweight materials are developed and tested for bikes (e.g. carbon fibres) that can be used in other areas. This is especially true for electric bikes and their innovative components like batteries and new power trains, making electromobility a reality in the EU. Cycling is also becoming more and more connected, using ICT for applications like route planning, public bike systems or GPS tracking. With these new services, cycling becomes an integral part of the transport systems of future smart cities’ [ECF, 2016].

In 2020, North America accounted for the largest revenue share of 34.9%. It is attributed to increasing awareness about health and the high adoption rate of fitness apps. The usage of fitness apps rapidly increased during the COVID-19 pandemic. During the COVID-19 related lockdown, 74% of Americans used at least one fitness [GVR, 2020].

The Asia Pacific will be the most lucrative regional market during the forecast period. Key factors such as growing smartphone penetration, rising health awareness, and an increase in the penetration of fitness apps drive the market in the Asia Pacific. Moreover, during the COVID-19 pandemic, the region saw a significant increase in the downloading of fitness apps. According to an article published in the World Economic Forum, health and fitness app downloads increased by 157% in India, equivalent to 58 million new users. Health and fitness app downloads increased by 47% in the Asia Pacific [GVR, 2020].

6.13 Conclusions

The considerations made confirm the initial assumption: the cyclist, and cycling practice, takes on a particular characteristic in the ‘dialogue’ between the individual, space, and means. This triadic relationship is the basis of the cyclist’s self-perception. The cyclist perceives himself and is socially perceived as an individual who always practices a sporting activity. When he does it as a tourist, when he does it as a ‘citizen’ and when he does it as a competitor. A practice that is ‘antagonistic’ to the typical ways of defining space in production-efficiency models. As a unique object, both social and technical, the bicycle has a retroactive effect on the individual. Together, the individual and the means of transport redefine the experienced and perceived relationship between social agent and space (*performative* practice). In particular, the urban space (the place where the city cyclists act most heavily) in which the sharing of space and time with other actors “practitioners” is continuous, necessary and not deferrable. This, we believe, is where the *transformative* power has always accompanied cycling as a sport lies. Indeed, it was one of the first sports to take on a professional form; it soon became a means available to the masses for recreation and travel; and it became, again among the first, a sport for the masses (practitioners at all levels and those who did not become spectators of heroic deeds). Finally, it assumed the role of an instrument of proletarian redemption, of a social and political claim, from its inception.

As defined in this work, the practice of sport sees above all the city cyclers as the witness and protagonist of transformation of the space used in a multifunctional sense. The bikers start from a request for recognition of a possible alternative relationship with space and time. It is no coincidence that the current issues of ecological sustainability and the crisis of post-industrial models have in cycling an element of support for a transformation initiated whose outcome does not seem obvious. The upward trend in the various aspects of cycling (increases in use, in the propensity to use, in sales of bicycles, in the greater regulatory attention of public decision-makers, in the growth of the spaces allocated to cycling, in use of fitness app), which began before the current pandemic phase, if confirmed once the events caused by Covid 19 are behind us, can only call on public decision-makers to assume specific responsibilities.

In a broad sense of politics, it is possible to say that the cyclist and the bicycle, as a sporting practice, are *political agents* in themselves. The needs of the sportsperson, in general, are fully experienced by cyclists in particular as their own. The bicycle, starting with the choice of type of bike, implies a thematization, often implicit but not infrequently explicit, of the practice of sport, which becomes the manifestation of a relationship with space in slowed-down modernity. The practice becomes a meaning experienced by cyclists as a sort of commitment to testimony and representation. But the cyclist is also a 'healthy carrier' of a model of relationship with space that Augè, as seen, has lucidly and romantically represented.

6.14 Skaters: Re-Signifying Places

The recent Milan Triennale exhibited an installation by Korean artist Koo Jeong A entitled OooOoO. It is a large multi-sensory fluorescent skatepark, animated by the music of Koreless, a Glasgow-based music producer (Fig. 6.6).

During an interview, Koo Jeong A stated that he "wanted to stimulate in the visitor a physical and mental participation in the space that would challenge the relational dynamics between human beings and objects, between individuals and collectivity". One of the curators of the installation, Julia Peyton-Jones, who shared with Lorenza Baroncelli the realization for the Triennale, said that "The Skatepark is a demonstration of what it means to play: to play with real determination and concrete skills. The skateboarders move with the grace of dancers, masters of space, speed, and movement. For me, it is as if they are drawing in space. Like choreographers, they define the movement of the human body, and, as dancers, they manage to pull off remarkable feats involving enormous effort and endurance.+.

" The interest in the reflections that, according to the artist, the body produces in that space makes possible a knowledge of space that can tell us that the sky is "Glue" and not necessary "Blue", and the lawn "Breen" and not necessary "Green". During the same period, the Triennale hosted a photographic exhibition on skaters curated by Roberto D'Agostino, a well-known Italian critic and opinion leader in the television world, with photos by Polo Cenciarelli on display.

Fig. 6.6 OooOoO skatepark by Koo Jeong. Source: https://www.nssmag.com

The installation is part of a larger project. Another one has already been created, in collaboration with L'Escault Architectures, on the island of Vassivière in France, called OTRO. It is another space dedicated to skaters, the metropolitan sports population made up, like tracers, mainly of young and very young people.

Skaters would thus be, first and foremost, producers of the geometry of motor experience whose action is not necessarily constrained by pre-constituted, pre-programmed, or pre-planned ways of using space. For the tracers, for skaters, space is a place of the "possibility" of interaction, imagining in power a project of dynamic occupation that certainly challenges the common imagination on the use of space.

Perhaps nothing represents the minimalist and postmodern use of space better than skateboarding. It is the blasé way of using normal and interstitial spaces, of those who, in an exemplary manner, "recode" urban spaces. Spaces that can become "Glue" or "Breen" depending on the meaning they take on for those who experience them by moving around in them, for those who observe them while they see them come alive through the vaults of those who use them.

Only recently have cities worldwide begun to design spaces for skaters to vault, for those who want to project their bodies into space, intertwining them with movement and speed, using talent, imagination, and technique. And using the resources at their disposal: body, technology, imagination.

Machemehl and Roult (2019) argued that the relationship between these sports, the urban system, and the processes of institutionalization of sports practice has changed over time. The change is due to the changing supply of dedicated spaces and the changing search for new spaces by skateboarders.

> First of all, urban board sports are at the heart of an institutionalization process through which disciplines are backed by federal authorities at the local, national and international levels. Skateboarding, which has just become a prestigious Olympic discipline, is a good example of this. [. . .] Secondly, democratization (which benefits the young, adults and women in particular) contributes to the transformation of the sociability of the practitioners; the elitist spirit of pioneers is replaced by that of popular sport. Finally, this rise in popularity of urban board sports is also explained by the support of local and national political authorities, who do not hesitate to inject public funds to promote the demand for leisure activities, particularly in order to encourage physical activity and active travel among various population groups. In fine, if urban agglomerations have their own skate parks, it is because the communities of practitioners bring them alive, but also because these facilities, on the beaches of Marseilles or Los Angeles, have become real symbols of the city and urban life. As a vector of urban transformation and development, urban board sports are now emerging as true standard-bearers of a new urban character or at least a renewed urban character centered on citizen aspirations where the notions of community and experience are central (ibidem, 322–323).

Moreover, skateboarding constitutes the most striking example of the use of space in a different way and for entirely other activities than those for which it was designed (ibid.). It appears as a 'subversive' practice precisely because it 'breaks' the logic of ordered space designed according to different criteria (Laurent, 2012). Skating, skateboarding—but we can add scootering—are still often seen as a "marginal practice", which is unique. It interferes in urban spaces, places, and other "interstices," which are often designed for entirely different activities. As Machmelh and Rout claim,

> We could say that roller sports renew the way we see the city and de facto how we plan it. [. . .] They certainly require that these urban fabrics are their "decor" and "playground" (ibidem, 323)

The research of "wild" environment starts to be how skateboarders try to imagine "new spaces" for their performance. Opening up to "wild" use in a wild environment means learning to use every little piece of concrete as a tool for a challenge. The use of 'interstitial' spaces helps these tightrope walkers of the wheels to construct that meaning of identity through their activities and what they want to represent: a 'lifestyle' centered on well-being, understood as such only if 'outside the box', outside the standards of life and institutional sports practice. That is outside the rules other than the technical ones imposed by the use of the skateboard itself.

It is a mode of "appropriation of interstitial spaces" that is placed among the performative and transformative practices of the space itself, physically marking it as one's own and also making it an object of "claim" in that its use becomes a "right of citizenship" (Nemeth, 2006; Stratford, 2016).

Spaces thus become a more general "message" on the part of those who use the body as a vector of ideal and real vaulting between spaces of the possible and "impossible" spaces. Practicing skateboarding means giving a message that wants to communicate that spaces can be used "freely," even giving them different meanings.

Fig. 6.7 Skater. Source: https://images.pexels.com

It is a call for tolerance concerning the different meanings that each person wants to give to the space they occupy with their body and with the practices implemented with their body, always respecting the community and the rights of others. Knowing how to accept the different uses of space means, for skateboarders, accepting innovation, change, the world of possibilities of use. But also tolerance towards those who surround space with other categories and construct other meanings (Fig. 6.7).

6.15 Skateboard Subculture and Skateboard Studies

As Luison claims (Louison, 2011, p. 2) and recalls in other papers (Machemehl & Roult, 2019), the first roller derby skateboard debuted in 1959 and had a short, narrow wooden deck with trucks and wheels made of steel. It cost just 1.90$.

However, the evolution of the skateboard is long and complex. Depicted in contradictory ways as 'child's play', or as an object that accompanied the misdeeds of gangs of youngsters—and criminalized for this reason—it has evolved through various phases (Borden, 2001). But it was born as a surrogate, alternative to another board and practice, surfing. The oldest skateboarders in the 1960s were commonly surfers and used skateboards when the surf was flat. So, the terrains on which to skate were particularly the gentle banks found in many Californian schoolyards. And they transcribed surfing techniques in it (Borden, 2001). California first established itself as the mythical place, where surfers start to surf concrete, starting the era of Urban board sports, de-institutionalized sport, and opening to sports experience as a lifestyle and a political and social *counter-culture* (Machemehl & Roult, 2019).

The counter-culture of skating refuses sports institutions and particularly the spirit of competition that reigns in it. And, overall, this *counter-culture* promotes a new way to "live" sport as a *counter-cultural* way of life, individualized, de-institutionalized, and "freedom centered". Recently, this way of conceiving sport gave birth to a meaning of some sports as a lifestyle sport, including skateboard. So this kind of sport constructs a meaning of sport as "a central component of the practitioners' identity" (Machemehl & Roult, 2019, p. 325). This practice leads some practitioners – first of all, who is considered "the founder" of street skateboard and freestyle, John Rodney Mullen—to affirm that.

> skateboarding should be regarded more as an art or mode of expression than as a sport, and it is an inherently innovative practice that works to create transformative relationships between environment and body, community and individual, brain and body.

As written before, about the relationship between city spaces, skateboarding, and skateboarders, Bordon identifies four eras: a) sidewalk surfing, b) the pool era, inspired by the Z-Boys, c) skateparks and d) street skating. And Lombard claims that from this diverse era, four differents meanings of skateboarding developed too, since.

> varying terrain means varying modes of engagement and forms of repression – changing the meaning of skateboarding (Lombard, cit., p. 8).

In these diverse phases remain some aspects of the board sub-culture, as, for instance, the spirit of community and comparison with others (not necessarily in a competitive way).

And this kind of consideration reflects how sporting populations implementing performative practices in interstitial places contribute, directly and indirectly, to giving new meaning to places. They contribute to constructing counter spaces and colonizing interstitial spaces through tactics and strategies, quoting De Certeau (1980), which highlight the "specific" reuse of practitioners, a "fabrication" of spaces and their meanings. The "recoding" of spaces connotates the "piercing" work referred to by De Certeau. Strategies and tactics, to use De Certeau's terminology, are therefore implemented by the skateboarders now concerning the spatial dimension—reusing and re-signifying the logos and above all the "interstitial", anonymous, undesigned, residual, marginal spaces, etc.; now concerning the

Fig. 6.8 Skaters during a training session. Source: https://www.pexels.com/

temporal dimension—inhabiting the places at unofficial times, even these "when others are not using them" or in a different way from how they are used at other times.

What is the motivation for people to start skateboarding and thus imagine urban spaces? Many studies speak of specific dimensions involved in the choice, namely the perception of autonomy, safety, pleasantness in use and the development of skills of use, and above all of the *flow* (Csikszentmihalyi, 1990), the positive aspects of human experience—joy, creativity, the process of total involvement with life. In the words of Csikszentmihalyi (Fig. 6.8),

> Yet we have all experienced times when, instead of being buffeted by anonymous forces, we do feel in control of our actions, masters of our own fate. On the rare occasions that it happens, we feel a sense of exhilaration, a deep sense of enjoyment that is long cherished and that becomes a landmark in memory for what life should be like. This is what we mean by *optimal experience* (ibidem, p. 3).
>
> [...] "Flow" is the way people describe their state of mind when consciousness is harmoniously ordered, and they want to pursue whatever they are doing for its own sake. In reviewing some of the activities that consistently produce flow—such as sports, games, art, and hobbies—it becomes easier to understand what makes people happy (*ibidem*, p. 6).

It has been argued that the representation of skateboarders as "transgressors" is fundamentally linked to the concept of "normoconstituted" space, i.e., designed according to an idea of order that would be challenged precisely through practices considered "inappropriate". These include the performances of skateboarders (Nemeth, 2006, p. 298). And this feeds the demand for youth identity. A made an

Fig. 6.9 Skater in urban context. Source: https://101da.ru/

explicit request by using the body and the body in a precise, irregular, innovative space.

In many cities worldwide, skateboarding has often been seen as a problem of 'public order' (ibid.). On the other hand, it has been argued that the presence of skateboarders constitutes a structural innovation. It is an effect of the gentrification of previously disused urban areas, which has been able to generate a new image of cities, centered on the creativity and performance of its 'creative class' (see also Lombard (ed.), Lombard, 2016).

In a recent work analyzing the subculture of skateboarders, Lombard cites Borden's well-known article on the relationship between them and the city, or rather, on the new culture of the emerging town's relevance to these issues (Lombard, cit., p. 2). Some scholars talk of skate urbanism and skate cities about the new demand of the town from this metropolitan population over the last 15 years. This new demand has become so articulated that it has become an "influential culture" (Lasane, 2015) (Fig. 6.9).

6.16 Some Data

There is not much data available on the use of skateboards in cities around the world. For the United States, a ranking of cities was made by counting the number of skateboard parks per 100 000 inhabitants.

The highest concentration of parks is found in cities where skateboarding is a broader range of entertainment in public and private spaces (Table 6.2).

We also know that the turnover around the whole chain of production and consumption of goods and services is significant and does involve not only children but also adults (Graph 6.14).

The trend is also considered growing, and the number of park-goers and practitioners has been increasing over the years (Graph 6.15).

Table 6.2 Cities with the Most Skate Parks per 100 000 Residents in the U.S. 2019

Cities with the largest number of skate parks per 100 000 residents in the United States in 2019	
Laredo, TX	3,7
Sacramento, CA	3,4
Chula Vista, CA	2,9
Reno, NV	2,3
Henderson, NV	2,3
Long Beach, CA	1,9
Anaheim, CA	1,9
Las Vegas, NV	1,7
El Paso, TX	1,7
Albuquerque, NM	1,6

Source: Statista

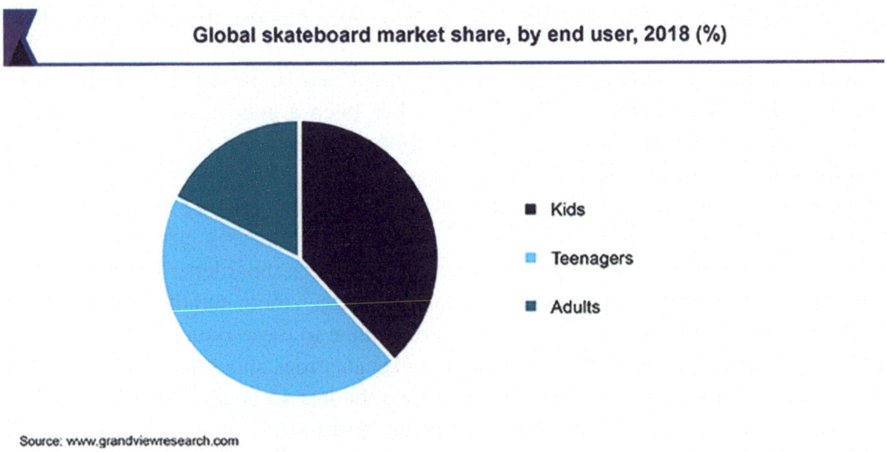

Graph 6.14 Global skateboard makert share

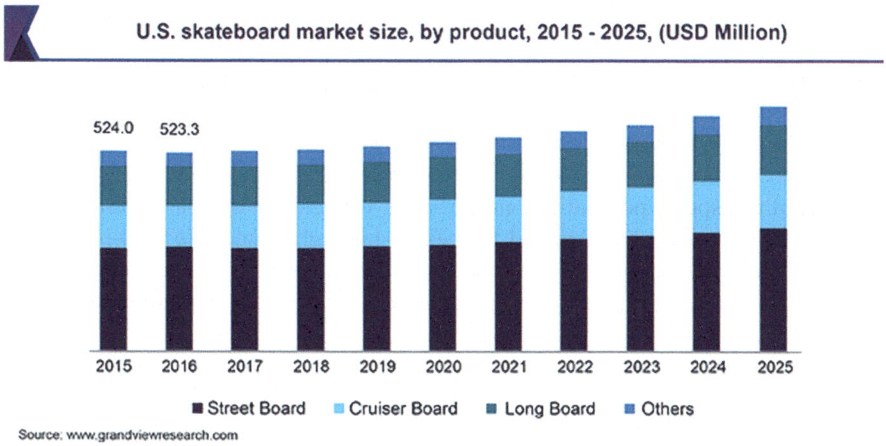

Graph 6.15 U.S. skateboard market size

Finding a specific "architecture of skateboarding" as a concrete metaphor that characterizes contemporary urban design Borden (2001) argues that

> The architecture of skateboarding falls into two interdependent categories, one closer to the conventional realm of architecture as the conceptualization, design, and production of built spaces, the other closer to the realm of the user and the experience and creation of space through bodily processes.

It is no coincidence, referring to Lefebvre's classification, that we mentioned at the beginning, he identifies three different ways of occupying the territory: (a) the physical or natural space; (b) constructed space; (c) the space of representation, which give rise to different phases in the evolution of the relationship between space, the body, and technology, but also, we would add, to the different construction of meanings that urban spaces take on about the demand for well-being.

This third phase represents today the most interesting way to explore precisely because the physical space—demanded or reused by skateboarders—also becomes a symbolic space that tends to give voice to interstitial spaces and the metropolitan populations frequent them. In the quadrant of our model in which those who use interstitial spaces in a perceptive way are placed, skateboarders are certainly the most striking example of a "reaction" to the normal city designed on order, calculation, and synchronicity and transformed instead into the city of play and artistic expression. The demand for the city becomes a demand for well-being linked to bodily practices. And physical practices are now the symbol of a new form of participation that translates into civic engagement by claiming spaces, the protection of spaces, the possibility of reuse, the possibility of redefinition. Today, these practices are the only ones that still manage to intercept this demand. They appear as an apparent concreteness, which seems linked to the superficiality of an "aesthetic of the body". But they are much more profound because the meaning of the aesthetics of the body today is deeper.

In short, fitness culture goes beyond the confines of the gymnasium to occupy urban spaces, all of them both established and interstitial. It now populates the city and circulates among the urban population, not only among gym-goers. In this way, it becomes the supporting structure to which demand for well-being and quality of life is anchored, which uses sport with the same spirit of claiming as the occupation of the squares was used in the past as a form of protest or participation. We must look at metropolitan sports populations in the same way as we looked at professional populations in the past: the demand for citizenship rights linked to well-being and quality of life remains strong. However, how it is expressed is intercepted by new "urban types", of which the sporting population is a politically influential group.

6.17 The Space of Well-Being, the Well-Being of the Space: A Sociological Approach to Quality of Life

We wanted to imagine a space that can take on connotations polarised with respect to strategically or socially constructed dimensions that involve three urban sports populations, runners, cyclers, skateboarders (Fig. 6.10).

We did not deal with other urban metropolitan populations such as parkour tracers, skaters, kids playing football on the road or in a square, as in many towns of the "global south", etc. Each activity can also 'spill over' into another quadrant or partly spill over into another quadrant. Each urban sports population can therefore develop an action of use or transformation of urban space. Use can take the form of "predation". The change, as a dysfunctional distortion. Upstream there is a difference in considering space as an object of attention that develops positively into a *space cared for*; or, as a space of use that develops negatively, as a *predated* space. Increasingly, therefore, because of the weight that the culture of fitness has assumed, urban spaces and practices in spaces are also giving rise to populations whose demand for well-being, gradually becomes not only aimed at improving their physical and mental conditions, but also the environmental conditions. The conditions in which they carry out the activities that generate that well-being. These are

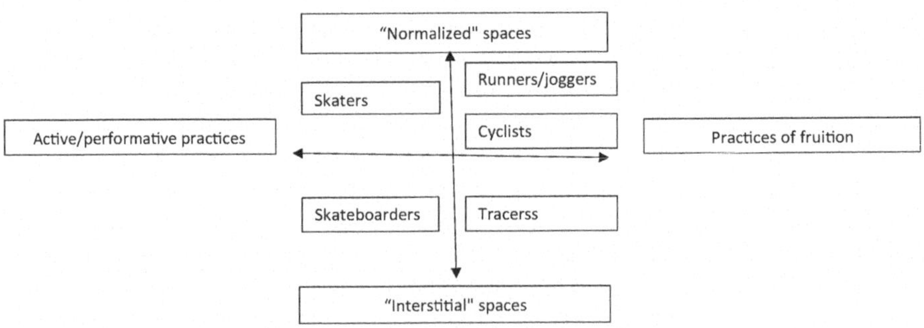

Fig. 6.10 Conceptualization of the space of well-being (By Authors)

new populations that demand new tipe of well-being. And which will most likely *coagulate* the interests of such pleasant activities into political demand.

Bibliography

Asimakopoulos, S., Asimakopoulos, G., & Spillers, F. (2017). Motivation and user engagement in fitness tracking: Heuristics for mobile healthcare wearables. *Informatics, 4*(5), 1–16.

Augè, M., (2008). *Eloge de la bicyclette*, Paris, Payot e Rivages, trad. it. , *Il bello della bicicletta*, Bollati Boringhieri, Torino, 2009.

Bale, J. (2004). *Running cultures. Racing in time and space*, Frank Cass.

Barsella, S. (1999). Bicycle. *Il mito e la poesia, in Italica, 76*(1), 70–97.

Barthes, R. (1957), *Mythologies*, Editions du Seuil. trad. It., *I miti d'oggi*, Einaudi, Torino, 1974.

Bijker, W. E. (1995). *On bicycles, backlites, and bulbs*. MIT Press.

Borden, I. (2001). Body architecture: Skateboarding and the creation of super-architectural space In J. Hill (Ed.), *Occupying architecture: Between the architect and the user*. Routledge, 1998.

Borgers, J., Vos, S., & Scheerder, J. (2015). Belgium (Flanders). Trends and governance in running. In J. Scheerder, K. Breedveld, & J. Borgers (Eds.), *Running across Europe. The rise and size of one of the largest sport markets* (pp. 28–58). Palgrave-McMillan.

Brand, C., Dons, E., Anaya-Boig, E., Avila-Palencia, I., Clark, A., de Nazelle, A., et al. (2021). The climate change mitigation effects of daily active travel in cities. *Transportation Research Part D: Transport and Environment, 93*, 102764.

Bridel, W., Pirkko, M., Denison, J. (Eds.). (2016). *Endurance running. A socio-cultural examination*, Routledge.

Cavazza, S. (2009). *Viva l'ozio. Il tempo libero nell'età contemporanea*. In S. Cavazza, & E. Scarpellini, *Il secolo dei consumi* (pp. 85–116), Carocci.

Chatterjee, K., Chng, S., Clark, B., Davis, A., De Vos, J., Ettema, D., Handy, S., Martin, A., & Reardon, L. (2020). Commuting and wellbeing: A critical overview of the literature with implications for policy and future research. *Transport Reviews, 40*(1), 5–34.

Collins, R. (2004). *Interaction ritual chains*. Princeton University Press.

Csikszentmihalyi, M. (1990). *Flow: The psychology of optimal experience*. Harper & Row.

D'Ovidio, M., & Nuvolati, G. (2011). Mobilità, classe creativa, popolazioni urbane. *Sociologia urbana e rurale, 94*, 43–61.

Dallinga, J. M., Mennes, M., Alpay, L., Bijwaard, H., & de la Faille-Deutekom, M. B. (2015). App use, physical activity and healthy lifestyle: a cross sectional study. *BMC Public Health, 15*(833), 1–9.

De Certeau, M. (1980). *L'Invention du Quotidien* (Vol. 1). Union générale d'éditions.

ECF. (2016). *The EU cycling economy.*

ECF. (2018). *The benefits of cycling.*

Elia, D. F. A. (2009). *Lo sport in Italia. Dal loisir alla pratica*. Carocci.

Ettema, D. (2016). Runnable cities: How does the running environment influence perceived attractiveness, restorativeness, and running frequency? *Environment and Behavior, 48*(9), 1127–1147.

European Commission. (2014). *Special Eurobarometer 422a. Quality of Transport.*

European Commission. (2021). *Gli europei vogliono andare in bicicletta*, disponibile sul link https://ec.europa.eu/info/strategy/recovery-plan-europe/recovery-coronavirus-success-stories/environment-and-climate/europeans-want-ride-their-bicycles_it#relatedlinks.

Eurostat. (2018). *Archive: Statistics on commuting patterns at regional level.* https://ec.europa.eu/eurostat/statistics-explained/index.php?title=Statistics_on_commuting_patterns_at_regional_level&oldid=403318#General_overview.

Favole, A. (2015). Augè's bicycle. *Anthropology of Sport, 60*, 45–46.

Fotopoulou, A., & O'Riordan, K. (2017). Training to self-care: Fitness tracking, biopedagogy and the healthy consumer. *Health Sociology Review, 26*(1), 54–68.

Franceschini, E. (2021). *Tutti in pista, con la pandemia cresciute le ciclabili in Europa*. Repubblica, https://www.repubblica.it/green-and-blue/2021/03/15/news/tutti_in_pista_con_la_pandemia_cresciute_le_ciclabili_in_europa-292309904/ (15 marzo 2021).

Frissen, V., Lammes, S., de Lange, M., de Mul, J., & Raessens, J. (2015). *Playful identities. The ludification of digital media cultures*. Amsterdam University Press.

Fujiki, Y., Kazakos, K., Puri, C., Buddharaju, P., Pavlidis, I., & Levine, J. (2008). NEAT-o-Games: Blending physical activity and fun in the daily routine. *Computer Entertainment, 6*(2), 1–22.

Gell, A. (1998). *Art and agency. An anthropological theory* (pp. 41–42). Oxford University Press.

Gouveia, R., Karapanos, E., & Hassenzahl, M. (2015). *How do we engage with activity trackers? A Longitudinal Study of Habito*, manuscript, Ubicomp (pp. 1–12). http://experiencedesign.m-iti.org/Ubicomp15_Engagement.pdf.

Gratton, C., & Henry, I. (Eds.). (2001). *Sport in the city*. Routledge.

GVR. (2020). *Fitness app market size, share & trends analysis report*. https://www.grandviewresearch.com/industry-analysis/fitness-app-market.

Hallmann, K., & Wicker, P. (2012). Consumer profiles of runners at marathon Races. *International Journal of Event and Festival Management, 3*(2), 171–187.

Hitchings, R., & Latham, A. (2016). How 'social' is recreational running? Findings from a qualitative study in London and implications for public health promotion. *Health & Place*, 1–7. https://doi.org/10.1016/j.healthplace.2016.10.003.

IJsselsteijn, W., de Kort, Y., Westerink, J., de Jager M., & Bonants R. (2004). Fun and sports: Enhancing the home fitness experience. In *Entertainment computing–ICEC 2004, LNCS* (Vol. 3166, pp. pp. 46–56). Springer.

Ilich, I. (1973). *Energie et équité*, Editions du Seuil, trad it., *Elogio della bicicletta*. Bollati Boringhieri, 2006.

Isfort. (2021). *17mo Rapporto Audimob*.

Istat. (2018). *Urban environment*, data tables.

Janssen, M., Walravens, R., Thibaut, E., Scheerder, J., Brombacher, A., & Vos, S. (2020). Understanding different types of recreational runners and how they use running-related technology. *International Journal of Environmental Research and Public Health, 17*(7), 2276–2294.

Jensen, M. M., & Mueller, F. F. (2014). *Running with technology: Where are we heading?* OzCHI '14, December, https://www.researchgate.net/publication/292986639_Running_with_Technology_Where_Are_We_Heading.

Kass, A., (2007). *Transforming the mobile phone into a personal performance coach*. In B. J. Fogg & D. Eckles (Eds.), *Mobile persuasion. 20 perspectives on the future of behavior change*. Stanford, Stanford Captology Media.

Kuru, A., & Forlizzi, J. (2015). *Engaging experience with physical activity tracking products*. In A. Marcus (Ed.), *Design, user experience, and usability: Design discourse*, DUXU 2015, (Lecture Notes in Computer Science, Vol. 9186). Springer.

Kuru, A. (2016). Exploring experience of runners with sports tracking technology. *International Journal of Human-Computer Interaction, 32*(11), 847–860.

Lasane, A. (2015). *Atiba Jefferson talks the cultural influence of skateboarding and the art of skate photography*, Complex, 31 March. Quoted in Lombard, 2016. Retrieved November 10, 2020, from, https://www.complex.com/style/2015/03/atiba-jefferson-talks-influence-of-skateboarding-and-the-art-of-skate-photography.

Latour, B. (2005). *Reassembling the social. An introduction to actor-network-theory*. Oxford University Press.

Latour, B. (2006). Where are the missing masses? Sociology of some everyday objects. In A. Mattozzi, *Il senso degli oggetti tecnici*. Meltemi.

Laurent, J. (2012). *Le skateboard: analyse sociologique d'une pratique physique urbaine*. L'Harmattan.

Lazendorf, M., & Geertsema, A. B. (2014). The cycling boom in large German cities—Empirical evidence for successful cycling campaigns. *Transport Policy, 36*, 26–33.
Lefebvre, H. (1974). La production de l'éspace. *L'Homme et la société, 31-32*, 15–32.
Lega, A. (2020). *1° rapporto sull'economia della bici in italia e sulla ciclabilità nelle città.*
Lepetit, B., Ozouf, M. V., & Salvemini, B. (1993). Pratiche dello spazio e identità sociali: temi e problemi di una riflessione in corso. *Meridian, 18*, 141–150.
Lo Verde, F. M. (2014). *Sociologia dello sport e del tempo libero*. Il Mulino.
Lombard, K. J. (Ed.) (2016). *Skateboarding. Subcultures, sites and shifts*. Routledge.
Louison, C. (2011). *The impossible. Rodney Mullen, Ryan Sheckler and the fantastic history of skateboarding*. Lyons Press.
Lupton, D. (2014). Apps as artefacts: Towards a critical perspective on mobile health and medical apps. *Societies, 4*, 606–622.
Lupton, D., & Jutel, A. (2015). It's like having a physician in your pocket! A critical analysis of selfdiagnosis smartphone apps. *Social Science & Medicine, 133*, 128–135.
MacBride Stewart, S. (2019). Atmospheres, landscapesand nature: Off-road runners' experiences of well-being. *Health, 23*(2), 139–157.
Machemehl, C., & Roult, R. (2019). Urban skating sport: Current research on sports-related urbanity. *Loisir et Société/Society and Leisure, 42*(3), 321–335.
Martin, A. (2005). Agents in inter-action. Bruno Latour and agency. *Journal of Archaeological Method and Theory, 12*, 283–311.
Martinotti, G. (1993). *Metropoli. La nuova morfologia sociale della città*. Il Mulino.
Meloni, P. (2013). Objects of everyday life and social relations: A reflection on Daniel Miller's studies. *Lares, 79*(2–3), 353–362.
Millington, B. (2014). Smartphone apps and the mobile privatization of health and fitness. *Critical Studies in Media Communication, 31*(5), 479–493.
Nemeth, J. (2006). Conflict, exclusion, relocation: Skateboarding and public space. *Journal of Urban Design, 11*(3), 297–318.
New York Times. (2020). *Thinking of buying a bike? Get ready for a very long wait*. https://www.nytimes.com/2020/05/18/nyregion/bike-shortage-coronavirus.html?action=click&module=Spotlight&pgtype=Homepage&fbclid=IwAR1edcp3Jig-OulJCmJhJu4_A1Yrp4cT9l0L6PFCrGrX6yO-YtyBoUmdGdk (04 maggio 2021).
Norman, D. A. (2003). *Emotional design: Why we love (or hate) everyday objects*. Basic Books.
Nuvolati, P. (2006). *Lo sguardo vagabondo. Il flâneur e la città da Baudelaire ai postmoderni*. il Mulino.
Pepe, V. (2014). La vita activa dei giovani anziani. In F. M. Lo Verde (Ed.), *Sociologia dello sport e del tempo libero*. Il Mulino.
Pucci, A. (2008). Agency, oggetto, immagine. L'antropologia dell'arte di Alfred Gell e l'antichità classica. *estratto da Ricerche di storia dell'arte, 94*, 35–40.
Reckwitz, A. (2002). Toward a theory of social practices: A development in culturalist theorizing. *European Journal of Social Theory, 5*(2), 243–263.
Ritterfeld, U., Cody, M., & Vorderer, P. (2009). *Serious games: Mechanisms and effects*. Routledge.
Saelens, B. E., & Handy, S. L. (2008). Built environment correlates of walking: A review. *Medicine & Science in Sports & Exercise, 40*(7, Suppl. 1), 550–566.
Sam, M., & Hughson J. (2013). *Sport in the city: Cultural connections*. Routledge.
Sassatelli, R. (2010). *Fitness culture. Gyms and commercialisation of discipline and fun*. Palgrave MacMillan.
Saunders, P. (1981). *Social theory and the urban question*. Hutchinson University Library.
Schatzki, T., Knorr Cetina, K., & von Savigny, E. (Eds.). (2001). *The practice turn in contemporary theory*. Routledge.
Scheerder, J., Breedveld, K., & Borgers, J. (Eds.). (2015). *Running across Europe. The rise and size of one of the largest sport markets*. Palgrave-McMillan.

Scheerder, J., Vandermeerschen, H., Van Tuyckom, C., Hoekman, R., Breedveld, K., & Vos, S., (2011). Understanding the game: Sport participation in Europe. Facts, reflections and recommendations. *Sport Policy & Management,* 10. University of Leuven/Research Unit of Social Kinesiology & Sport Management.

Shimano. (2020). *State of the nations report. Examining attitudes towards e-bike usage in 11 European countries.*

Shipway, R., & Holloway, I. (2013). Health and the running body: Notes from an Ethnography. *International Review for the Sociology of Sport, 51*(1), 78–96.

Smith, R. (2020, July 8). *How bicycles changed the world*, https://www.nationalgeographic.it.

Smith, S. (1998). Athletes, runners, and joggers: participant-group dynamics in a sport of "individuals". *Sociology of Sport Journal, 15*, 174–192.

Stebbins, R. A. (2002). Leisure Reflections...No. 1: Choice and Experiential Definitions of Leisure, LSA Newsletter No. 63, November 2002.

Sthephens, J., & Allen, J. (2013). Mobile phone interventions to increase physical activity and reduce weight. *A systematic review. Journal of Cardiovascular Nursery, 28*(4), 320–329.

Stratford, E. (2016). Mobilizing a spatial politics of street skating: Thinking about the geographies of generosity. *Annals of the American Association of Geographers, 106*(2), 350–357.

Tallarita, L. (2017). Sport e benessere corporeo. il fitness italiano punta sul pilates. *Studi di Sociologia, Anno 55*(Fasc. 1), 103–120.

Tholander, J., & Nylander, S. (2015). Snot, sweat, pain, mud, and snow—Performance and experience in the use of sports watches, wellness & wearables «CHI '15». *Proceedings of the 33rd Annual ACM Conference on Human Factors in Computing Systems 18* (pp. 2913–2922).

Tumminelli, G. (2010). *Sovrapposti. Processi di trasformazione degli spazi ad opera degli stranieri*. Franco Angeli.

United Nations. (2019). *The world cities 2018*. https://www.un.org/en/events/citiesday/assets/pdf/the_worlds_cities_in_2018_data_booklet.pdf

Van Hooren, B., Goudsmit, J., Restrepo, J., & Vos, S. (2019). Real-time feedback by wearables in running: Current approaches, challenges and suggestions for improvements. *Journal of Sports Sciences*. https://www.researchgate.net/publication/337732005_Real-time_feedback_by_wearables_in_running_Current_approaches_challenges_and_suggestions_for_improvements.

Volontè, P. (2017). Il contributo dell'Actor-Network Theory alla discussione sull'agency degli oggetti. *Politica&Società, 1*, 31–58.

Warde, A. (2005). Consumption and theories of practice. *Journal of Consumer Culture, 5*(2), 131–153.

Wilcox, R. C., Andrews, D. L., Pitter, R., & Irwin, R. L. (2003). *Sporting dystopias the making and meaning of urban sport cultures*. State University of New York Press.

Zenger, N. (2013). *Appropriate Fitness and the CyberRunner: Governing the body through mobile media* [Master thesis, Concordia University]. http://spectrum.library.concordia.ca/977829/.

Zichermann, G., & Cunningham, C. (2011). *Gamification by design: Implementing game mechanics in web and mobile apps* (1st ed.). O'Reilly Media.

Chapter 7
"From Whom Comes the New Question of Well-Being in Italy? Practitioners of Sport and Physical Activity"

Stefano Martelli and Giovanna Russo

7.1 Introduction: Towards a "Wellness Culture"

In the last decades, the physical and mental well-being of the population has become one of the primary goals of "advanced" societies. The concept of well-being is now a "concept-guide" for innovative actions for health, consumption and sustainable lifestyles. Daily life is becoming the object of "care" as never before. With a view to a better "life-time value" (Rifkin, 2000, p. 11), individuals are becoming more aware of themselves and their needs, which leads to question of well-being that goes beyond overcoming the disease or pain, or the indication of a specific social status.

The notion of health is strongly intertwined with that of a healthy lifestyle, intercepting in sports practice and physical activity one of the keys to interpret the socio-cultural change that goes under the wider term of "wellness". It is not just a matter of putting together fitness and well-being, but of going further. Nowadays, wellness refers not only to the idea of improving/preserving the health of the individual in order to increase wellbeing, but also to spread this vision to the community and the environment (Russo, 2018b).

The approach and work strategy presented in the document of the World Health Organization "*The European health report 2012: Charting the way to wellbeing*" (Who EU, 2013a) states this key point. The report involves the broad perspective of well-being as a frame to achieve improvements for the psycho-physical, social and relational health of the population. Pursuing and maintaining these goals is part of the social contract that connects Governments to the citizens they represent. Health

---

The chapter is the result of the joint work of the authors; in specific S. Martelli wrote par. 3; G. Russo par. 1 and 2.

S. Martelli · G. Russo (✉)
Department of Education Studies, "Alma Mater Studiorum", University of Bologna, Bologna, Italy
e-mail: s.martelli@unibo.it; giovanna.russo6@unibo.it

P. Corvo, F. M. Lo Verde (eds.), *Sport and Quality of Life*, Social Indicators Research Series 84, https://doi.org/10.1007/978-3-030-93092-9_7

and wellbeing are therefore the most meaningful aspects of a social transformation in which integration, social cohesion and security are requirements to the European welfare state. They are particularly important not only themselves, but also because they reduce inequalities in health that still are one of the main challenges for civilized countries.

The most well-known international documents aimed to promoting health and active lifestyles lie on these premises—from Ottawa Charter (1986), to Jakarta Declaration (1997), up to the Toronto Charter (2010)—specifically and strongly support physical activity as a tool of advocacy and invite people to adopt active and sustainable lifestyles. In this context, health promotion represents a global, social and political process, including actions aimed to strengthening the skills and abilities of people both at an individual level, and at a macro level, thus changing social, environmental and economic conditions.

In other words, it is necessary to create favourable conditions for health and healthy lifestyles in terms of *advocacy* for health (ibidem), mass media and the new subjects of public and social communication becoming strategic instruments for empowering people.

One of the *advocacy* main priorities is therefore, to counter the population's tendency to overweight and obesity, mainly reducing people's sedentary habitus (Bourdieu, 1979) by promoting healthy and active lifestyles. The sedentariness is in fact the main reason for several diseases (chronic non-communicable diseases, including cardiovascular diseases) that cause about 600 000 deaths per year in 53 European WHO countries only. In these areas 30–80% of adults are obese and/or overweight; about 20% of children are overweight, among which 1/3 are obese (WHO, 2015). Obesity, especially among children and elderly people, is a key issue for health organizations. Since 2000 «for the first time in human evolution the number of adults with excess weight *(has)* surpassed the number of those who were underweight" (Caballero, 2007, p. 1).

This condition is mainly due to three interconnected factors, the following:

1. Rapid globalization and urbanization**:** the growth of economic, social and cultural integration between different areas of the world has led to a change in lifestyle, involving nutrition and physical activity, which are often defined as unhealthy. The scientific community defines the so-called *obesogenic environment* (WHO, 2007) referring to the plurality of causes (economic, technological and political factors) that increase the chances to gain weight and become obese. The exposure to the obesogenic environment «is increasing in both high-income countries and low- and middle-income countries and across all socioeconomic groups» (WHO, 2016, p. 4);
2. Changes in food availability and type: over the last decades, food production and distribution of always cheaper fatty food and therefore more easily accessible for a lot of people (ibidem);
3. Decline of physical activity: decreasing opportunities for physical activity, and more time spent on sedentary leisure activities. Sedentary work and modern transportation imply that most of our life is spent while sitting (EU, 2014, p. 6).

The direct consequences of a sedentary habitus are very important at an economic level, in terms of both private and public spending for hospital treatment, but the social, cultural and environmental effects are even worse (Edwards & Tsourus, 2008). Therefore, between "macro" effects (welfare policies) and individual trajectories, cultural parameters are established to redefine the concept of well-being by stating the importance of sporting activities in order to keep fit/healthy.

The evolution of sports practices with a view to the pluralisation of sports choices, together with a conception of preventive and pro-active health, has highlighted the importance of sport and physical activity, their diffusion and ability to pursue a better quality of life. Physical activity plays a double role in health promotion strategies. On one hand it contributes to countering obesity and chronic diseases; on the other, it is part of the broader project of promoting an active lifestyle among the population, encouraging people to walk, use a bicycle, move around the city, etc., with environmental advantages such as decreasing air pollution and reducing the risk of getting involved in traffic accidents. This in a perspective of sustainability and implementation of collaborative and relational dynamics (WHO, 2016). This way, sports policies and widespread physical activity become instruments of social integration which are essential for health, environmental and sustainable mobility policies. Moreover, they also appear useful social "devices" for planning of urban spaces, design of infrastructures, mobility, social and educational services (Edwards & Tsouros 2008).

Following these standards, the *European Gaining in health* strategy promoted by WHO Europe (autumn 2006), was included in Italy in the 2007 National Health Prevention Plan. The main objectives of the program were the following: promoting healthy eating, encouraging regular physical activity, controlling one's own weight and abandoning behaviours that are harmful to health. Therefore, a set of basic actions have been implemented for the well-being of citizens to improve their lifestyle (IstiSan, 2016, p. 118).

The socio-cultural change behind these transformations concerns the progressive expansion of the concept of sustainable well-being in the global society, which appears increasingly linked to life chances (Dahrendorf, 1989) and the spread of "*wellness culture*" (Foster et al., 2011; Russo, 2018a). Exploring the wellness phenomenon nowadays it's particularly interesting because it helps to broaden the concept of well-being, whereby through sports practice it implies improving the "quality of life". Hence the assumption that wellness relates to a concept of healthy life, in which sporting activities are the main means of staying healthy, physical and psychic. Wellness as practices and knowledge, oriented towards a "good life" (Soper, 2007): a healthy existence, that is aimed to a more authentic and socially adequate concept of *well-being*.

The new challenges of the politics of well-being and health of the population are increasingly played on the awareness of the importance of active, healthy and socially participated lifestyles on an individual and collective level. This means considering the importance of sport practices not only in relation to the amount of people doing sport or physical activity; but rather, for the proposed and spread values. The broader goal of sport and physical activity is pursuing a better quality of life, being healthier from both a psycho-physical and environmental and relational point of view (Russo, 2018a).

The following paragraphs discuss the core reflection of wellness culture and the strategies for physical activity at European and Italian level starting from WHO Global Action Plan 2013–2020 (Who 2013b) (non 2015) to confirm the diffusion of the process of "sporting health".

On these premises, the chapter analyses the theme of promoting sport for health and well-being in Italy, through the following aspects:

(a) the evolution Italian people who practice sport and physical activity recently (par. 2);
(b) the emerging portrait of "Fan for health" (par. 3). This kind of description makes it possible to distinguish those who play sports for wellness reasons only (health-conscious), and those who do so for other reasons. On the overall, this analysis highlights the characteristics of "wellness Italian people" (who they are, how many they are, for what reasons they practice physical activities wellness oriented), giving a socio-cultural portrait of sportsmen motivated by the health goal.

In short, the aim of the chapter is to highlight the main and recent trends taking place in sports and physical activity in Italy.

7.2 "Keep on Moving and Stay Healthy": A Portrait in Europe and Italy of Sporting Practices

A series of legislative and regulatory measures for sport and physical activities have been developed in the new millennium, in order to go beyond the merely economic dimension of sport and enhance its social, cultural and political aspects. The White Paper on Sport (2007), as well as the Treaty of Lisbon (2009), have in fact formalized the interest in sport at the European level due to its important social function and the ability to promote a shared cultural identity.

Mainly the strategies of the European Region of the WHO consider sport and physical activity as a fundamental tool to promote good health for all citizens through a culture of movement aimed to combine physical activity, well-being education and citizenship rights.

The document "Physical Activity strategies for the WHO European Region 2016–2025" (WHO, 2015) was prepared in view of the main objectives of the WHO Global Action Plan (WHO, 2013b), in which the increase in daily physical activity for the population is considered one of the main nine targets at global level. The aim is a 10% reduction in prevailing insufficient physical activity by 2025; in addition, an increased level of sporting practice could play an important role for three other goals (ibidem, p. 1):

- a 25% relative reduction in the risk of premature mortality because of cardiovascular diseases, cancer, diabetes or chronic respiratory diseases;
- a 25% relative reduction in the prevalence of raised blood pressure or containment of the prevalence of raised blood pressure, according to national circumstances;
- halt the rise in diabetes and obesity.

Despite the known benefits of physical activity, there is a worldwide trend towards lower global daily physical activity par day. Globally, 1/3 of adults do not achieve the recommended levels of physical activity. In Europe, estimates indicate that more than 1/3 of adults are insufficiently active; 1/6 of teens (15 y.o or above) never/rarely exercise or play sport; more than half never or seldom engage in such physical activities (dancing, cycling, gardening) (ibidem, p. 2).

The consequences of sedentary life are impressive in terms of deaths (one million, about 10% of the total), burden of coronary heart disease (5%), type 2 od diabetes (7%), obesity (more than 50% of adults, about 70% adult population) and so on. Given these data, there are many strategies implemented in the Health 2020 Plan—the WHO European policy for health and wellbeing: the ongoing debate on sport and physical activity suggests and promotes different guiding documents[1] to enhance it for people, organization and whole country.

Therefore, many studies and researches have been carried out to investigate these issues starting from the demand and supply of sports, but also the impact of active participation in the various European countries. The last survey of Eurobarometer (2018) shows a heterogeneous picture, in line with the latest surveys from 2005 to date. The proportion of Europeans that state to do exercise or play sport with at least some regularity is only 40%, including 7% who exercise or play sport regularly. Conversely, the amount of those that never exercise or play sport continues to increase. Almost half of Europeans (46%) say that they never exercise or play sport, while 14% only seldom do so. Compared to 2013, the proportion of those who never exercise or play sport has increased (+4 percentage points, from 42% to 46%), while the proportion that does so seldom has decreased (from 17% to 14%). This has kept being the longer-term trend since 2009, when 39% of the interviewed said that they never exercised or played sport.

In general, it is important to note, with respect to the 2013 survey (Eurobarometer, 2014), the awareness of the importance of physical activity: 42% of the interviewees stated they were interested in it. The tendency to carry out physical activity in an informal manner (bicycles, walks, dancing ...) is confirmed, involving 44% of the European population at least once a week. Performing outdoor activities (40%), at home (32%) or in sports centre (12%) is an increasingly popular trend that highlights a new "people" of practitioners who want to combine distraction, relaxation and movement in the name of good health. In fact, this is one of the individual

[1] In this sense, see for example: *Step to Health a European framework to promote physical activity for health* (2007); *A healthy city is an active city* (2008); *Eu Action Plan on Childhood Obesity* 2014–2020 (2013).

motivations for physical-sporting practice in Europe to reap the greatest consensus (ibidem, p. 5, and p. 51): 54% of European citizens interviewed say that they carry out a physical activity in order to preserve and improve their health status.[2]

This summary of European sporting practices explains the different welfare demand of the population. The phase of pluralization of sports practice (from the 1970s onwards), is no longer connect to the competitive nature of sport. The spread of outdoor sports, the emphasis on the playful dimension, the emergence of the acrobatic component, fitness, sports tourism, gentle exercise shows evidence of the success of the "post" -modern sport culture.

Above all, it emerges the importance of "keeping fit", the result of a "good work" on themselves (not only physical) and the pleasure of leisure.

The scene of sports practice traced at European level shows strong discrepancies between the member states of the EU. The most physically active countries are in particular those of northern Europe, while the percentages of physically active European citizens belonging to the so-called Mediterranean countries, including Italy, are lower.

Over the last decades, Italians have changed their attitude with sport and physical activity, but the ambiguous approach of social policies (in sports) does not really promote healthy and active cities, in which citizens can improve their habitus.[3]

Nevertheless, a briefly view on the latest ISTAT report (2017: 1) shows that the numbers of sports practitioners have increased considerably in all age groups, in both genders and in all regions. From 2013 to 2016 (+ 4.2 points), two "new" million and 519 000 Italians approached the sporting practice. Overall, the active population in Italy is composed of 35 million 593 000 individuals who do one or more sports or some physical activity in their free time.

In specific, a long-term tendency to participate more in sport seems to emerge: in 1982 the share of participants aged over six was only 15.4%. This increase affects both men and women and, although in a differentiated manner, all age groups. Nevertheless, the number of sedentary citizens remains very high over time: after a decrease between 2006 and 2010 (from 42.0% to 38.8%), since 2010 the share of inactivity is stable at around 39% [ibidem: 2].

According to Istat (2017), in 2015 there were 20, two million people aged over three practising one or more sports (34.3% of the population) in their spare time, of which 24.4% with continuity and 9.8 percent occasionally. On the other hand, the 26.5% of the population, while not practicing a sport, carry out physical activities

[2]This is followed by motivations such as: "fitness improvement" (47%), "relaxation" (38%) and "fun" (30%). The aesthetic improvement of the body instead appears a secondary motivation: 28% are trained to improve their physical appearance, 14% to counteract the effects of aging, 12% to strengthen their self-esteem (Eurobarometer, 2018, p. 51).

[3]A deeply analysis of the different welfare policies on sport and PA in Europe is carried out by Pioletti A. and Porro N. (2013), *Lo sport degli europei*, Franco Angeli, Milano [*European's sport. Citizenship, activities, motivation*]. In this study the sporting European system emerge in all its contradictions and differences between all the countries about the Union.

such as walking, swimming, cycling or others (15.64 million). The inactive people are 23.05 million (39.1% of the population).

The attitudes to participate in sport are not homogeneous across the different regions of the country. This is also due to a different availability of organized structures, habits, and cultures. In the North-East there is the highest rate of people practising sport (40.4%), followed by the North-West (39.5%) and the Centre (35.3%). In the South and in the Islands the rate of sport participation is 26.2%. The participation in sport is the highest for the group age 11–14 (70.3%, of which 61% regularly and 9.3% occasionally) and tends to decrease with the age. Predominantly, Italians participate in sport and physical activity for passion or pleasure (60.3%), to keep fit (54.9%), for leisure (49.5%), and to reduce stress (31.6%). A strong gender difference emerges: participating in sport and physical activity for passion or pleasure is more common among men (67.8% vs. 49.6% of women), as well as considering it as a source of leisure (50.8% vs. 47.7%).

In specific keeping fit, reducing stress and improving physical appearance are the motivations privileged by women (59.8%, 32.6% and 22.3% vs. 51.4%, 30.9% and 17.4% respectively). Moreover, while women attribute greater value to the therapeutic potential of sport and fitness (15.9% vs. 8.8% of men), the values that sport transmits and the contact with nature are motivations declared above all by men.

Motives of sport participation vary considerably by age. The youngest live mainly sport as a pleasure (76.9% in the age group 11–14 and 75.7% among those aged 15–17). Children and adolescents highlight the socializing aspect (more than a quarter of the boys 6–19 practice sport to "to be with others") and the importance of the sport values (over 26% between 3 and 14). Young people over the age of 20 consider sport related to playfulness and pleasure, but the desire to keep fit, indicated by over 65% of people aged between 25 and 44, seems to be the most important motivation. People between 35 and 44 state a decrease in stress (44.5%) as a major motivation. The therapeutic features of sport are related with ageing: it gets value from the age of 45 to become prevalent over 75.

For Italian people, these data show a growing awareness of the importance of physical activity and sport as a tool for health and wellbeing (even if not yet turned into a habitus: data on inactivity remain high). In this framework, the practice of fitness and wellness is evolving. Over the last years fitness (including gymnastic, yoga, aerobic and body building) involves 25.2% of the active population (5.97 million people; 38.7% females, 15.6% males). In particular it represents the first sporting activity (23%, 4642 million people), overcoming football as most participated sport since 2006.

Physical activity is therefore a vehicle of growing awareness aimed to the health and well-being process of the individual, but not yet turned into current practice in the lifestyle of both European and Italian citizens.

7.3 "Fan for Health": A Socio-Cultural Profile of Italian People *(Who Practice Sport for a Healthy Life)*

What motivations push many Italian persons to practice sports or physical activities, with continuity or occasionally? In the special editions of its 'multiscopo' survey, Istat prepared a list of nine motivations to do sport and other activities in the leisure time, which the Institute conducted in the last 20 years.[4]

So one can see that Italian people practice sport and physical activity more frequently because these three motivations (the frequencies in brackets show the findings of last Istat survey (2015):

1. to *keep fit* (62.9%),
2. for *pleasure, passion* (59.1%), and
3. for *recreation* (49.8%).

Less frequent motivations to practice sport are the following: the *chance to relieve stress* (37.5%), the *desire to improve its own physical appearance* (22.4%), the *desire to meet other people* (19.6%), the *therapeutic purpose* (18.6%), the *opportunity to live in synthony with nature* (12.7%), *to practice for the values that sport transmits* (10.8%), and—the last diffused motivation –, *to keep up with the times* (1.9%).

One can ask if there are hidden structures in the motivations, useful to explain these findings. And if there are evidences such as to reinterpretate sport as a movement for physical and mental well-being or wellness; or if other motivations stay in the background and affect the overall wellness demand.

By a factor analysis, repeated for each survey conducted in the four already mentioned years, the "Alma Mater" SportComLab has looked at this hidden structure in the motivations to do sports or physical activities (Martelli, 2018; Martelli et al., 2020). One studied the statistical correlations among these motivations and discovered that those Italian persons who practice sports for healthy or therapeutic purposes, namely wellness, form a distinct group on the three extracted clusters.[5] Another very different group is shaped by sportsmen/sportswomen *for the wish to*

[4]Istat conducted these four surveys in 1995, 2000, 2006, and 2015: this motivations list has never changed. These surveys are "a special edition", because a wide section of their questionnaire has a lot of queries on sport and physical activities; on the contrary, in the annual ('normal') 'multiscopo' survey the questionnaire has very few indicators on movement practices. These 'special' surveys were performed on a sample of about 20 000 Italian families, living in about 840 Italian municipalities of different demographic size; the amplitude of each sample was more than 60 000 people, who were statistically representative of about 60 million of Italian citizens (from 3 to 75 and more years old). Their data has been collected by mixed ways: the CAWI technique (computer-assisted web interviewing), or the PAPI one (paper and pencil interviewing). For further information: http://schedefontidati.istat.it/index.php/Indagine_cittadini_e_tempo_libero

[5]This group was shaped by the *factor 3* (obtained by rotated factor loading, in the pattern matrix, and unique variance: 0.8284); it identified 209 Italian persons on 4.562 of sportsmen/sportswomen (4.58%).

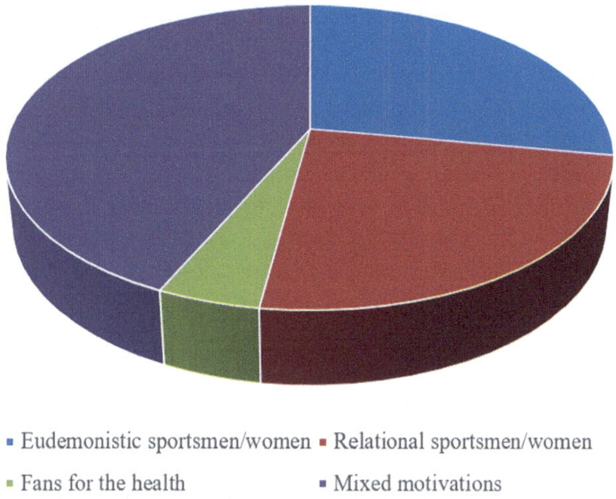

Fig. 7.1 The four groups of Italian sportsmen/ sportswomen, extracted by the factor analysis according to their motivations at movement practices (2015). *Source*: Istat, 2015. *Processing*: the "Alma Mater" SportComLab

achieve a better physical fitness.[6] The extracted third group of respondents gathers Italian persons who *practice sport for the implicit values which it spreads*, and *better relate oneself with others* and *with the nature.*[7] Moreover, the most numerous group is composed by Italian sportsmen/sportswomen *with mixed up motivations*, which is to say persons who are moved by motivations belonging to two extracted factors, or even all of the three of them.

Figure 7.1 shows the rate of these four extracted groups on Italian sportspeople, according to the most recent survey. In the year 2015, the amplitude of these four groups was been the following one:

1. Eudemonistic sportsmen/sportswomen (27.7%),
2. Relational sportsmen/sportswomen (24.5%),
3. Fans for the health (4.6%), and
4. Sportspeople with mixed motivations, that is the 'residual' group (43.2%).[8]

The profile of each of these four groups, drawn by the usual socio-demographic variables, reveals well characterized types. In short, one can see that the "Fans for

[6]This group was shaped by the *factor 2* (0.7255, and other two values); it identified 1.266 Italian persons (27.75%).

[7]This group was shaped by the factor 1 (0.6588, and other four values); it identified 1.118 Italian persons (24.51%).

[8]The consistency of each group is good and one can observe that the four groups have been extracted in each survey, conducted by Istat in the period 1995–2015. Obviously, their amplitude varies according to the survey; for instance, in the year 2006 it was the following one: "Eudemonistic sportsmen/sportswomen" (27.9%), "Relational sportsmen/sportswomen" (16.2%), "Fans for the health" (2.4%); and Sportspeople with "mixed motivations" (53.5%). Moreover, I have proposed [Martelli, 2011] to interpret the first three clusters as distinct sporting styles; indeed, each of them could be interpreted as the effects in the sport of more wide socio-cultural trends, which are transforming the modern society in a 'post'-modern one.

health" are a small minority of Italian sportsmen/sportswomen (4.6% in last Istat survey). Their amplitude has grown in the considered period, moving from about 350 000 Italian people in 1995, to more than 1.6 million in 2015. Most frequently they are: females; adults (+45 years); married persons; inhabitants in a northern region of Italy, such as Valle d'Aosta and Alto Adige; and most commonly they practice postural gymnastics, walking and footing.

It also is possible to complete the socio-demographic profile of the "Fans for health" with many other details, useful for a better understanding of this group of sportsmen/sportswomen; e.g. in the field of cultural and media consumption, their choices are most frequently the following ones:

(a) *According to their exposure at television broadcasts:*

- The "Fans for health" are the less frequently *viewers of 'mediated' sports* (Martelli, 2010) among Italian sportsmen/sportswomen: less than one out of four of them (21.5%) watches sporting games on Tv; indeed, more frequently they prefer to watch *other Tv programs*. Furthermore, they expose themselves at television broadcasts for a *number of hours* a day that is higher than the average of Italian sportsmen/sportswomen (2.80 hours, +0.23 hour on average).
- Among those who turn on the Tv set *exclusively to see sporting events*–not watching anything else, such as movies, fiction, quizzes etc.—the "Fans for health", especially if females, expose themselves less frequently to sports-related broadcasts (−19.7 percentage points on average).

(b) *According to their exposure to newspapers and magazines*:

- Less frequently than the other extracted groups, the "Fans for health" *read newspapers daily* to *look at sports news* (−19.5 points): no other explanatory variables such as sex, age, or residence seem to affect their choice;
- As a confirmation of this less frequent orientation to the reading of sport newspapers, no "Fan of health" *reads* the "Gazzetta dello sport" or other *Italian sporting newspapers* (indeed these magazines seldom offer news about health or wellbeing);
- Unlike the other groups of Italian sportsmen/women, the "Fans for health" do not even *read weekly sports magazines*.

(c) *According to their exposure to radio broadcasts:* The "Fans for health" *listen to sport news on the radio set* less frequently than the other groups of Italian sportsmen/women (−11.8 points), and Italian women make this choice less frequently than males;

(d) *According to their use of a personal computer*:

- Among the heavy users of the *on-line personal computer*, the "Fans for health" appear to be the least frequently represented ("I use Internet every day": −16.3 points). This less frequent propensity of this group of Italian sportsmen/women to frequently surf the Internet strictly depends on the main independent variables, such as age: and the "Fans for health", being more frequently *adult*

persons and the *elderly ones* ("45 and more years old": 81.3% of this group), are therefore less accustomed to frequent use of their pc;
- Even among the surfers in the sports websites, the "Fans for health" are the least commonly represented among the four groups of Italian sportsmen/women (−6.4 points);
- If the computer is off-line, the "Fans for health" use it for gaming less frequently than other groups (−11.8 points). Distributing their answers according to the indipendent variables, one can note that the age affects the choices of these sportsmen/women very much: the younger "Fans for health" use pc for gaming most frequently (+10.5 points), while the adult persons and the elderly ones are far below the average of this group (−6.4 and −4.5 percentage points on average, respectively);

Now, if one looks at the choices of the "Fans for health" to spend their free time, one can observe that:

(e) *Presence of "Fans for health" in a stadium*: in the year 2015 the sportsmen/women of this Italian group were less frequently present at *competitions or sports events* than the ones of the other three extracted groups: only about one out of "Fan for health" four persons went there: 22.3% (while 35.3% of the second group, the "Eudemonistic" ones, and 55% of the first group, the "Relationistic" ones went at the stadium). Among the "Fans for health", this happened more frequently if males, young people, and inhabiting in Southern Italy;

(f) *Participation of "Fans for health" in cultural activities*:

- In 2015 the "Fans for health", most frequently than the other extracted Italian groups, *visited museums or other historic and artistic locations* (+1.6 percentage points on average). Even in this case, the influence of independent variables –such as gender, age and education title– was felt: indeed in that year males, young people or graduates, visited a museum or another historic monument more frequently, than females, elderly people, and people with lower education titles (for instance: the "Fans for health" graduates: +20 percentage points on the average of educational titles);
- On the contrary, in 2015 the "Fans for health" *read books* less frequently than the other extracted groups (−3.1 points); they also *went to a library* less frequently than the other ones (−6.3 points on average);
- Furthermore, in 2015 the "Fans for health" listen to *heard music* less frequently (−6.9 points).

(g) *Their social relations in free time:*

- In 2015 the "Fans for Health" went for walks with their own friends more frequently than the average of Italian sportsmen/sportwomen (+2 percentage points);
- In the same year they *practiced sport with friends* much less frequently than the average (−1.3 points);

- In the same year the "Fans for health" *went to a stadium or to other sporting facilities with their own friends* less frequently (−0.9 points);
- The "Fans for the health" *went also dancing with their friends* less frequently than the average (−1.4 points).

In short, the choices of the "Fans for Health", both in the field of exposition to mass media, and in the field of cultural activities and social relationships in free time, confirm the set hypothesis, i.e. that this Italian sportsmen/sportswomen group shows the emerging transformation of modern sport as itself, to a means of keeping healthy or wellness. The aim to prevent the risks for health, which are often related to aging or therapeutic treatment of joint diseases, is a powerful motivation, even if such aim is shared by few, compared to the majority of Italian sportsmen. The "Fans for Health" group, indeed, seems to be the bearer of one of three main trends in the 'post'-modern culture; it shapes a motivational "pure" type, easy to spot in the widest range of Italian sportspeople.

It's clear now the relevance of the nexus that the "Fans for health" have established between sport and lifestyles, and the importance to study the movement for health in all its socio-cultural implications.

In short, the emerging and the choices made by Italian "Fans for health" in the field of cultural activities and mass media, confirm their undiscussed relevance for the emerging well-being society in Italy. At the same time, it's evident the importance of strengthening the scientific observations on relationship between healthy lifestyles and movement practices to answer the wide and growing demand-making of well-being.

References

Bourdieu, P. (1979). *La distinction. Critique sociale du jugement*. Les Édition De miniut.

Caballero, B. (2007). The global epidemic of obesity: An overview. *Epidemiol Review., 29*, 1–5.

Dahrendorf, R., (1989). *The modern social conflict: The politics of liberty*. California University Press.

Edwards, P., Tsouros, A. (2008). A healthy city is an active city: A physical activity planning guide. Word Health Organisation Europe

EU. (2014). *EU action plan on childhood obesity 2014–2020*. https://ec.europa.eu/health/sites/health/files/nutrition_physical_activity/docs/childhoodobesity_actionplan_2014_2020_en.pdf.

Eurobarometer. (2014). *Sport and physical activity*. Report, Bruxelles, Special Eurobarometer 412/Wave EB80.2—TNS Opinion & Social.

Eurobarometer. (2018). *Sport and physical activity*. http://ec.europa.eu/public_opinion/archives/ebs/ebs_472_en.pdf..

Foster, L. T., Keller, C., McKee, B., & Ostry, A. (2011). *British Columbia atlas of wellness* (2nd ed.). Western Geographical Press.

Istat. (2015). *Indagine multiscopo sulle famiglie: I cittadini e il tempo libero*, elaborazioni sui dati raccolti tramite accesso al Laboratorio per l'Analisi dei Dati ELEmentari ADELE. https://www.istat.it/it/informazioni-e-servizi/per-i-ricercatori/laboratorio-adele.

Istat. (2017). *La pratica sportiva in Italia* «I cittadini e il tempo libero» Anno 2015. http://www.istat.it/it/archivio/204663; and http://dati.istat.it/.

IstiSan—Istituto superiore di Sanità. (2016). *Salute in Italia e livelli di tutela. Approfondimenti sulle indagini Istat sulla salute*. IstiSan rapporto 16/26, Roma http://www.iss.it/binary/publ/cont/16_26_web.pdf.

Martelli, S. (2010). *Lo sport "mediato". Le audience televisive di Olimpiadi, Paralimpiadi e Campionati europei di calcio (2000–2008)*. FrancoAngeli.

Martelli, S. (2011). *Sport, media e intrattenimento. Emozioni in/controllate e struttura sociale emergente*. FrancoAngeli.

Martelli, S. (2018). Italian sportsmen and sportwomen, in search for their own wellness. In G. Russo (Ed.), *Charting the wellness society in Europe. Social transformations in health, sport and consumption* (pp. 65–99). FrancoAngeli.

Martelli, S., Porro, N., & Testa, A. (2020). *Sport, welfare and social policy in the European Union*. Routledege.

Rifkin, J. (2000). *The age of access*. Penguin Putnam, Inc.

Russo, G. (2018a). *The wellness society: Towards a new demand for wellbeing*. In G. Russo (Ed.), *Charting the wellness society in Europe. Social transformations in health, sport and consumption* (pp. 17–34). FrancoAngeli.

Russo, G. (Ed.). (2018b). *Charting the wellness society in Europe. Social transformations in health, sport and consumption*. FrancoAngeli.

Soper, K. (2007). Re-thinking the 'good life': The citizenship dimension of consumer disaffection with consumerism. *Journal of Consumer Culture, 7*, 205–228.

WHO. (2016). *Ending childhood obesity*. WHO.

WHO Europe. (2007). *The challenge of obesity in the WHO European region and the strategies for response*. Summary, WHO Regional Office for Europe.

WHO Europe. (2013a). *The European health report 2012: Charting the way to wellbeing*. Who -Regional Office for Europe.

WHO Europe. (2013b). *Who global action plan for the prevention and control non comunicable desease 2013–2020*.

WHO Europe. (2015). *Physical activity strategy for the WHO European Region 2016–2025*, Who Publication. https://www.dgs.pt/ficheiros-de-upload-2013/pnpaf-who-eu-physical-activity-strategy-2016-2025-final-2016-pdf.aspx.

Chapter 8
Atalanta, a Contemporary Myth that Challenges "Big Football"

Paolo Corvo

> *Who else but a football fan would use a fumble on a muddy field 300 miles away to recall a wedding? Obsession requires a commendable mental agility. (Hornby, 1992)*

8.1 Football as a Grassroots Sport

Writing about football in a scientific way is quite a recent achievement: in the past, in fact, there was a sort of distrust in those who approached sports academically, particularly football. This attitude reflected the unhappy relationship that for a long time football had with the world of culture and science. The writer Galeano compared football to God, for the devotion held by a multitude of believers and the concurrent mistrust of many intellectuals (Galeano, 2012). In truth, this snobbish attitude was not shared by all cultured men, to the point that some intellectuals, also in the past, have argued in favor of conferring the right social importance to sports. To this end, Pier Paolo Pasolini, writer and poet among the most authoritative of the twentieth century, contended that sport is such an important cultural phenomenon that it would be negative for the ruling and intellectual class to ignore it (Pasolini, 2020). In fact, in 1933, the great poet Umberto Saba had already written his *Cinque poesie per il gioco del calcio* (Five poems for the game of football).

The reflection about the social value of football is especially founded on the identification of the game as a religious phenomenon. Still Pasolini saw in football the last sacred representation of our times, fundamentally a ritual, even if also a spectacle meant for diversion (Pasolini, 2020). More recently, the anthropologist Marc Augé reaffirmed that football still 'works' as a religious phenomenon, and that the relationship between sport for the masses and religion is far from being metaphorical (Augé, 2016). Some even blew the dust off the old definition applied to religion, to speak about football as 'opium of the people', i.e. instrument to distract

P. Corvo (✉)
University of Gastronomic Sciences, Pollenzo, Italy
e-mail: p.corvo@unisg.it

P. Corvo, F. M. Lo Verde (eds.), *Sport and Quality of Life*, Social Indicators Research Series 84, https://doi.org/10.1007/978-3-030-93092-9_8

the masses from social and political commitment. It is undoubted, however, that within a few decades football has become one of the most central elements of the entertainment industry and, concurrently, a source of extraordinary profits (Michea, 2014; Tomlinson, 2005).

As a matter of fact, the set of relations existing among football supporters shows many traits commonly ascribed to the religious dimension: the sense of community and, sometimes, of territorial identity; the game as a sacred ritual that differentiates special occasions from everyday life; chanting as an accompaniment to the ritual; urging on the team and the players as if they were super-human entities. Nevertheless, there also are dynamics that distance football from sacred, such as victory and loss happening in the same context, thus dividing the state of mind of the audience, part of which is winning and part of which is losing. Indeed, one of the great merits of sport is its 'capacity for truth': if you are a poor player, you will definitely be unmasked (Hornby, 1992). At all rates, studying the ways in which people live football is undeniably worthwhile: for its unfolding along an apparently uninterrupted continuum of events and comments, the social life of football really promises to offer every sort of information about our society and our culture (Hornby, 1992). It is this perspective that attracted the world of social and human sciences.

One of the most interesting research fields deals with the introduction of individuals to their passion for football. Usually, it works as an intergenerational transmission: fathers bring their children to see a game and they eventually fall in love with their favorite team. It is a feeling not far from the one backing up the relationship of a couple. The author Hornby wrote that he fell in love with football in the same way he would later fall in love with women, without minding the pain and emotional turmoil that goes along with it (Hornby, 1992). He added that football taught him many important things, such as a good share of his knowledge of places in the UK and in Europe, thanks to away games and international competitions. Also, he wrote, it is thanks to football that he learnt the value of investing in things he could not control or belonging to a community where aspirations are shared in a totalizing and uncritical way.

These statements describe what it means to be a football supporter and root for a team (which in Hornby's case is Arsenal) from the point of view of an intellectual, but they hold true for any individual belonging to whatever socio-cultural segment. On the one side, Hornby admits that due to his education and work he inadequately represents most of the stadium population, but on the other, he affirms that for his passion, knowledge about the game and devotion to the team he is nothing different than his fellows supporters (Hornby, 1992). In effect, football has always been an interclass sport. Everybody goes (or better, *used to go*, as we will see) to the stadium and, except for those who populate VIP stands, there small and medium entrepreneurs sit next to their workers (Fini & Padovan, 2019). Football constitutes a total social fact because it regards (to a varying extent) all elements of society and, also, because it lends itself to being scrutinized from a multiplicity of standpoints (Augé, 2016; Porro, 2008).

It is important to underline that football still constitutes *a "regno della lealtà umana esercitato all'aria aperta"* (kingdom of human loyalty practiced outdoors), as defined by the politician and sociologist Antonio Gramsci. This explains the enthusiasm that football keeps sparking among working classes, to the extent of being called 'people's game' by British workers already at the end of the nineteenth century, despite having been invented, like many other sports, by young English noblemen (Michea, 2014). It is a game that does not require money to be played, and all it needs is a ball and a patch of grass, a street, or a beach. Galeano, for instance, remembered creole and migrant boys who improvised football games employing balls made with old socks filled with paper and rugs, and a couple of stone to create the goal (Galeano, 2012; Turnbull et al., 2008).

In addition, supporters experience a thorough identification with their teams, which they desire to be always united and compact, as a large single force that defeats the opponent. In fact, the most spectacular and offensive football happens when the team works as a sympathetic collective, in which every player enjoys playing in support of the others. Players must never find themselves abandoned, without a teammate ready to support them (Michea, 2014). The victory of a team, as much as its defeat, are first and foremost the victory or defeat of the supporters of the team. It is not by chance, indeed, that it is common to say 'we won' or 'we lost'. With their constant support and incitement, supporters 'get on the pitch' along with their players, especially in the hardest moments of a game. That is why the supporter is often addressed as the 'twelfth man on the field". Players can feel the heat of the crowds and many admitted suffering from its lack in the empty stadiums of these Covid19 pandemic years.

Lastly, the physical presence of supporters is fundamental to transform the game into a 'spectacle'. By chanting and realizing choreographies, organized supporters create a lucky combination between the show enacted in the field and the one performed on the stands (Goldblatt, 2006; Spagnolo, 2020). Within this frame of awe, the climax moment is obviously the goal, which in football, differently than in other sports, is relatively rare. Following with Hornby, the goal is described as the thrilling sensation deriving from seeing someone doing something that can only be done three or four times in a game, if you are lucky, or not even once, if you are unlucky (Hornby, 1992). Pasolini instead defines the goal as an invention, a subversion of the code: every goal is ineluctability, dazzle, astonishment, irreversibility (Pasolini, 2020). The crowd rooting for the team that scores a goal rejoices with unstoppable happiness, feeling sensations that are hard to describe. At the same time, supporters of the conceding team remain still, in a silence overwhelmed by disappointment. Moments later, anyway, they gather up again and hope for the comeback. It is within this sequence of emotions that a football game develops before the eyes of spectators: the constant alternation of moments of joy and sufferance produces a tension that is psychological but also physical. At the end of the game, merit and luck will have provided the two crowds with opposing sensations (Hopcraft, 2006).

8.2 What Future for 'Modern' Football?

In the last decades, football underwent substantial changes. It acquired an increasingly global characterization, featuring a progressive prevailing of economic interests over sporting ones and of the interests of TV audience over those of stadium supporters. Many scholars and observers define this model of football as 'modern', in order to distinguish it from the game of the early ages, perhaps connoted by greater authenticity (Robertson, 2009).

The turn towards a more international football was spurred by the 'Bosman ruling' of the Court of Justice of the EU, issued in 1995 to regulate the transfer of football players within the federations belonging to the Union. The ruling prevented national federations to set a limit of footballers with an EU passport who can play for a certain team. In consequence, the so-called foot-ballers market has become increasingly important and teams have turned into truly international entities, to the point that in several instances the starting 11s do not feature any domestic player. The mobility of players—who change teams more frequently than ever—also strongly increased. Concurrently, the 1-to-11 numbering disappeared, making it harder for the fan to memorize line-ups and players' field positions. Today, players can choose whatever number from 1 to 99, according to their preferences and motivations.

However, the phenomenon that most revolutionized the world of football is the progressively reinforcing interdependence between media and sport, which caused profound transformations to the organization of this game. Today we witness a threefold interconnected system of dependency: firstly, a dependence of media on businesses, because sales of advertisement represent a fundamental element of multimedia enterprises; secondly, a dependence of media on sport, for the crucial role played by champions and winning teams; thirdly, a dependence of sports teams on media, being the latter the main source of income for the former (together with advertisement and sponsorships) (Doidge, 2015; Martelli, 2011).

Teams have thus found new opportunities for profit, even though ideas have rarely been generated by teams themselves. Managers from other industries have in fact been more able to understand the potential to derive profits from selling sportswear, gadgets and television rights (Kuper & Szymanski, 2014). Only recently, indeed, the bigger teams have adopted a managerial strategy, usually associated with large companies from other sectors. In some cases, this led to stock exchange listing, which realized the most direct connection between football and finance and, concurrently, raised the most pressing concerns about football as a people's sport open to everybody.

At any rate, football teams have become extremely dependent on the needs of media, to the extent of allocating league games over different days and time slots, in order to allow TV broadcasts to overlay as little as possible. Even European tournaments adjusted to these prerogatives, by incrementing the number of group stage matches; while world and continental cups, for the same reason, have extended the number of teams partaking in the final stage. On the whole, the number of games played during the season considerably incremented, causing a series of physical as well psychological problems to players. The unprecedented amount of injuries recorded over the last years is probably a reflection of such changes.

The 'modern' player, however, is thoroughly aware of the new role football has taken on within the current mediatized society. The best and most famous ones have often managed to create a real brand of themselves, the upkeep of which require them to pay scrupulous attention to all aspects related to their personal image (Foot, 2007; Lupi, 2017). Differently than in the past, today footballers can deliberately decide what team they want to play for, usually entrusting their destiny to their agents. These professionals have in turn become prominent characters on the modern football scene, having accumulated large bargaining power in dealing with teams on behalf of their clients, and thus realizing large profits.

Even coaches underwent a process of modernization. Nowadays, coaches must be able to manage a differentiated set of relations, with the team board, the players, the media, and the audience. Coaches need to possess ability and subtleness of thought, which is generally not required to most players. They must have a wide understanding of their role, which in turn leads them to reach a high degree of popularity (Lupi, 2017).

Certainly, in addition, a new figure is born: that of the 'tele-supporter'. The possibility to follow all games from home made many supporters accustomed to such comforts, therefore slowly and progressively emptying out stadium (Spagnolo, 2020). Concurrently, new generation stadiums seem to be built in accordance to principles of social control management. They are smaller than their predecessors and therefore easier to surveil. Such a reduction in audience is justified by the new prevalent vision of modern football as a media phenomenon (Lupi, 2017). It is also important to underscore that the spaces for consumption new stadiums offer are meant to attract individuals with a higher spending capacity than traditional supporters. The modern fan is like the *homo consumens* described by Zygmunt Bauman: his/her needs must never be fully satisfied, in order to avoid economic stagnation (Lupi, 2017). Substantially, there has been a transformation from supporters to customers, who are provided with bars and restaurants where to eat and have fun, shops where to buy merchandise and other leisure spaces to spend their free time. The stadium has thus become a place of opportunity for business and public relations, where space is offered to enjoy the game but also to arrange business meetings and events (Caruso & Tosi, 2016).

Modern football also spurred the development of a scientific vision of sports. A host of specialists and technicians has entered the scene (physicians, psychologists, nutritionists, motivators, etc.), while big clubs have reached a level of statistical knowledge that is substantially renovating the game (Kuper & Szymanski, 2014).

Beside these profound transformations, however, some fundamental aspects of traditional football have been able to survive. The football scene is therefore more varied and complex than how it is commonly depicted by media. Firstly, supporters do resist, and they often claim a little more respect, since they are still spending time and money in a world in which all other actors gain increasingly exorbitant incomes (Spagnolo, 2020). Then, the identification of a team with its territory is still alive, especially in provincial contexts. Passion is still there, and during competitions for national teams it is shown at its maximum height. Furthermore, grassroots football is far from extinct. Its panorama is composed of myriad small teams, either newly founded or long established, at times acquired and revived by supporters themselves, who sign them up for amateur leagues (Spagnolo, 2020).

The persistency of fans underlines the need for sacred that permeates society. Maybe it also reflects the need for ethical values that political parties, family and religions are failing to satisfy. The consumer society has flattened ethical values, and everything that could be converted into a commodity has been commodified (Bottiglieri, 2020). Surely football is not going to step out of the prevailing turbo-capitalist dynamics, yet the resilience capacity of people's passion—recently highlighted by the protest wave that followed the proposal by 12 of the most influential European teams to create the SuperLeague—demonstrate that it is possible to envision an alternative solution to the growth problems that have been affecting football in the last years. Undoubtedly, economic and political interests as strong as counterpart's motivations determined the opposition to the SuperLeague. Nevertheless, the reaction of fans was real and genuine, distant from that empty false rhetoric that some commentators described as its source.

Maybe it is possible to imagine a more balanced world of food, avoiding falling into utopia. An environment in which *aficionados* keep playing their crucial role and a durable balance is stroke to overcome the dichotomies between sport and mediatized spectacle, and between the game and its economic interests. The experience of the football club Atalanta of Bergamo seems to demonstrate that moving towards such a direction is possible. We shall now address the Atalanta's growth model to try to grasp its most innovative elements and significant dynamics.

8.3 Atalanta, One Step from Sky

In order to study the case of the football team Atalanta of Bergamo, setting off from the comprehension of its corporate structure, we made use of documentary material complemented by qualitative research, based on several in-depth interviews. In the following, we will list our interviewees, who are privileged witnesses of the growth path undertaken by Atalanta in the last 5 years. We also found useful to interview the supporter of another team who nonetheless feels sympathy for Atalanta, as a representative of those football enthusiasts who approached Atalanta in the last years, due to game performances and results obtained. We would like to warmly thank our interviewees for their kind availability and precious contribution.

List of interviewees

1. Roberto Belingheri (rb) Journalist, editor of *Corner*, sports blog of *L'Eco di Bergamo*
2. Diego Colombo (dc) Journalist, editor of *L'Eco di Bergamo*
3. Giorgio Gori (gg) Mayor of Bergamo

4. Cesare Malnati (cm) Journalist, collaborator of *L'Eco di Bergamo*
5. Raffaele Matacena (rm) Food sociologist, supporter of Reggina
6. Nando Pagnoncelli (np) CEO of *Ipsos Italia*
7. Arturo Zambaldo (az) Journalist, collaborator of *L'Eco di Bergamo* and *Bergamo TV*

8.3.1 A Brief History

A first noteworthy aspect regards the origin of the team's name. In the last decade, the team has been often referred to with the sobriquet *dea* (goddess). Such an epithet, though, is inappropriate:

> Secolarization causes the boundaries of sacred to fade. Until not so many years ago, no one would have ever felt like calling Atalanta 'the goddess'. It's wrong, because Atalanta, in Greek mythology, is not a goddess but a nymph or heroine (dc).

In classical mythology, Atalanta is a nymph devoted to hunting who had taken a vow of chastity. The myth tells that a young man named Hippomenes who was running a race against Atalanta, was helped by Aphrodite who gave him three golden apples. He dropped the apples during the race, thus preventing Atalanta from overtaking him three times: out of curiosity or perhaps because she wanted the boy's victory, Atalanta stopped every time to pick the apples and was defeated.

Atalanta is the team of Bergamo, an Italian city in Lombardy, northeast of Milan, of about 120,000 inhabitants. The oldest area is called *Città Alta*, which houses the *Duomo*, the Romanesque *Basilica of Santa Maria Maggiore* and the *Colleoni Chapel*. Surrounded by Venetian Walls, it can also be reached with a funicular. The people of Bergamo are considered very hardworking, tenacious and men of few words. The province of Bergamo is quite large and inhabited by 1108 million people.

The football club Atalanta was founded on October 17, 1907. The idea of the name came to five founding members who were completing their classical studies at the *Liceo Classico Paolo Sarpi*, from which they probably derived their mythological inspiration.

Along the seasons played in the Italian leagues, Atalanta has always been considered a *squadra di provincia* (provincial team), which is a term used in Italy to refer to teams that do not represent a large city and draw their audience from their peripheral regions (Losapio, 2020).

> Atalanta is the expression of a whole province where more than 1.1 million people live, the eight most populated of the whole country (dc).

In terms of appearances in Serie A, the top Italian football league, Atalanta enjoys the eleventh place of the all-time ranking (it took part in 60 seasons out of the total of 89). Among provincial teams, Atalanta holds the record of appearances. Before the last five winning years, the best result achieved was the conquest of the Italian Cup in 1963. At the European level Atalanta reached the semifinals of Cup Winners' Cup

Table 8.1 The last 5 years: the big leap

2016–2017:
Fourth in Serie A, direct qualification to the group stage of Europa League.
2017–2018:
Seventh in Serie A, qualified for Europa League preliminaries; eliminated in the round of 32 of Europa League by Borussia Dortmund.
2018–2019:
Third in Serie A (best result in its history) with qualification for Champions League; second in Italian Cup final (lost the final 2-0 to Lazio); eliminated in the last qualifying round of the Europa League by Copenhagen.
2019–2020:
Third in Serie A with record of points (78), and goals scored (98, best attack in the league), qualification for Champions League; eliminated in the quarterfinals of Champions League by Paris St. Germain.
2020–2021:
Third in Serie A; second in Italian Cup (final lost 2-1 to Juventus); eliminated in the round of 16 of Champions League by Real Madrid.

in 1987–1988 and the quarterfinals of Uefa Cup (the current Europa League) in 1990–1991. In addition, the team had won four Italian Primavera championships (the national league reserved for youth teams).

In the last 5 years, instead, Atalanta has made a qualitative leap by becoming a team that fights for important achievements and is no longer satisfied with avoiding relegation to Serie B (the second-tier Italian league) (Table 8.1).

These results were achieved thanks to the interplay four components: the company, the coach, the players, the city and the public.

> Atalanta is living a favourable "astral conjunction": surely the owners and the board deserve great credit, [ranging] from the way they cared about the economic aspects, to the unconditional trust accorded to the coach, to the 'backseat' profile adopted by Antonio and Luca Percassi (which is very different from the attitude of many managers, whose hypertrophic egos prompt them to wanting to be visible at all times). Furthermore, we need to give merit to Gasperini, Sartori, and the athletic trainers. Even supporters have done their part, but this is not a novelty. Then, there also is Lady Luck: when things go well, it always means she kissed you (np).
>
> I think the management really did a great job, also showing to be well far-sighted—let's think about the purchase of the stadium, for instance—and also organizational ability: without a responsible management achieving sport results would be unthinkable. The project was built around the character of a charismatic coach such as Gasperini, who really stamped his own mark on the team. Plus, our supporters are among the best in the country and gave that extra-thrust for the team to get on the field always motivated and aware of its possibilities. You don't get these results out of chance: there is a lot of work behind the success of Atalanta (gg).
>
> The presence of Sartori, the "market man" of the team, is not to be underestimated. His intuition has been often winning, he bought quite unknown players who then revealed to be medium-high level, also thanks to Gasperini's work (cm).

It is relevant to remind the great importance of the youth academy, onto which the bergamasque team has always put a large effort and is now considered one of the best in Italy:

> It was precisely Percassi, during his first years of presidency, to bring Favini to Bergamo. He was considered the best in the sector. It's not a chance, in fact, that Atalanta won the Primavera [youth] league in 2018–2019 and 2019–2020 (rb).

8.3.2 The Club and the Turning Point

The fundamental continuity of the sports club Atalanta is guaranteed by the president Antonio Percassi and his son Luca, CEO of the company. The Percassi family is originally from Clusone, a little town in the province of Bergamo. A former grim and tenacious defender who played for Atalanta from 1970 to 1977, today Antonio Percassi is a successful entrepreneur, whose net worth is estimated around 1 billion dollars. The main business of the family holding, called Odissea, consists of operating retail chains, either owned (the most famous is the make-up and cosmetic brand Kiko) or under license from world-level corporations (i.e., the Italian branch of Lego and Starbucks stores). In total, it operates more than 1200 stores spread across 17 countries, with an annual turnover exceeding 850 million euros (Gennari & Riscassi, 2020).

Antonio Percassi became the president of Atalanta in 2010. After immediately bringing the team back to Serie A in 2010–2011, a few consolidation seasons were quickly followed by a real turning point during the 2016–2017 season, when the team hired Gian Piero Gasperini, a coach coming from Genoa where he had lived a series of excellent seasons showing a brilliant and innovative game. In the meantime, the Percassis had invested 40 million euros in the youth sector and in the sports center of Zingonia, which is now considered among the best in Europe. In the period, as said, the youth team won two Primavera championships, in 2018–2019 and 2019–2020.

Another decisive step was the purchase of the Bergamo stadium in 2017, for 8.6 million euros. In the turn of a couple of years the stadium was largely renovated. This made it possible to finally play European tournaments in Bergamo. In fact, until the stadium was approved by UEFA, Atalanta had to play Europa League matches in Reggio Emilia and Champions League in the prestigious San Siro stadium in Milan (Gennari & Riscassi, 2020).

The board realized the stadium operation also thanks to the good relationship with the municipality, which helped surmounting long-standing obstacles:

> A very fruitful collaboration, which lately strengthened with the renovation of the Gewiss Stadium. Atalanta won the public tender to buy the structure; since then we have been working side-by-side to modernize the stadium. Both the municipality and the team wanted to have a modern infrastructure able to satisfy the ambitions of the city and the team; we are working hard on this and I think our results are evident (gg).

The club is also strongly committed to taking care of the relationship with its fans. The objective is to further tighten the very strong bond of identity and belonging that exists between Atalanta and the people of Bergamo. In this direction, the team launched the 'Atalanta newborn babies' project', which provides for the distribution in all hospitals of the area of mini-kits containing a newborn version of the shirt team.

8.3.3 The Coach

The coach Gian Piero Gasperini is the other great architect of Atalanta's growth over the last 5 years. His inspiration, he claims, derives partly from Dutch football and Arrigo Sacchi (former Milan and Italian national team coach.) His football is offensive, aimed to goal through a game that starts from the defense and involves the whole team. In his game, a strategic role is played by wing players (wingbacks, wide midfielders and wingers) who are often called to penetrate centerfield and score important goals. In Atalanta all players have the chance score, often even the defenders. Three main merits of the coach are detectable:

1. having been able to enhance young players, especially during his first year in Bergamo (Gagliardini, Caldara, Conti)
2. having revitalized players from other teams who seemed to be struggling in their careers (such as Cristante, Zapata, Ilicic, Muriel).
3. having been able how to transform semi-unknown players into national team players (Gosens, Hateboer, Freuler, De Roon, Papu Gomez).

The persistency of game's style revealed itself as a winning factor, which Gasperini was able to maintain in spite of the frequent turnover of players that happened especially in his first years with the team.

> The way Atalanta plays stayed the same, even with different players on the field, thanks to the aggressive and winning tuning the coach gave the team since the beginning. Merit is to be given also to those who have known how to substitute departing players with others almost always better; and to those who have been able to make players who were desired by richer clubs stay (dc).

8.3.4 The Players

Atalanta players have been offering a well-suited interpretation of the spirit and values that characterize the team: always extending the utmost effort with determination (Corsi & Serpellini, 2017). It is no coincidence that the sentence "*La maglia sudata sempre*" (always sweating through the shirt) is inscribed on the shirt itself. After qualifying to the quarterfinals of Champions League by beating Valencia, players celebrated holding a t-shirt showing the following sentence: "*Bergamo, è per te. Mola mia*", which in a mix of Italian and Bergamasque dialect means "Bergamo, this is for you. Never give up". At that time Bergamo was the most affected city in the world for the Covid19 pandemic, with an impressive number of deaths:

> The *Atalantino* spirit is lived also by the majority of players, most of which are foreigners: it's a rather unusual aspect, in an era when footballers are often accused of being mercenaries. I was strongly impressed by the harmony of values, emotions and characters between the team and Bergamo's population, especially during the hardest peak of the sanitary emergency. It created a sort of osmosis (np).

8.3.5 The City and the Fans: Bergamo Identity

There is a strong identification between the city and the team. It is almost impossible for a Bergamasque not to be *Atalantino*. In Bergamo, people going to the game say "*vado all'Atalanta"*, i.e. "I'm going *to the Atalanta*", rather than "to the stadium" or "the game". The Covid 19 pandemic, as said before, acted to further strengthen this link: the successes of the team have rapidly become the symbol of a possible rebirth for the city. Atalanta brought the name of Bergamo throughout Europe, with important repercussions on the image of the city.

> In Bergamo we don't say "I'm going to the stadium", we say "I'm going to the Atalanta", because Atalanta represents a trait of Bergamasque identity, incarnating the principal values that characterize our territory: hard-working industriousness, 'low profile', concreteness, proximity (np).
>
> Atalanta and our territory have always been in symbiosis. Such a feeling also expands geographically, reaching all Italy and crossing over to Europe and the world, because of migrants in the past and their sons today (az).
>
> Atalanta and the spread of Covid have bounced Bergamo into the world's conversation. It's difficult to foresee what will be the economic return from such a popularity spike. Without any doubt, Atalanta is a symbol, a symbol the gives value and strength to the identity of our citizens and our businesses (np).
>
> I think that, once again, it will be the mirror of the rebirth of the city; once again, sports achievements will go hand-in-hand with Bergamo's own. I'm sure, however, that people will talk about Atalanta and Bergamo for a long time, definitely not because of the Covid19 episode.

The identification between the Bergamasque spirit and the team materializes in a series of shared values, such as the awareness of one's own limits but also own potential, obstinacy and desire for redemption after a defeat.

> It's easy to jump on the winning train when things go well; more difficult to have fans welcoming you at the airport or in Zingonia after a harsh defeat (np).

We are also witnessing a growth of the city that is parallel to that of the team, a concurrency demonstrating that nothing is determined by chance and that the link between football and the socioeconomic dimension is particularly valuable.

> The team, in addition, is a little bit the mirror of our city: in the last years—I believe—Bergamo and Atalanta have been growing in parallel. Football success reflected the emancipation and consolidation of our city. The UNESCO award as much as the Champions League, the 2017 gastronomic region award as much as the qualification to Europa League, the growth in attractiveness to foreign tourists as much as climbing the league chart: I think there are many common points between the team and the city (gg).

Clearly, there are also many other symbols of Bergamasque identity, which demonstrate the existence of a vital and innovative socioeconomic fabric, despite the dramatic Covid experience.

> Atalanta is a pivotal element, albeit not the only one left, of the Bergamasque identity: the mountains, the Walls, work, the love for your own land. I think [these] are still preponderant and were never placed on the backburner (gg).
>
> A research conducted in the Covid period provided a portrait of a region shaped, despite its internal differences, by the fruitful relationship between institutions, local administrators (regardless of political colors), unions, Church and third sector. Identity, differently than in the past, is like a mosaic composed of many pieces: Atalanta is one of those (np).

This shared framing of thinking and living the sports life expressed itself, in Bergamo, almost exclusively in relation to the football team. Indeed, Bergamo almost always lacked teams achieving success in other sports (with a few brilliant exceptions in some specific periods, such as the Foppapedretti in women's volleyball and the Lyons Club in American football). As a consequence, at a sports level the identification with Atalanta has always been the easier road to follow. In addition, all sponsoring businesses have always financed primarily Atalanta. In truth, however, many football fans in the region are supporters of more rewarded teams, especially Milan and Juventus, although recent Atalanta's successes prompted younger fans to increasingly favor their domestic team over big clubs. The crowds are happily getting used to seeing their team among the top tier of the league, even though some are struggling to adapt to the new situation:

> Passion for Atalanta is really transversal. It is difficult to point out a typology of *Atalantini* supporters. Undoubtedly, results from last years have brought many 'lukewarm' people to discover or rediscover their passion for the black-and-blue colors: they are "come-back" *Atalantini* (np).
>
> Sometimes there is too much provincialism among *Atalantini* fans, and a lot of self-reference, which bring many to imagine conspiracies from the so-called 'Palace' [the Italian football federation and league association] about the team being constantly given a disadvantage by referees when playing big teams. We probably need a quantum leap also on the side of supporters: they should get comfortable with reasoning in a different way (cm).
>
> Actually, conspiracy theories and victim complexes are often just alibis to avoid recognizing the superiority of other teams, which in some games may emerge (gb).

Besides these problems of awareness and growth, we must observe that Atalanta fans come from all socioeconomic and cultural tiers of society, as a testimony to what said earlier about the transversal nature of football. This large group, then, does not lack celebrities who proudly declare their *Atalantina* faith:

> I will cite one explanatory case, that of a great artist, deeply Bergamasque. He owns a studio in New York and exposes his art and works all over the world but he's never lost his relations with the stadium stand. He celebrates every week from New York and always puts a little piece of Atalanta in his works. It is difficult to draw a typology of *Atalantino* supporter, we range from the bank director or corporate manager to the factory or agricultural worker. The Sunday game is a big social 'level' (gg).

In the last years, it seems evident that Atalanta's game—always offensive and driven to victory—brought football fans to develop a certain sympathy towards the team. For some of them, it has become a second team to support. It is also worth reminding the long-standing twinning between Atalanta and Ternana, the team from Terni, Umbria. We will now report in full length the response of a Reggina supporter—the team from Reggio Calabria—to whom we asked the reasons why Atalanta is increasingly appreciated by other teams' fans. His words brightly highlight why Atalanta has become a symbol and a model for both other teams and fans:

(rm) Because it collects affection from supporters of small teams—from the province—of which it represents the revenge. It demonstrates that with the right amount of commitment, reliability and far-sightedness it is possible to get to hear, in the turn of 5 years, the anthem of Champions League.

Because the performance improvement came with seriousness, without clamor or sensational declarations, without media fanfare and without the typical controversies of Italian football.

Because it plays a football that is funny, sparkling, fast but at the same time very orderly. There are neither 'prima donna' nor star players but just some 20 good footballers who score a crazy amount of goals just playing their position well together with their teammates. It is an "understandable" type of football; it is recognizable: the defender plays as defender, central midfields play as central midfields, and the striker plays as striker. At the same time, though, it is a well-conceived type of football, refined and, above all, effective. The true football lover, who plays or played it—but is unfortunately born without Messi's feet and is very accustomed to not being able to afford fancy dribbles or supersonic runs (the punishment for that would be coach and teammates yelling at you)—can't help but identify with those [Atalanta] players. I mean, everybody vainly dreams to score with a bicycle kick like Cristiano Ronaldo, but real football practitioners do recognize the magic alchemy that lays behind Atalanta's well-organized drives.

Because it is guided by a coach who's the bearer of a peculiar and definite football style, which in some places didn't work, while it found at Atalanta a thorough consolidation. Once again, we're not speaking of a "big shot" with the power to demand the best champions on the market; we're speaking of a very specific idea put into practice in an enjoyable and effective way.

Because it is known that Bergamasque people are strongly passionate about their team, and this—keeping rivalries aside—usually generates empathy, especially among those who are aware of the peculiar sociocultural dynamics that characterize the relationship between the inhabitants of a small town and their football team.

Because it manages an exceptional youth academy, often able to launch onto the scene new Italian talents, which is something becoming rarer and rarer in our national football.

Because it is a strong yet imperfect team. Differently than bigger teams, when Atalanta loses a game it is not because it played poorly (for instance,

(continued)

underperformance of the single champion, inability of the team to organize nice drives, 'slacker' attitude, and so on) but because in that specific game—more than in others—the shortcomings ('structural', so to speak) of the team emerged. The same shortcomings that in other games seem to be overcome by the unity of the group.

Lastly, a look at financial aspects also differentiates Atalanta from many other teams. Keeping the balance sheet in order, in fact, is a fundamental point that guarantees a bright future for teams. For some years, Atalanta has been producing profits, which reached about 25 million in 2019. In the period, there has been an increase in expenses but also a growth in revenues: turnover has grown from 147 million in 2017 to around 200 million in 2019 (also due to the participation in European cups). Until 2019, revenues from sales of players exceeded 280 million. This enabled the club to avoid selling any major player before the 2020–2021 competitive season, which embodied a very significant change of direction. In terms of salaries, in Serie A Atalanta is twelfth with 36 million annual total. Atalanta's balance sheet demonstrates that there is no need to cover players in gold to make great teams and get great results. For example, Juventus spends 294 million on salaries, Inter follows with 139, Roma 125, etc. Anyway, many of these teams are in deficit and face many difficulties to pay players regularly.

8.3.6 The Last Challenge

However, not everyone looks with sympathy at the Atalanta model (or at the Atalanta 'fairytale', as some have called it). The president of one of the most important Serie A clubs once said in an interview that teams like Atalanta should not take the place in Champions League away from big city teams with a more solid tradition, such as Roma. He was among the proponents of the SuperLeague, a European tournament in which participation was granted by right to the teams with the longest history of success. The plan was to play international matches on the weekend, leaving a Wednesday slot to national leagues.

The SuperLeague proposal was brought about by 12 European clubs in order to obtain greater revenues from television rights and sponsorships, as a mean to sustain increasingly weighty management expenses. These clubs are heavily debt-ridden, due to exorbitant salaries and transfer money paid to acquire top players. It is a sick system that tries to survive by creating new exclusive and elitist organizations, often overlooking sporting merits.

Within this scenario, what role can Atalanta undertake, both at a national and international level? There appear to be divergent opinions, even among our interviewees:

Money makes the difference and it seems really difficult to stay on top for a long time. There's been a lot of debate about the enormous budget differences between Paris Saint Germain and Atalanta, both qualified to the quarterfinals of Champions League (np).

I find it difficult to believe that we will win the league. Cagliari, Verona and Sampdoria did win the league, but it was many years ago. Juventus has been the winner for nine times straight and, in nineteen years, only two other teams from another Italian city, Milan, won. [It's] An oligopoly that became a monopoly (dc).

With each passing year, it becomes harder and harder to obtain the same sports results. The other teams are no longer underestimating us, everyone knows our game and potential. We're no longer a surprise and they all want to defeat us. But we can still get some satisfaction, I'm pretty sure (gg).

The high profile the team built for itself is bound to last. I don't think we will be a one hit wonder, both because of the results on the ground and for the very solidity of the club (az).

Atalanta is a strong company. It will stay at the top for a long time, thanks to the Percassi family—father and son—who guarantee a much-needed continuity (cm).

It is hard to foresee the future, even though it appears that Atalanta's managerial concreteness together with those values inspiring the team may grant it a bright future among the most important teams of Italian football, perhaps with some good continued results on the European scene. Much will also depend on the development of projects such as the SuperLeague or other elitist leagues that do not take into account sporting merit. Our hope is for an inclusive logic to prevail, one that recognizes the glorious past of some clubs while allowing all other financially viable and managerially virtuous teams to emerge and reach the top of competitions. Indeed, erasing the chances for a provincial team like Atalanta to accomplish the unexpected probably means depriving the game of football from its charm. What is at stake is the unpredictability, uncertainty, popularity, and simplicity of this sport. The nymph Atalanta, on 'her' side, faces a defying challenge: finding her way to the top, among the greatest football teams of the world. This is an issue that does not only concern football, but also politics, economics, media and leisure. And especially, it is a sociological issue!

References

Augé, M. (2016). *Football: il calcio come fenomeno religioso* (Vol. 15). Edizioni Dehoniane.

Bottiglieri, N. (2020). Il gran teatro del mondo. In M. Lupo & A. Emina (Eds.), *Visioni di gioco. Calcio e società da una prospettiva interdisciplinare*. Il Mulino.

Caruso, L., & Tosi, L. (2016). Scelte, modelli e retoriche della città sportiva. Una riflessione comparata tra "ITALIA '90" e i processi sistemico-strutturali oggi in corso. In N. Porro, S. Martelli, & G. Russo (Eds.), *Il Mondiale delle meraviglie. Calcio, media e società da "Italia '90" a oggi*. Franco Angeli.

Corsi, S. & Serpellini, S. (2017). *La dea della giovinezza. Atalanta, un vivaio di uomini e di campioni*. Bolis Edizioni.

Doidge, M. (2015). *Football Italia: Italian football in an age of globalization*. Bloomsbury.

Fini, M., & Padovan, G. (2019). *Storia reazionaria del calcio. I cambiamenti della società vissuti attraverso il mondo del pallone*. Marsilio.

Foot, J. (2007). *Calcio: A history of Italian football*. Harper Perennial.

Galeano, O. (2012). *Splendori e miserie del gioco del calcio*. Sperling & Kupfer.

Gennari, F., & Riscassi, A. (2020). *Favola Atalanta. Bergamo alla conquista dell'Europa, tra sogno e realtà*. Novecento Media.
Goldblatt, D. (2006). *The ball is round: A global history of football.* Viking.
Hopcraft, A. (2006). *The football man: People and passions in football.* Aurum Press.
Hornby, N. (1992). *Fever pitch*. Victor Gollancz. Italian Translation: Febbre a 90', Milano: Guanda.
Kuper, S., & Szymanski. (2014). *Soccernomics*. HarperCollins.
Losapio, A. (2020). *1001 storie e curiosità sulla grande Atalanta che dovresti conoscere*. Newton Compton.
Lupi, R. (2017). *Fenomenologia del calcio moderno*. Edizioni Bepress.
Martelli, S. (2011). *Sport, media e intrattenimento. Emozioni in/controllate e struttura sociale emergente*. Franco Angeli.
Michea, J. C. (2014). *Le plus beau but était une passe*. Flammarion.
Pasolini, P. P. (2020). *Il mio calcio*. Garzanti.
Porro, N. (2008). *Sociologia del calcio*. Carocci.
Robertson, R. (Ed.). (2009). *Globalization and football.* Sage.
Spagnolo, P. (2020). *Contro il calcio moderno*. Odoya.
Tomlinson, A. (2005). *Sport and leisure culture*. University of Minnesota Press.
Turnbull, J., Satterlee, T., & Raab, A. (Eds.). (2008). *The global game: Writers on football.* University of Nebraska Press.

Chapter 9
Authenticity as Element of Connotation in Sport Tourism Activity. Some Empirical Elements from the Italian Arena

Nico Bortoletto

9.1 Introduction

The aim of this chapter relies in the attempt to show how the narrative dimension of sport tourism must be boosted at the aim to find a sort of balance between its denotative dimension and its connotative dimension. For doing this we have to start from a classical conceptualization of Sport-Tourism. This could be the one used by Gammon and Robinson (1997) assuming that 'Sport Tourism' is different from 'Tourism-Sport'. The first, basically, are related to the practice of sport by different levels of involvement (from a professional sport practice to an amateurial one). The second rely in the different level of involvement of spectators, starting from the engagement in some minor forms of sport and/or leisure (mini-golf, bowls, swimming) to a simple reinforcement of a pure tourist activity (i.e. sport cruises, centre parks walks, etc.). Giving that, in recent times we are facing an increasing mix of this forms of sport-tourism with an increasing involvement of local communities always hovering between the search for a significant tourist attraction and the need to maintain forms of identity that preserve them from dissolution.

In fact, one of the criticisms of sports tourism is sometimes that it leads to the construction of events and pseudo-events that, to some extent, cannot reflect—or, better express—the culture of a place (Boorstin, 1964; Fredline, 2005). This kind of criticism suggests that the process of creation of tour packages for these types of events results also in the construction of places where to host the tourists, with the consequent risk to alter the authenticity of the localities.

Communities that happen to be in the heart of these events try to counterbalance the public exposure of their own "being" a community by creating a structure that divides *front and backstage,* in order to protect from extemporaneous visitors, the

N. Bortoletto (✉)
Department of Communication Sciences, University of Teramo, Teramo, Italy
e-mail: nbortoletto@unite.it

P. Corvo, F. M. Lo Verde (eds.), *Sport and Quality of Life*, Social Indicators Research Series 84, https://doi.org/10.1007/978-3-030-93092-9_9

sphere of relations inside of the community, together with their own reference environment (King & Stewart, 1996).

The continuous increase in visitors in specific tourist sites (the case of Arco, ITA, international sport climbing centre, is –for instance– emblematic) makes this strategy of community survival more and more difficult.

Basically, a destination risks to be destroyed by its own success, uniqueness and suitability as centre of excellence for certain sports (see Mowforth & Munt, 2015).

In this respect, the concept of commodification of a place necessarily alters also the culture of the destination. The so-called claim of authenticity in tourism destinations is then significantly compromised. When tourists perceive this loss of authenticity, they are in the condition of having to decide if they should either change destination or sport activity. Even from the community's point of view, paradoxically, the loss of the demanded cultural authenticity—inevitably linked to the collective identity—represents a problem.

Communities can try to avoid this type of development, that risks wearing out a place from the core, by adopting strategies aiming at protecting or at least preserving a centre of cultural integrity.

This concept follows the so-called *sight-seeing* theory (to see what is supposed to be seen), based on the belief that the essence of tourist experience is altered when it is pre-packaged (Burgelin, 1967). Paradoxically, this goes also for sport tourism, although to a lesser extent. The so-called *hallmark event,* the New York marathon for example, is an event ichnographically well-defined and often very well recognisable: the starting point on Verrazzano bridge, the finish line at Central Park, the New York skyline. However, as discussed later in this rows, the element that differentiates sport tourism from *sight-seeing* tourism is the mix of the personal involvement with the locality where the sport performance takes place. This mix, a sort of Heideggerian *Dasein*, represents the core of the contemporary sociology of sport tourism, and, as personal opinion, it is one of the most interesting aspects to form post-modern keys to read the entire tourism phenomenon.

9.2 Sport as Tourism Attractor

Sport represents a very particular type of tourism attractor. Leiper (1990) is among the first to talk about sport in this perspective and starting from the definition of tourism attraction (a system composed by a human element, a core and an informative element or maker) gives the coordinates to frame the phenomenon, also from the empirical point of view.

Considering the sport phenomenon indeed, the human element includes travellers driven by sport interests, and, indirectly, people accompanying them (families, staff, technicians, referees, etc.). In general, from for classification purposes, there are no significant differences between professional athletes and amateurs, except for the fact that professionals, in case of bigger events, attract the interest of a wider public, creating significant income in all the related sectors. The Olympic Games in London,

EXAMPLE ITINERARY

DAY 1	DAY 2	DAY 3	DAY 4	DAY 5
Arrive In Madrid Check into National Training Centre	Atletico Madrid Training Session	Real Madrid Training Session	Morning Fixture vs Local Opposition	Morning Fixture vs Local Opposition
La Liga Fixture	Tour of Ciudad Deportiva de Majadahonda Evening Fixture vs local Opposition	Bernebeu Stadium Tour Sightseeing Tour of Madrid Evening Activity	Ciudad Real Madrid Facilities Tour National Football Museum Tour	Hotel Check Out Flight Home

Fig. 9.1 Example of thematic itinerary for a sport tourism travel

for example, produced an increment of 1% in the number of visitors from abroad and 9% in the number of visitors from Great Britain.[1]

According to Leiper, the informative element finds its expression both in the classic way through advertising campaigns, and in the diffusion of sport news (via traditional media and new media). This continuous diffusion of informative elements introduces a social construction, in the sense of sport community, that translates into the creation of a tradition, especially important to generate tourist flows (Holt, 1990).

The last coordinate proposed by the academic from New Zeland is the place, the *nucleus*, meant as what the visitor specifically admires or uses. Obviously, the concept of nucleus in terms of sport is wide, and most of all has not strictly defined boundaries.

Figure 9.1 shows a table taken from an English website (*Complete Sport Solution*), exclusively specialized in sport tourism, proposing a week in Madrid during which sport activities are combined with a more traditional tourism and culture itinerary.

This table introduces, as will be better explained later, an interesting insight of a symbolic path to feed a myth: city, museums, sport infrastructures and teams become an *unicum*, making the invention process of a place semiotically indistinguishable.

Among the most accepted definitions of sport tourism, there are the ones of Hinch and Hingham (2001), highlighting elements such as the limited duration, the

[1] https://www.telegraph.co.uk/travel/destinations/europe/united-kingdom/england/london/articles/Londons-Olympic-legacy-the-results-are-in/

magnitude of the travel, the sport as main motivation either as fun pastime or organized event.[2]

It is evident that this definition perfectly fits the general framework suggested by Leiper, most of all in terms of sport as a link between formal and informal nucleus of the tourist activity itself.

There are of course many more definitions of sport tourism, such as, for example, the ones of De Knop (1990) and Gibson (1998), originated from the extreme fluency of the phenomenon in terms of heterogeneity and change (a table like the one shown in Fig. 9.1 would not exist only 10 years ago).

The taxonomy proposed by Gibson (1998: *event, activity or nostalgia*) is widely accepted and is in line with the majority of studies about sport tourism. However, also in this case, literature distinguishes and classifies different types of attractor events (mega-events, big events, regional events, local events), also in terms of income in all sectors related to tourism.

The path for the recognition of authenticity depends also on the ability to avoid the denaturation of the places caused by sports with high environmental impact (for example, ski mountaineering). The consequent modification of the places is an element that inevitably causes a loss of charm, at least concerning the experience-based tourism. On the other side, sport tourism in urban areas risks to diminish the charm of a place by standardizing it (i.e. stadiums), although, as already underlined (Bortoletto, 2008), there is a tendency to build up new sport centres, with the reintegration of design elements, sometimes with retro style [see for example the stadium Luis II in Monaco (F) and the Stadium of Light in Sutherland (UK)].

Bale was one of the first scholars suggesting—in 1994—that sport events are essentially cultural experiences and cause a change in the perception of the host location. Golf resorts, for example, require a permanent modification of the landscape, and also sail racing fields: significant examples of this process are the urbanistic modifications made for the America's Cup, the most famous sailing race, in the case of Valencia 2010 and, yearly, the gulf of Trieste for the s.c. *Barcolana*.

Place identity is obtained through the sedimentation of community values giving to sport a predominant role: sporting attractions, and sport's vocation reflect indeed the culture of the place. The little alpine locality Kranjska Gora (SLO)—historical location of one of the stop-overs of the worldwide ski mountaineering, in the same way as Arco (TN) and the stadium in Manchester city (Etihad Stadium), are not only expression of the physical, but also cultural environment composed of people, sport and landscape or infrastructure, which assume the role of mediators between *ludum* and *homines*.

Nauright (1996) affirms that in several cases sport events and public relations are inevitably expression of a collective culture of the society. In general, sport

[2] Sport-based travel away from the home environment for a limited time, where sport is characterized by unique rule sets, competition related to physical prowess and play" (Hinch & Higham, 2001, p. 49)

represents an exceptional mean to access the "backstage" of a community: visitors are not perceived as intruders (or at least not only) that participate but are unable to grasp the deep meaning of what is happening in that place, as it often occurs in case of other cultural events (i.e. the carnival "*Su Carresecare*" in Mamoioda—Sardinia Region), but they are seen as part of the phenomenon itself, regardless if they participate as athletes or public. The difference is that in this case the private sphere of the community is not (allegorically) damaged, but is placed on a public level, shared between participants and host community.

9.3 The Commercialization

Considering that tourism is a financial matter for Mediterranean countries—and in general for all countries that are relatively developed in economic-industrial sectors—(the United Nations Organisation for tourism estimated that in the whole planet, tourism-related business volume reaches USD 1,330 billions, half of which concerns only Europe (UNWTO, 2018))—the commodification process of the tourist offer is in fact at the base of this phenomenon.

Cohen (1988) describes the commodification as a process evaluating things and activities first of all in terms of their exchange value in a business context, becoming in this way goods and services. Since local culture is necessarily involved in this business, the backstage of the community is again an important issue, representing that central nucleus identified by MacCannell (1973), where the community has to give the impression to consider and value the presence of the tourist, but also preserve and protect its culture, in order to not disappear as moral community.

Sport, as cultural phenomenon, is obviously subjected to commodification and association to tourism, suggesting that an annihilation of the culture of the community can happen.

Even admitting this risk, it is anyway necessary to underline that local offers related to tourism business, included sport tourism, bring new elements of signification to the community value. Although sport, and tourism in general, is perceived by the community as a tool to fight depopulation of the places (even from a symbolic point of view) or the abandonment of the old production models, there might be contaminations of values belonging to the two different communities (the local and the tourist ones), and this is not necessarily negative.

Values (mostly, but not only, hedonistic) spread by Western media are anyway individuum-centric, and also permeating and homologating by definition. Sport tourists look for places in the host community where they can stay in a useful way instead of being considered a "*someone*", more and more difficult to understand in the process of self-realization. Tourist-oriented cultural products made (or reproduced) by a place, acquire a new meaning for the local community, becoming a diacritic representation of its ethnic and cultural essence, as a way to transmit a portrayal of the locality to the external public (see Fig. 9.2).

Fig. 9.2 Turin, candidate city to host the Winter Olympic Games 2026

This is particularly true in case of local sport events, both the ones existing by tradition and the competitive ones: these events sometimes reflect unique styles, founding values and a landscape context. An easy example is the already cited New York Marathon, where the skyline accompanies the participation to a unique sport event, in a multi-ethnic and multistyle context, reflecting the essence of the host city. Participants join the event moved by different reasons, but most of all, athletes give a big value to the elements discussed above (place, sport nucleus, symbolic nucleus).

The public, representing the first type of sport tourism since the dawn of time, is a natural component of sport events, starting from competitive highly attractive events that create expectations related to identity and values. For this reason, people travelling to attend a sport event can be divided into two categories: the ones attending leisure events or anyway non-elite sports, and the ones going to highly competitive sport events requiring a complex organization process. The first type of events involve most of all small communities and give back a different dimension of identity compared to the second ones, linked more to the places and the athletes, which are often relatives or friends of someone in the public, remaining in this way—as described by Mead's theory—an entity that socializes only with its own proximity, particularly connected to the game as an element able to recombine daily experiences.

The big event, or anyway the public event with larger dimensions, has an impact on the psychological (and sociological) dimension of the public: it represents a moment of break from reality inside of which groups of people, often disconnected in the everyday reality, find a common symbolic set, sharing emotions and experiences (Curi et al., 2011). These emotional sections act at different levels and can integrate daily personal dimensions sometimes irreducible (the ministry official that comments the basketball game with a student and then they both join a group of supporters celebrating the victory, 'talking with gestures', and networking).

This condition of Husserlian *epochè* fits the problem of the authenticity of the tourist experience, how it is perceived and how it influences the quality of the relationships.

9.4 Authenticity

The authenticity issue in tourism exists since almost half a century in the field of sociology. In the 1970s, MacCannell (1973, 1976) underlined that the search for authenticity is one of the main elements giving motivation to the tourism.

Its contribution is particularly interesting considering the concept of *staged authenticity*, known to derive by the application of Goffman's idea of stage and backstage of the social spaces.

A clear example demonstrating the modernity of this theory is the itinerary shown above (Fig. 9.1): the visit to the changing rooms of the Santiago Bernabeu is an obvious extension of the main scene of the show; or better, it is a show in the show from the moment in which the backstage, thanks to the pay-tv, has been monetized and sold as the rest of the main show or "stage show".

This gives rise to a question: does a backstage still exist? Of course, it does, but it is a backstage that is more and more contaminated by elements belonging to the main scene: values, trends and even effectual data.

In the end, the tourist brings a vast range of different experiences that—through the search of authenticity—produce, according to Cohen (1988), an *emerging* authenticity, different from what expected.

It is indeed a problem of perception of the authenticity of the reality, which refers to the reality as social construction (Koski, 2008).

This impossibility to define authenticity outside of the synchronic social construction, induced Urry (1990) to hypothesize that the tourist looks for pleasant experiences, having however an intrinsic meaning. For example, in the case of the cruise industry or pure invention such as the one of the theme parks, the meaning of the experience is certainly not represented by the authenticity but by the personal perspective of entertainment and game.

Therefore, we need to consider two things: first of all, the underlying, persistent demand of real (authentic?) experience offered by famous tourist guides, and also the activity of travelling seen from a mere phenomenological perspective.

Harvey (1990) introduces a new element to understand the problem of authenticity. He talks about the concept of simulacrum[3] (derived by Baudrillard) as a copy of a non-existent original, present only in a hyper-reality in which true or false are substantially indistinguishable. True and false depend on the dimensions of time and place and, for example, support the relevant theory of the non-places as decontextualized, duplicated and even simulated sites.

9.4.1 An Epistemological Approach

The main focus of these pages relies in the well-known work of Ning Wang (2000), in which he proposes, among the other things, an interesting taxonomy incorporating the concept of authenticity, explaining it in a post-modern key which is inclusive, not exclusive, and introducing the experience of the tourist as a yardstick, interpreted as *existential authenticity*.

Wang suggests three types of authenticity that can be applied to the tourism context:

- The first type is linked to what we can define "*goal*" of authenticity: authenticity as something belonging to the field of originality. It is the typical case of authenticity of museums or historical places: tourist and curator face a problem of inclusion/exclusion in a given field of knowledge (for example: is it or not a Bronze Age relic? Is it or not a building belonging to Hadrian's Wall?).
- The second type of authenticity, defined by Wang as *constructive authenticity*, is intriguing. It refers to a process via which tourists (or operators) project the authenticity to the objects in terms of images, expectations, preferences, beliefs, etc. It is a form of authenticity based on the existence of a projection process of the touristic experience, referring not (or not only) to the historical or geographic substance of an object, but most of all to its situational features.

Most of all in sport, this symbolic driving force, often fostered by media, reveals a great internal power. The invention of a tradition that does not exist but has a strong symbolic meaning (for example the Champions League anthem) gives back to the public a feeling of historical authenticity of the event, that would instead be difficult to grasp because non-existent in the everyday life.

The trekker that goes to Nepal to climb Annapurna Massif, place that man has always travelled by foot, performs however a very modern discipline, that symbolically derives from a merely touristic market such as the one of the sport-adventure.

- The third type of authenticity is defined by Wang as *existential authenticity*: the concept of authenticity is not anymore based on the reality of the destination, but on the reality of the tourist experience, on a special way of feeling and being (a *mood*) that does not link this form of authenticity to the object of the travel. Indeed, it consists in the spirit of the travel. The travel consists in an overturning, or anyway a change, of the role of the tourist: according to Wang, there would be a contrast between tourist and ordinary existence, in which the tourist—forced in pressing social roles—does not find an expression of the reality until the moment of, or during, the travel.

The travel creates then a state of transcendency from the daily life (Pernecky & Jamal, 2010) and authenticity is perceived as a suspension of the roles of the everyday life.

Considering these three types of authenticity, we can say that the last one can be further divided in intra-personal and inter-personal. The first one concerns the construction of an identity through physical perception. The body is seen as something with a strong identity, in terms of canonical beauty, health and physical strength. As indicated by sport sociology, the body is situated at the intersection between nature and culture, individual and society, space and time, substance and mind. The athletic body becomes the instrument to elaborate and spread lifestyles, role models inspired to the complex and variable sport culture (Besnier & Brownell, 2012).

The tourist, often locked in his ordinary sedentary lifestyle, experiences through the travel the existence of his own body as instrument to experience life. Authenticity is therefore found in this self-experimentation, which suddenly becomes real. The existence of risk factors, the uncertain outcome of the interaction with the surrounding nature, convert people into sport tourists: this is both valid for the fit triathlete and the beginner skier facing the red piste for the first time.

The interpersonal dimension can be easily identified, for example, in the typical family holiday, where the bonds are strengthened by the time spent together—time that in the everyday life is more claimed than real. Vacations for touristic or sport communities are even more meaningful in this sense: for example, groups walking through religious trails or athletes performing a specific sport (such as skippers) in which the teamwork or joint participation is essential to feel integrated in a sub-culture. According to Coakley (2004), this happens most of all in sports following the concept of "participation and fun", instead of sports based on power and performance.

9.5 The Italian Case of Outdoor Tourism: Some Evidences of Analyses

Beyond being a country with a very high concentration of touristic, historical and archaeological resources, Italy is a country naturally suitable for outdoor tourism, thanks to the impressive geomorphological diversity of the territory.

A recent report from the Italian Observatory for outdoor tourism (Aa.Vv., 2018) showed that outdoor tourism gives an important economic contribution to Italian tourism, most of all considering that the majority of these activities does not require investments in infrastructures, using places that either already exist in nature or were created for other purposes.

This report analysed 245 outdoor sports, performed by almost 21 million people, of all age ranges, but most of all 44 years-old in average, moment in life when the sportsmen usually have significant economic possibilities.

The classic bicycle touring for example, was chosen by 837,000 Italians in 2017 as outdoor activity. In general, 6,672,000 Italians spent an average of three nights away from home for outdoor sport activities in 2017.

The economic value of this sector is of course very relevant.

Table 9.1 Prediction for arrivals and presences in 2018—values express thousands of units

Outdoor tourists in Italy, 2018	Arrivals	Departures
Italians	5552	16,100
Foreigners	7288	23,322
Total	12,840	39,422

Adapted and modified from Aa.Vv. (2018), *Osservatorio italiano del turismo outdoor: situazione congiunturale del turismo outdoor focus tendenze e discipline 2018*, Faenza–RA, http://www.outdoorexpo.eu/media/outdoor/documents/comunicati/05_OUTDOOR_2018_Osservatorio.pdf

Table 9.2 Outdoor sport activity and derived sociality

Preferred company for sport activities	Percentage
Friends	57.8
Family	27.2
Acquaintance	3.6
Alone	11.4

Adapted and modified from Aa.Vv. (2018), *Osservatorio italiano del turismo outdoor: situazione congiunturale del turismo outdoor focus tendenze e discipline 2018*, Faenza–RA, http://www.outdoorexpo.eu/media/outdoor/documents/comunicati/05_OUTDOOR_2018_Osservatorio.pdf

The equivalent economic value of the participation in tourism described in the report corresponds to EUR 4.32 billion. Table 9.1 shows the prediction for 2018, expected to present an increase of about 4% in tourism presence, according to the first evaluation of the observatory, corresponding to about EUR 157 million.

The Italian regions mainly involved in the phenomenon of tourism entry are Trentino-Alto Adige (11.4% of the entries), Sardinia (10% of the entries), Emilia-Romagna (9.8%) and Veneto (9.2%). Tourists interested in outdoor sports are instead coming from Lombardia (12.9%), Veneto (10.2%) and Piemonte (7.4%).

Unlike other tourism phenomenon, outdoor sports keep a constant distribution of departures during the whole year, reaching however a peak during warm seasons (for example March 10.2%, July 13.8%, September 12.6% and October 9.3%).

Table 9.2 supports the theories about the importance of sport subculture described before.

This synthesis of the work that we cite shows that the Italian case and also sport tourism phenomenon (at least the actively performed one) are linked to a condition of sociality (one person out of ten individually performs outdoor sports); moreover, this activity involves most of all regions characterized by geo-diversity (Veneto and Trentino) or by effectual territorial policy supporting outdoor sports in rural areas (for example Emilia-Romagna and Tuscany).

In all cases, the volume of sport tourist movement here focusing only on Italy, indicates that this phenomenon is becoming more and more relevant both from an economic and sociological perspective. The different hypotheses about the importance of experiential authenticity take up a role, if considered as part of a more general picture of the development of sport tourism. In particular, the topics of subculture and created authenticity are the core of future investigations about tourism, a phenomenon that is continuously changing and varying.

9.6 Conclusions

Sport tourism, as other attractions belonging to the cultural sector, is subjected to the risk of commodification and loss of authenticity (Roberts & Pointing, 2018). Sport presents the big advantage of being able to "align" collective identity and image of the places, building up a strong symbolic authenticity and providing in this way experiences that are perceived as culturally authentic, since they involve typical elements characterizing the sport: the uncertainty of the outcome, the morphogenetic nature of the relations and the kinaesthetic nature of sport activities become the strength elements in the projections of authenticity typical of sport tourism (Hinch & Higham, 2005).

Obviously, the construction of sport tourism itineraries, both in case of outdoor activities and sport competitions, represents a potential element for the strategic development of tourism in a certain locality. Some suggestions can come from trends in outdoor sports. First of all, there is a significant increase in the participation to multisport disciplines (Triathlon, Iron Men, Cliffhanger, etc.), that often go with an increase, although to a lesser extent, in the attendance to adrenaline sports such as bungee jumping, paragliding, canoeing, etc. Sport is therefore intended as a challenge: as anticipated by Guttmann (2004), the record (generally speaking) becomes a basis for comparison that cannot be avoided. Overcome self-limitations as guide for social existence. The limitation is seen as a modern form of immortality: it is a paradox, modern way to distinguish between "right" and "wrong", the "self" and the "me", the "us" and the "them".

In retribution, slow, non-competitive and almost contemplative sport disciplines are becoming more and more popular: amateur slow cycling (the real one, often off-road), equestrian tourism, multi-stage excursionist tourism, are all ways to approach the type of sport authenticity aiming not to a widespread sociality (although this is what inevitably happens), but a self-exploration, a detachment from a repetitive and urban routine, difficult to stand. Travel authenticity is therefore represented by its inner perception and, regardless of its adventurous nature, the more this perception provides an escape from the daily routine, the more the travel will be perceived as authentic (Savelli, 2008).

In semiotics, we know, denotation and connotation are terms unfolding the relationship between the signifier and its signified, and an analytic distinction is made between two types of signifies: a *denotative* signified and a *connotative* signified. Meaning embraces both denotation and connotation (Silverman, 1983). The proposal of this paper relies in the necessity to highlight that—especially researching Sport Tourism—connotation, in short, produces a sort of illusion of denotation where the signifier and the signified is treated as identical. From such a perspective denotation can be seen as no more of a 'natural' meaning than is connotation but rather as a process of *naturalization*.

The protagonist of the famous science-fiction movie 'Total Recall'[3] goes to a private provider of memory implants for recreational purposes, choosing a trip to Mars as a secret agent. This subject (and the follow up of the movie) show the ambiguity and the impossibility of an inner travel only, but, at the same time, reveal the effectiveness of the perception of authenticity of the travel itself.

The future of tomorrow's tourism lies—very likely—in this search for a synthesis between authenticity, artificiality and community.

References

Aa.Vv. (2018). Osservatorio italiano del turismo outdoor: *situazione congiunturale del turismo outdoor focus tendenze e discipline*. Faenza—RA. Retrieved February 15, 2019, from http://www.outdoorexpo.eu/media/outdoor/documents/comunicati/05_OUTDOOR_2018_Osservatorio.pdf.

Bale, J. (1994). *Landscapes of modern sport*. Leicester University Press.

Besnier, N., & Brownell, S. (2012). Sport, modernity, and the body. *Annual Review of Anthropology, 41*, 443–459.

Boorstin, D. (1964). *The image: A guide to pseudo-events in America*. Harper & Row.

Bortoletto, N. (2008). Identità sportiva e comunità locale. In N. Bortoletto & B. Mazza (Eds.), *Sport al grandangolo: L'evento sportivo tra metafora e pragmatismo* (pp. 149–170). Rubbettino.

Burgelin, O. (1967). Le tourisme jugé. *Communication, 10*, 81–96.

Coakley, J. (2004). *Sports in society: Issues and controversies*. McGraw Hill Higher Education.

Cohen, E. (1988). Authenticity and the commoditization of tourism. *Annals of Tourism Research, 15*, 371–386.

Curi, M., Knijnik, J., & Mascarenhas, G. (2011). The pan American games in Rio de Janeiro 2007: Consequences of a sport mega-event on a BRIC country. *International Review for the Sociology of Sport, 46*(2), 140–156.

De Knop, P. (1990). Sport for all and active tourism. *World Leisure & Recreation, 32*(3), 30–36.

Fredline, E. (2005). Host and guest relations and sport tourism. *Sport in Society, 8*(2), 263–279. https://doi.org/10.1080/17430430500087328

Gammon, S., & Robinson, T. (1997). Sport and tourism: A conceptual framework. *Journal of Sport Tourism, 4*(3), 11–18. https://doi.org/10.1080/10295399708718632

Gibson, H. J. (1998). Sport tourism: A critical analysis of research. *Sport Management Review., 1*(1), 45–76.

Guttmann, A. (2004). *From ritual to record: The nature of modern sports*. Columbia University Press (orig. ed. 1978).

Harvey, D. (1990). *The condition of postmodernity*. Blackwell.

Hinch, T. D., & Higham, J. (2001). Sport tourism: A framework for research. *The International Journal of Tourism Research, 3*(1), 45–58.

Hinch, T. D., & Higham, J. (2005). Sport, tourism and authenticity. *European Sport Management Quarterly, 5*(3), 243–256.

Holt, R. (1990). *Sport and the British: A modern history*. Oxford University Press.

[3]The movie was released in 1990, directed by Paul Verhoeven, and is freely inspired by a story by P. W. Dick, *We Can Remember It for You Wholesale*, 1966.

King, D. A., & Stewart, W. P. (1996). Ecotourism and commodification: Protecting people and places. *Biodiversity and Conservation, 5*(3), 293–305.
Koski, P. (2008). Physical activity relationship (PAR). *International Review for the Sociology of Sport, 43*(2), 151–163. https://doi.org/10.1177/1012690208095374
Leiper, N. (1990). Tourist attraction systems. *Annals of Tourism Research, 17*, 367–384.
MacCannell, D. (1973). Staged authenticity: Arrangements of social space in tourist settings. *American Journal of Sociology, 79*(3), 589–603.
MacCannell, D. (1976). *The tourists: New theory of the leisure class*. Schoken.
Mowforth, M., & Munt, I. (2015). *Tourism and sustainability: Development, globalization and new tourism in the third world*. Routledge.
Nauright, J. (1996). A besieged tribe? Nostalgia, white cultural identity and the role of rugby in a changing South Africa. *International Review for the Sociology of Sport, 31*(1), 69–89.
Pernecky, T., & Jamal, T. (2010). (Hermeneutic) phenomenology in tourism studies. *Annals of Tourism Research, 37*(4), 1055–1075.
Roberts, M., & Pointing, J. (2018). Waves of simulation: Arguing authenticity in an era of surfing the hyperreal. *International Review for the Sociology of Sport., 53*(1), 1–17.
Savelli, A. (2008). Alla ricerca di nuovi spazi per il turismo. In id. (Ed.), *Spazio turistico e società globale*. FrancoAngeli.
Silverman, K. (1983). *The subject of semiotics*. Oxford University Press.
UNWTO. (2018). *World tourism barometer* (Vol. 16, Issue 5). UNWTO ed.
Urry, J. (1990). *The tourist gaze*. Sage Publications.
Wang, N. (2000). *Tourism and modernity: A sociological analysis*. Pergamon.

Chapter 10
Social Capital and Paths of Inclusion Through Sport Practice. A Closer Look at Immigration in Italy

Loredana Tallarita

10.1 Introduction

What characterizes the migration phenomenon in Italy? In what spaces is possible to implement prospects for intercultural coexistence between local population and migrants themselves? The immigrant experience all the condition of uprooting, he doesn't belong to the reality of the reception process and he certainly faces a processor of resocialization which puts his identity in crisis. Integration is a complex path (Ambrosini, 2017, 2020) at territorial level (Fukuyama, 1995, Lin et al., 1986) and positive results obtained using sport as a mean of inclusion has led to the consideration of amateur football (Gasparini, 2013; Gasparini & Beaud, 2018; Vinnai, 2003) which has sorted positive effects also in other European countries. Football is a sport with a high educational value, the social capital produced (Bourdieu, 1988; Coleman, 1988, 1999; Martelli, 2015, 2020; Putnam, 2000; Russo, 2016, 2019; Vinnai, 2003) in sports has been effective for integration purposes. The relational environment (Donati, 2008; Martelli, 2020; Tallarita, 2014) of sport allowed the construction of paths of inclusion (Elling et al., 2001; Caperchione et al., 2011; O'Driscol et al., 2014) characterized by a high regulatory power thanks to binding rules and values (Elias, 1988; Elias & Dunning, 1989).

L. Tallarita (✉)
"Kore" University of Enna, Enna, Italy
e-mail: loredana.tallarita@unikore.it

P. Corvo, F. M. Lo Verde (eds.), *Sport and Quality of Life*, Social Indicators Research Series 84, https://doi.org/10.1007/978-3-030-93092-9_10

10.2 Methods and Techniques

This research was conducted in Sicily in 2018, in the province of Ragusa, specifically in the municipalities of Comiso and Vittoria: two places where with a high frequency immigrant arrivals. Four reception centers were considered for this study: two for minors (reception centres) and two for adults (SPRAR). A set of 60 in depth interviews[1] were conducted with reception centre operators, cultural mediators, and hosted immigrants. Two football coaches involved were also interviewed in the cities of Vittoria and Comiso (RG). The interviews introduced the "symbolic provinces of meaning" (Schütz, 1982) built by immigrants in their experience of reception. The case study (Glaser & Strauss, 1967; Yin, 2013) highlighted how the influences of "institutional social capital" (Coleman, 1988, 1999; Putnam, 2000) and football (Gasparini & Beaud, 2018; Vinnai, 2003) has been effective on the paths of inclusion of immigrants.

10.3 Results. Migrant Flows: Welcome, Reciprocity and Integration

Today's immigration phenomenon is interconnected with institutional realities like immigrant reception, health care, crime prevention and social integration. The current status of these interconnections determines the socio-institutional capacity to create opportunities for inclusion in the host communities, reflecting the cultural and linguistic diversity of which migrants are the bearers. Land migration raises the sensitive issue of respect for cultural and ethnic diversity and social inclusion (Ambrosini, 2017, 2019). Immigrant live in a value system far from the culture of belonging: therefore they experience a condition of "double absence" (Sayad, 1999) and faces a complex path of resocialization that involves restructuring one's identity. The immigrant is a marginal, subjected to xenophobic and racist attitudes (Dal Lago, 2004; Siebert, 2003). Overall the migratory experience is a fracture event in the biografic path, and landing countries are usually places transit places for other destinations. This is one of the most important reason for the difficulties experienced by immigrant in the integration process, in addition to the cultural and linguistic barriers already faced during reception.

[1] Interviews were numbered and ordered progressively: from 1 to 9, interviews with the operators of the four first reception centers and Sprar of Comiso and Vittoria; 10–12, interviews with the two instructors of the two football schools considered; 13–60, interviews with foreign immigrants who are guests of the four reception centers and Sprar.

10.4 Relief and Welcome in Sicily. The Regulatory Framework

The issue of immigrant's reception has led Italian institutions to face immigrant acceptance values and to employ a suitable social capital (Bourdieu, 1986, 1988; Coleman, 1988; Putnam, 2000) in order to produce positive effects for integration. In Italy the first law that regulating migration flows is the Martelli Law (L. 39/1990). This law re-examined the issues of political asylum, entry, residence and expulsion, planned entry of flows and reclassified the foreign population. With the Martelli Law the authorization for landing is connected with the so called *Intervention Plans* implemented through the collaboration of State, Regions Municipalities and with the support of local voluntary associations. However, soon the fragility of the law manifested itself and it was replaced by the Turco-Napolitano Law. This passage represented a discontinuity in approach with the previous, focusing more into repression and expulsion against immigrants present illegally on the territory. The Turco-Napolitano Law was then replaced by the Bossi-Fini Law (L.189/2002) which established the release of entry authorization to immigrants only in the presence of a regular working relationship. The aim of these laws was to coordinate a national reception plan leading to a fair distribution of migrants between European countries. The Minniti Decree (13 April 2017 Law 46) in this sense highlighted the need for a closer cooperation between State and Municipalities to which the responsibility together with local police districts mainly fall in order to control migrants distribution. The increasing frequency of flows of incoming migrants during the most recent years has determined a critical point in the regulatory framework which has often turned out to be not adequate. In Italy with the 142 Decree of 2015, immigrant reception is organized in two processes: a first reception implemented with the assistance of government centers parts of the national assistance plan; and a second reception implemented by centers belonging to SPRAR (i.e. protection systems for asylum seekers and refugees protected by Law 46 of 2017 which identifies measures for *immigrants health screen checks,* health care assessment and protocols for international asylum seekers applications). The Ministry of the Interior established that due to the increased migration flows the number of migrant in Italy raised from 22 000 in 2013 to 181 436 in 2017. Immigrants requiring international protection are usually sent in reception centers for asylum seekers initially and then to identification and deportation centers (CIE) and when applicable detained by law enforcement in order to avoid dispersion in the territory. Immigrants are then assigned to regions based on each region availability of national policies funds. In Sicily in 2017 there was a higher number of immigrants compared to other regions. This data relates to the presence of protection systems for asylum seekers (SPRAR) having an higher availability (4374 positions for immigrants) than other regions. Five hotsposts (gathering centers for early identification practices) were organized in locations around the main ports: Pozzallo, Lampedusa, Porto Empedocle and Augusta. Pozzallo is historically the first italian port opening to migrants. ISTAT data (2017) shows that net migration is 8.4% and that Italy populations grew by 6.5% compared to other European countries thanks mainly to positive net migration (8.4%) rather than birth rate (−1.4%).

10.5 Migration Networks and the Impact of Social Capital on Inclusion Pathways

Analyzing the paths of inclusion of immigrants means paying attention to the influences that a *reception network* already present in the territory generates on the construction of behaviors. The quality and type of relational ties are essential for the success of integration protocols. Migrants build a dense network of relationships and some of them already have family ties that sometime hamper the work done by institutions. If the host community is unable to support the migrant's needs, the parental *migration network,* already present in the *host territory,* can actually adversely affect behaviours. The positive impact of *institutional social capital* for integration is therefore related to the influences of the migration network. The reception environment determine success or failure of the migration experence. **Not all *relationships* generate** *positive* ***social capital*** (Bourdieu, 1988; Tallarita, 2014).

> Immigrant illegal work is now spread in many centers and is almost physiological in a too long reception system process. Managers of work-training projects would like to counteract this phenomenon, but they are not succeeding (Int. n. 6, reception center operator, Vittoria).

The social capital produced by Institutions in contrast to that produced by the migration networks represent a resource able to consolidate the cultural heritage of the immigrant, connecting them with the opportunities presented by the reception process. Employment segregation often leads to the exclusion of the immigrant (Decimo & Sciortino, 2006) from legitimate employment opportunities, on that front migration networks produce a negative influence on the work and social integration of migrants. The arising discrimination is often related to the economic and social inequalities experienced by immigrants. While family networks (Ambrosini, 2019, 2020) determine community memberships it is the *habitus* defining the role that the immigrant will assume in the receiving territory, therefore the institutional social capital is crucial for the purposes of integration. Such institutional networks positively influence the search for work and enable the immigrant to find better positions in the host society. While strong social bonds tend to limit contact with different environments it is the weak social bonds (Granovetter, 1973, 1985) that lead to explore norms and values of other networks by stimulating fiduciary attitudes (Fukuyama, 1995) and reciprocity.

10.6 Paths of Inclusion/Integration in the Cities of *Comiso* and *Vittoria*

In the cities of Comiso and Vittoria, a set of actions were put in place to facilitate integration into the territory: from logistic organization of the reception process itself to language training, increasing participation through sport e and job training and counselling on the use of administrative services. Vittoria (RG) is a municipality of 65 000 inhabitants where there is a strong concentration of the Muslim community (Tunisia, Algeria and Morocco) mostly employed in the agricultural sector. Others are from Senegal, Gambia, Mali, Bangladesh, Nigeria, Libya, Somalia, Guinea, Eritrea and Syria. In reception centers, immigrants have learned Italian language and attended job-training courses; there are those who have found work in agriculture or even as *cultural mediator*. Social inclusion begins with the support of local associations that promote job-training courses such as painting, ceramics and cooking; inclusion in social activities such as assistance to dog shelters; or participation to agricultural activities like harvesting of olives and tomatoes, and distribution to the poor families in collaboration with voluntary associations:

> Initiatives that have increased dialog between local population and migrants with the common goal of care for the territory, the local parks, heritage sites, ultimately expressing the real meaning of social volunteering and its strong cultural significance (Int. 9 reception center operator, Vittoria).
>
> Immigrants are disheartened by the long wait for documents. Those who work do not have a regular contract. Our institutional partners say that there is no such thing as unreported employment in Vittoria and are the actual landowners who would go to a point in the city every morning to pick up the labor they need, while this is clearly not what is happening (Int. 5 reception center operator, Vittoria).

The reception center team in the city of Vittoria consists of four administrative managers; ten receptionists, two professionals of social, psychological and legal services, one consultant for active policies and job orientation and one cultural linguist mediator:

> Immigrants spend time attending Italian language courses and training in the gym but it is difficult to fill up entire days without doing anything. Some have been here for two years, and after waiting such a long time, they have been denied their asylum application and they are now appealing (Int. 7 reception center operator, Vittoria).

In the kitchen of the apartment housing one of the adult reception centers (SPRAR) in Vittoria, some immigrants have organized a catering service for a downtown restaurant. Immigrants usually cook and also assist restaurants in the area earning some money:

> The atmosphere here is more relaxed. I made many friends. I'm frustrated with the wait for identity document. It's not life just eating and sleeping. We spend our time thinking about documents that never arrive and the situation does not change. We need to think about our future (Int. 24 reception center guest, Vittoria).

Other integration projects aimed to guide immigrant towards more professional jobs:

> The digital literacy course is an educational and socializing moment. Training is the only way to be integrated into the territory. The meeting generated enthusiasm transforming the course into a moment of integration. Immigrant children responded well to the initiative (Int. 6 consultant for active labor policies, SPRAR Vittoria).

In Vittoria interaction experiences and dialogue with foreigners were realized thanks to the support of work grants. The project was born with the aim of inserting the immigrant beneficiaries of those grants into the social economic fabric of the territory, assessing activities of the children and their sense of responsibility.

> The project last four months and involved 40 immigrants in the city cleaning services, taking care of streets, the city cemetery and library, mounting stages for local events and shows, setting up facilities for sports competitions; cleaning up the port and beaches in the seafaring fraction of Scoglitti. The partecipants worked to install the beach access facilities, painting and cleaning up the coast. (Int.9 SPRAR operator, Vittoria).

The project was a positive example of a relationship/integration with the host community and has taken immigrants away from the practice of illegal work in the agricultural sector.

> Over the last year more than 78 asylum seekers have been involved in the immigrant reception and assistance activities of a volunteering association (of Civil Defence) taking place in the Port of Pozzallo during the landings (Int. 8 reception center operator, Vittoria).
>
> Immigrants together with young people from Caritas have collected oranges and tomatoes to be distributed to poor families with the support of voluntary associations. In Vittoria information projects and language certification training courses for foreigners have produced positive results (Int. 5 SPRAR operator Vittoria).

Comiso (RG) is a city of about 30,000 inhabitants that had numerous experiences on integrating immigrants, resulting from a close cooperation between the Prefecture, the Municipality and the volunteering world. In 2015 a *multifunctional information and services centre for migrants* was born as result of a complex path of interaction between institutions":

> The multifunctional centre assists immigrants in their administrative obligations with the Municipality, INPS (Italian social security services bureau), immigration office, territorial directorate of labour, national registry, social services and healthcare. Voluntary associations offer services for the prevention of discrimination and violence. There are also workshops and exhibitions of crafts and art. There is a space equipped with a multimedia platform to allow access to services via apps that can be downloaded on mobile phones (Int. 4 reception center operator, Comiso).
>
> I learned how to use a computer, to plant tomatoes, eggplants, potatoes and zucchini. Gardening is fun and I love spending time outdoors. We attended italian language courses and studied in the evening school (Int. 38 immigrant guest, Mali Comiso).

These projects for social inclusion in host communities and those for professionals development of immigrants have had excellent outcomes, allowing them to strengthen their language and professional skills and interact more fluidly with the territory. Areas of Sicily covered by the projects now reflects better their needs, satisfied through the use of structures managed through associations, with the support of solidarity networks. The positive impact was seen on the entire immigrant community in both cities.

10.7 Football: A Project for Immigrants Integration

In many European countries the experience of social inclusion through sport has had often positive results. Football is a *social laboratory* in which foreigners confront natives, is a tool for prevention and care of youth discomfort and it is able to produce a positive social capital (Vinnai, 2003) having a positive influence on behaviors through exposure to models of interaction based on respect for values and norms of sport (Gasparini, 2013). Football is also a relational space in which individual intentions and aspirations are realized in a climate of reciprocity and trust (Fukuyama, 1995) and where one confronts the management of negative experiences. Football facilitate the discharge of tensions and aggression (Elias & Dunning, 1989) through the game. Immigrants establish a trust relationship with sport coaches, learning the value of solidarity (Martelli, 2020, 2015; Russo, 2016, 2019). Coaches are also flanked by educators and psychologists of reception centers during training sessions. Football is a positive relational model (Bourdieu, 1986, 1988) because it promotes the value of universal brotherhood and breaks down linguistic and cultural barrier, offering valuable opportunities for confrontation with members of the community. Football is a psycho-physical wellbeing indicator (Gasparini & Beaud, 2018) and helps in the prevention of deviant behaviors.

10.8 Football, Multicultural Reality?

Sport is an instrument of participation in the activities of a civil *society* and is a practice of inter-ethnic confrontation. Non-competitive football tournaments are accessible to everyone. Training sessions create moments of reflection starting from your own experience. The dialogue during sessions allows the rise of reflexive thinking (Donati, 2008, 2009) that guides choices abiding to a set of rules. The best players are awarded football club memberships and play in regional teams, confronting themselves with a larger relational environments. Football is a laboratory that creates moments of interaction between young immigrants and the community that welcomes them (Caperchione et al., 2011; Elling et al., 2001; O'Driscol et al., 2014) because it educates at preventing xenophobic and racists behaviors. The interactions between coach and players are crucial for their development of feelings of trust in a positive relational climate and reciprocity. The relationships being based on the sharing of common values, generate integration paths:

> In Comiso football club team there are 17 non-EU members who have been with us for two years. The boys integrated well. Some misunderstandings are due to language. Our boys don't speak well foreign languages. As an instructor during matches I often scream: tackle the man, shorten the distance, dribble the ball, run diagonal or other technical words. If I try to use gestures, they think I am angry (Int. 10 football school instructor, Comiso).

The sport policies expert from Vittoria has proposed a project entitled: *In Sport Nobody is a Foreigner*, which facilitated integration in the local territory. The reception center *Spirito Santo* has organized a football tournament with the presence of 12 teams formed by guests of the various social cooperatives operating in Vittoria and those of Vittoria football club. The football club team has a large number of immigrants. The amateur football school championship has hosted young immigrant members who regularly attend training. Sport has had a positive impact on the socialization process between immigrants and natives:

> Integration through sport teaches solidarity for those who are less fortunate. For them, football is an opportunity to relish a pleasure lost along with their youth. At the Gianni Cosimo Stadium in Vittoria solidarity matches are held, between teams of non-EU nationals, police force, local administration directors, and there are woman football matches too (Int. 9 reception centre operator, Vittoria).

Football teaches the values of universal brotherhood and has a positive social capital (Tallarita, 2014; Vinnai, 2003) that promotes positive habits. In the city of Comiso many immigrants have been registered in the city's football club and attend regular training session and play in championship. Immigrants have clear ideas about their future and for many Italy is just a transit destination. They do not learn Italian because they hope to reach other European destinations. However football is the most practiced sport by immigrants in our country and is also the most followed in their country of origin, therefore many arrive in the country with a physiological predisposition and remarkable sporting skills:

> I wanted to be a professional footballer. I know this country has given me a chance. I have to respect the rules to make my dream come true. I miss my family. I have relatives in Dublin and I hope to join them. I am happy to train in the football school (Int. 26 immigrant guest, Senegal, Comiso).
>
> To play at professional level you need to have the right connections. When we arrived in Italy initially it was not easy. At the reception center you are not free to do what you want. Thankfully there is football. That moment of freedom and in which I feel myself again (Int 38 immigrant guest Mali, Vittoria).
>
> If you want to play you need to know who can introduce you in the right places. In my country I have always played on the street or on makeshift dust-filled play pitches. The football fields here are more beautiful (Int. 45 immigrant guest, Guinea Bissau, Comiso).

Sports initiatives facilitates acquaintances and improve relationships between locals and foreigners. The sport supports integration by involving institutions: schools, voluntary associations, sports groups, creating moments of solidarity on the topics of denied rights and rejection of racism. Sport is an easy to interpret language, even among individuals who do not speak the same language and that is why it is an extraordinary meeting space between languages, cultures and ideologies in its ability to stimulate paths of mutual coexistence:

> Last year one of the immigrant boys ended up in hospital and never played again. Some of the immigrants came walking from all the way from the reception centre and couldn't complete the training session because they have been working before coming to play. While Italian boys train with continuity, immigrant boys despite having the skills and abilities in the sports practice, they lack continuity (Int. 12 football school instructor, Vittoria).

Sport is a valuable tool of socialization and of peaceful coexistence between races. The model of integration through football aims at spreading the value of sport for everyone by facilitating relations with immigrant communities by creating paths of coexistence based on the recognition of differences:

> Sport is important for children living in reception centers and has always been a neutral place of respect between races and ethnic values, in which a sports citizenship is built, and it works as an effective tool of socialization. Thanks to sport, immigrants experience paths of contamination between cultures and reciprocity (Int. 11, football school instructor, Vittoria).
>
> There are those running away from hunger and personal tragedies for which migrating represent a journey of hope seeking a better life (Int. 4 reception center operator, Comiso).
>
> We have been walking for days suffering from hunger and thirst. We arrived in Sicily. I want nothing more than to be able to realize my dream: to play in a football team and wear the team shirt (Int. n. 22 Senegal immigrant, reception center Vittoria).

Only a few immigrants manage to meet the sports consultants who can place them into more prestigious teams. One of the instructors of Comiso football club when asked about talent discovery he reply that is often the fate to make him realize the excellent skills for some of them:

> The city council football fields are crowded all day by young black people. Some of them are very talented and that is why I have decided to allow them to join my club given the consent of their reception centre (Int. 10 football school instructor, Comiso).

Sports activities promote positive values and help building confidence. Interactions with a sport environment allows immigrants to learn the rules of the local society. With increasing frequency sport get included in integration programs for immigrants.

10.9 Sport Teams Social-Relational Dynamics and Coach Educative Role

There are many relational dynamics created in a sport team and the related comparison opportunities generated highlight the level of integration achieved by foreigners in a host community. The team creates moments of trust (Coleman, 1988, 1999; Lin et al., 1986) and the football field become a relational environment characterized by high level of social cohesion (Fukuyama, 1995; Putnam, 2000) in which players share the joy of winnings and the sadness of defeats. Immigrants like any player become involved technically, emotionally and relational. They learn to accept values of others and to respect rules. This kicks off a regulatory path of introjection allowing players to develop good practices (Tallarita, 2014, 2019) that will then be also adopted in other social environments. The coach evaluates performances on the field and he is an indispensable mean for transmission of educational and positive values to the players (Gasparini & Beaud 2018; Gasparini & Talleu 2000; Sferragatta, 2013):

> The coach keeps in check conflicts and differences threatening the team peace and harmony and in his educational role he directs the relational dynamics between players (Int. 11, football school instructor, Comiso).

> Matches represent a chance for the players to relate to different cultural environments and precious occasion opportunities to learn how to interact, discuss respecting each other. Coaches are responsible for the overall interaction climate arising during a match between players (Int. 12 football school instructor, Vittoria).

A Fotbool coach make decisions with authority and is equipped with a high assessment capacity on which he relay in order to perform appropriate functions for the benefit of his team. He encourages young people in the decision-making process and stimulates their ability for self-assessment of self behavior correction during the game:

> The coach will look into either motivate, reward or sanction every single behaviour or action during the match and will be able to assess the climate generated among members of the team (Int. 10 football school instructor, Comiso).

Sport allows immigrants to feel they are equal and to enter into a relationship by speaking the same language. This puts foreign and indigenous players at the same level therefore allowing immigrants to redeem themselves from the fragility of their present life situation and to face their condition of social marginality with positive attitudes.

10.10 Discussion

In both Sicilian communities (Vittoria and Comiso) the impact of social capital (Bourdieu, 1986, 1988; Coleman, 1988, 1999; Putnam, 2000) for integration (Caperchione et al., 2011; Elling et al., 2001, O'Driscol et al., 2014) and sports social capital (Gasparini & Beaud, 2018; Gasparini & Talleu, 2000; Vinnai, 2003) is positive. 70% of the children interviewed train on a daily basis and the motivations given are the importance attributed to "sport" and the "ability to establish themselves" as an "indicator of well-being". Football is a relationship environment in which the symbolic meanings built (Geertz, 1973; Schütz, 1982) revolve on the paths of socialization through sports practice to the sharing of egos and positive attitudes (Elias, 1988; Elias & Dunning, 1989). Immigrants took part in numerous solidarity matches organized by Vittoria and Comiso football schools. Sport environments develop positive socio-relational models leading to the application of the same behavioral practice and respect for the rules outside and create an intercultural perspective by overcoming ethnic barriers and differences. The positive effects of amateur sport can be seen in the ability to be tolerant, to understand own limits and to overcome them. In this sense football is a social laboratory through which it is possible to establish a universal dialogue between multiple dimensions: *human and cultural*. It is in the playing fields that one questions and experiences the intersections between cultures and builds identity (Bourdieu, 1986, 1988; Gasparini, 2013; Zoletto, 2010). Sport is a field of cultural experimentation in which social actors are confronted with different values and success in sports practices is a form of redemption for those living in a condition of social inferiority.

10.11 Conclusion

The increase and consistency of migration flows in Italy has stimulated reflections on the course implemented at regulatory and institutional level for the purpose of integration of immigrants. The themes addressed in this research are intertwined with the sport universe, and with its ability to stimulate concrete paths of inclusion. Institutional social capital (Coleman, 1999; Fukuyama, 1995; Putnam, 2000; Lin et al., 1986) together with sport social capital (Gasparini & Beaud, 2018; Vinnai, 2003) with which immigrants come into contact, represent two different models of integration. Football produces a sense of belonging and social mobility, it is a place where new forms of solidarity and dialogue are generated. Football facilitates in young foreigners the ability to build more balanced personalities and to measure their own resources and abilities. Its values create feelings of trust and brotherhood by educating player to avoid and even prevent racist attitudes. In a team, players share the same values and talk through the same cultural code. Football becomes a form of social redemption when the best player gets the chance to play at professional level but only in few cases it constitutes a chance of social mobility. Football is a unique space that allows us to overcome disadvantages and to experience significant moments of relationship/integration with the host community. This case study has provided a window into the lifestyle of immigrants of the two communities and showed how in Sicily institutional integration projects are complemented by the ability of sport to create a new forms of solidarity towards immigrants. Educational projects carried out through sport and intercultural projects implemented by institutions when implemented together have been a very effective mean of social integration for migrants.

References

Ambrosini, M. (2017). *Migrazioni*. Egea.

Ambrosini, M. (2019). *Famiglie nonostante. Come gli affetti sfidano i confini*. Il Mulino.

Ambrosini, M. (2020). *L'invasione immaginaria. L'immigrazione oltre i luoghi comuni*. Laterza.

Bourdieu, P. (1988). Program for a sociology of sport. *The Sociology of Sport Journal, 2*, 150–161.

Bourdieu P., a cura di (1986). The Forms of Capital. In J. Richardson (Ed.), *Handbook of theory and research for sociology of education* (pp. 241–258). Geenwood.

Caperchione, C. M., Kolt Gregory, S., Tennent, R., & Mummery, W. K. (2011). Physical activity behaviours of culturally and linguistically diverse (CALD) women living in Australia. *A Qualitative Study of Socio-Cultural Influences. BMC Public Health, 11*(26), 1–10. http://www.biomedcentral.com/1471-2458/11/26

Coleman, J. S. (1988). Social capital in the creation of human capital. *American Journal of Sociology, 94*, S95–S120.

Coleman, J. S. (1999). *Foundation of social theory*. Harvard University Press.

Dal Lago, A. (2004). *Non persone. L'esclusione dei migranti in una società globale*. Feltrinelli.

Decimo, F., & Sciortino, G. (a cura di) (2006). *Reti migranti*. Il Mulino.

Donati, P. (2008). Riconoscersi con la ragione relazionale. *Atlandide. Un Mondo che fa parlare di Altri Mondi, 14*, 59–64.

Donati, P. (2009). *Oltre il multiculturalismo. La ragione relazionale per un mondo comune*. Laterza.
Elias, N. (1988). *Il processo di civilizzazione*. Il Mulino.
Elias, N., & Dunning, E. (1989). *Sport e aggressività*. Il Mulino.
Elling, A., Knop, P., & Knoppers, A. (2001). The social integrative meaning of sport: A critical and comparative analysis of policy and practice in the Netherlands. *Sociology of Sport Journal, 18*(4), 414–434. https://doi.org/10.1123/ssj.18.4.414
Fukuyama, F. (1995). *Trust: The social virtues and the creation of prosperity* (p. 26). Simon and Shuster.
Gasparini, W. (2013). Ripensare l'integrazione attraverso lo sport: la partecipazione sportiva a livello comunitario dei migranti turchi in Francia. *M@gm@, II*, 1.
Gasparini, W., & Beaud, S. (2018). *Le Football Des Nations*. Éditions De La Sorbonne.
Gasparini, W., & Talleu, C. (2000). *Sport of discrimination en Europe. The perspective of young European research of journalists*. Council of Europe Publishing.
Geertz, C. (1973). *The interpretation of culture*. Basic Books.
Glaser, B., & Strauss, A. (1967). *The discovery of grounded theory: Strategies for qualitative research*. Aldine.
Granovetter, M. (1973). *La forza dei legami deboli*. Liguori.
Granovetter, M. (1985). Economic action and social structure: The problem of embeddedness. *American Journal of Sociology, 91*, 481–510.
Istat. (2017). *Rapporto del Paese*. Istat.
Lin, N., Dean, A. & Ensel, W. M. (1986). *Social support, life events and depression*. Academic Press.
Martelli, S. (2015). Religions and sports: Are they resources for integrations of immigrants in the host society? *Italian Journal of Sociology of Education, 7*(3), 2015–2238.
Martelli, S. (2020). *Migrants social integration through movement practices?* In R. Porro Nicola, S. Martelli, & A. Testa (Eds.), *Sport, welfare and social policy in the European Union* (pp. 9–28). Routledge.
O'Driscol, T., Banting, L. K., Borkoles, E., Eime, R., & Polman, R. (2014). A systematic literature review of sport and physical activity participation in culturally and linguistically diverse (CALD) migrant populations. *Journal of immigrant and minority health., 16*(3), 515–530. https://doi.org/10.1007/s10903-013-9857-x
Putnam, R. D. (2000). *Bowling Alone. The collapse and revival of American community*. New York: Simon and Shuster (trad. it. Capitale sociale e individualismo: crisi e rinascita della cultura civica in America. Il Mulino, 2004).
Russo, G. (A cura di) (2016). Sport e migrazione. *Africa e Mediterraneo*. **N 84.**
Russo, G. (2019). Integration by sport activities: Resource or only a paradox? *Journal of Mediterranean Knowledge-JMK, 4*(1), 17–29. https://doi.org/10.26409/2019JMK4.1.02. Retrieved from http://www.mediterraneanknowledge.org/publications/index.php/journal/issue/archive
Sayad, A. (1999). *La Double Absence. Des illusions de l'émigré aux souffrances de l'immigré*. Préface de Pïerre Bourdieu.
Schütz, A. (1982). *Life forms and meaning structure*. Routledge & Kegan Paul.
Sferragatta, F. (2013). *Le mete dell'allenatore*. Angeli.
Siebert, R. (2003). *Il razzismo. Il riconoscimento negato*. Carocci.
Tallarita, L. (2014). Social capital and governance styles in Italian professional football clubs. *Rivista Trimestrale Scienza dell'Amministrazione, 3*, 65–85. https://doi.org/10.3280/SA2014-003005
Tallarita, L. (2019). Il calcio come luogo di dialogo e di confronto interculturale. *Costellazioni, Anno III*, 9.
Vinnai, G. (2003). *Il calcio come ideologia. Sport e alienazione nel mondo capitalista*. Guaraldi.
Yin, R. (2013). *Case study research. Design and methods*. Sage.
Zoletto, D. (2010). *Il gioco duro dell'integrazione. L'intercultura sui campi da gioco*. Cortina.

Part III
International Perspective

Chapter 11
Social Representations of Physical Disability in Professional Environments. The Example of Disabled Employees High-Performance Athletes in a Service Company

Bernardeau-Moreau Denis

For many authors (Barel & Fremeaux, 2012; Blanc, 2006; Gardou, 1991; Le Dantec, 2004; Kerroumi, 2007), the integration of disabled people, particularly those with physical disabilities, in the workplace continues to be insufficient in our society. Although various studies (Mormiche and Goillot 2003, AGEFIPH 2013) indicate that there has been noticeable progress, the 2014 study by AGEFIPH and FIPHFP[1] highlights that only two-thirds of physically disabled persons who are capable of working are currently in employment.[2] The Le Houerou parliamentary report (2014, p. 9) states that the rate of unemployment among disabled people is 22%, which is double the national average. In spite of the 1987 and 2005 laws[3] that impose a financial penalty on employers with at least 20 employees that do not achieve the 6% quota of disabled workers, the share of disabled people in public and private companies is still low. Of the 100 100 private-sector establishments affected by this employment obligation in 2011 (2014 key figures from AGEFIPH and FIPHFP,

[1]AGEFIPH (French National Association for Managing Funds for the Inclusion of Disabled Persons in the Workplace—*Association Nationale pour la Gestion du Fonds pour l'Insertion Professionnelle des Personnes Handicapées*) and FIPHFP (Funds for Including Disabled Persons in the Civil Service—*Fonds pour l'Insertion des Personnes Handicapées dans la Fonction Publique*) aim to promote the inclusion of disabled persons in jobs in private companies, firstly, and in public companies, secondly.

[2]AGEFIPH's activity report (2013) establishes that in 2005, of the 938 820 disabled people who are able to work, 680 000 were actually in work and 570 000 of this number were employed in an ordinary working environment.

[3]**Law No.87-517 of 10 July 1987 in support of employing disabled persons.** Law No.2005-102 of 11 February 2005 for equal rights and opportunities, involvement and civic rights for disabled persons.

B.-M. Denis (✉)
Univ. Artois, Univ. Lille, Univ. Littoral Côte d'Opale, ULR 7369, Unitéde Recherche Pluridisciplinaire Sport Santé Société (URePSSS), Liévin, France
e-mail: denis.bernardeau-moreau@univ-lille.fr

P. Corvo, F. M. Lo Verde (eds.), *Sport and Quality of Life*, Social Indicators Research Series 84, https://doi.org/10.1007/978-3-030-93092-9_11

p. 2 and 3), only 41% of them meet or exceed the required threshold. Other establishments either have agreements with service providers regarding indirect employment (11%; +2 points compared with the previous year) or prefer to pay their contributions to AGEFIPH (47%; −2 points[4]). The report fares little better in the public sector. Of the 10 596 establishments listed, only 51% meet or exceed the required 6%. Furthermore, on a national level, AGEFIPH and FIPHFP (*Ibid.*, p. 4 and 5) report that in 2013, the percentage of disabled people recruited into direct employment increased to 3.1% in the private sector and to 4.64% in the public sector (3.56% in government civil service, 5.20% in hospital public service and 5.66% in regional civil service). However, despite clear legislation, it appears that many companies still prefer to pay the fine rather than employ disabled people. Although figures are certainly improving, there is still a persistent gap.

As a result, we are questioning the causes of this report. According to the authors, there are multiple causes stemming from economics, culture and sociology. For Davin et al. (2006), social inequalities facing disabled people are the result, in part, of inadequate facilities and insufficient financial means. It is the difficulties of adapting jobs and the costs of altering access to buildings and offices that make employers hesitate. According to a 2014 AGEFIPH study, it appears that only one in five disabled people benefit from a modification to their working hours or alleviated tasks. The 1999 HID study[5] also highlights that disabled people have a level of education that is too inadequate for jobs. The Le Houerou report (2014, p. 9) states that 78% of disabled persons have a level of education that is equal to or lower than BEP or CAP vocational qualifications (INSEE reports that on a national scale, this rate is 50.4%). Auerbacher (2007, p. 2) notes that disabled people do not receive proper training, and even less training, throughout their lives. For Kerroumi (2007), the difficulty is in conducting more research into social representations and the extent that companies still too often consider disability as a factor in unproductivity. This author continues that despite efforts by organisations and public bodies, disability is still associated with negative collective associations, including social issues that are imagined to be disruptive to a company's good operation (Kerroumi, 2007, p. 32). Point et al. (2010)) also observe that disability is rarely presented as an asset for companies and because of this, employers remain reluctant to hire disabled employees.

With regard to the current situation for disabled employees, our aim is to focus on social representations. More precisely, our aim is to provide some elements for reflection with regard to the imagined issues of physical disability in the workplace by focusing, in particular, on the social representations that they trigger among employees who work with disabled colleagues on a day-to-day basis. What are the representations of physical disability in the workplace? Do these change through

[4]For 2013, the total sum of penalties increased to €441 million.

[5]Mormiche, Pierre; Goillot, Catherine. (2003). "Enquête Handicap-Incapacités-Dépendances de 1998–1999", *société*, n°22.

contact with disabled employees? What role can the company play to encourage integration of workers with disabilities?

Methodological Framework For identify the elements that make up representations, we have opted for a multi-methodology approach (Abric, 1994). Firstly, we carried out exploratory interviews (22 in total Annex I), with social and medical managers responsible for matters regarding disability in France, enabling us to better contextualise our subject. We then selected several work situations at a branch of a large service company bringing together a total of seven people with a disability and all high-level athletes (Annex II) and 30 employees working in the same workplaces (Annex III). We then used De Rosa's method of the free association (De Rosa & Sophie, 2003). Our objective was to identify the elements that make up employees' representations (central core) based on the key term "disability in the workplace". For this, we created two groups differentiated according to whether the employees were or were not in direct and regular contact with workers with disabilities. This stage enabled us to identify the recurrent words and expressions used in discussions (frequency, meaning, classification). By combining the various methods (interviews, free association), we were able to have a more precise identification of the elements constituting the central core of those with disabilities are viewed at work in a service company.

Our paper consists of three parts. In the first part, we shall set out the legal framework and its incentive role. In the second part, we shall emphasize the social construction of disability and the evolution in the representations in social interaction situations. Finally, in the third part, we shall underline the importance for organizations to encourage internal dialogue capable of mitigating the impact of negative attitudes.

11.1 A Legislative Framework that Encourages Organizations to Employ People with Disabilities

In 1987, a law for the employment of disabled persons (law n°87-517 of 10 July 1987 in support of employing disabled persons) established the obligation for companies with more than 20 employees, whether full or part-time, to have disabled people make up at least 6% of their workforce. In 2005, France decided to modernize its legislation and promulgated the law of 11 February 2005 (law n°2005-102 for equal rights and opportunities, involvement and civic rights for disabled persons) that defines disability in all its diversity. Thanks to this law, disability is much more widely recognized in society. For Maryse Aïo (interview on 22 April 2014), the national head of the disability mission in the agricultural social cooperative (*mutuelle sociale agricole*), the employment obligation created by the 2005 law grants disabled people a status and, above all, rights. For Nicolas Janda (interview on 19 May 2014), head of training at the TH Conseil organization,[6] *"this judicial document offers disabled people a better opportunity to find a job or to be integrated into the workplace"*. Works by Barbusse (2002 and 2009), Blanc (2006) and Morin (2006) show that among disabled people, employment provides meaning and a feeling of usefulness. It is a place of activity and for creating social connections. Morin also remarks that work is a "*health provider*" (Morin, 2006, p. 66) as it encourages access to everything. For disabled people, integration in the workplace is therefore essential, even lifesaving. In addition, Blanc notes that it is "*a test that is indicative of existing solidarity within democratic societies that are now ruined by globalisation*" (Blanc, 2006, p. 49).

So, although the law contributes to promoting the professional integration of disabled persons, what is the reality? Various studies (CSA study for CED—"Disability in the workplace: perceptions in the French population" September 2014; IFOP study on "Perceptions, views and experiences of employees concerning disability in the workplace" carried out for ADIA and EURO RSCG C&O in October 2009) show a positive change in the perception of disability. However, this trend is not necessarily followed by an actual integration of disabled people in the workplace. The IFOP 2012 study (cited previously) also reports that 57% of disabled people questioned believe that the 2005 law has changed nothing about their day-to-day lives. Additionally, this survey highlights that 64% of this group thinks that integrating disabled workers into companies continues to be too difficult. For the majority of people we spoke to, effecting a deep change in society's view of disability remains a priority and a prerequisite. The matter of physical disability in the workplace is, of course, complex and involves all of the actors concerned fully: the national government, social partners, associations and also employers and employees.

11.2 The Role of Interaction in Improving How Society Views Disability

For Abric (2005), societal views and practices are inextricably linked and feed off each other: "views guide and determine the practices and the latter act by creating or transforming the views" (Ibid, p. 12) For verify that, we immersed ourselves in a service company. The department in question, situated in the Paris area, employs 300 people, 18 of whom live with handicaps (representing 5.8% of the total payroll). The disabled workers we met are engineers, technicians, consultants, physiotherapists or survey leaders. Their disabilities, both visible and invisible, are quite

[6] The TH Conseil is an organisation that provides consultancy, training and recruitment, specialising in managing diversity for organisations, particularly the employment of disabled persons.

diverse—these include varying degrees of restricted mobility, various debilitating diseases (Parkinson's disease, Little's disease, diabetes, leukemia, ankylosing spondylitis, functional dystonia) and sometimes require specific equipment (bags, hearing aids or catheters).

Having identified the employees working daily with or close by the members of staff with disabilities, we selected 30 of them. We then split them into two differentiated groups: Group A was comprised of employees who worked with a colleague with a disability only occasionally and often indirectly. These were employees who, in carrying out their duties, discussed, or collaborated with their disabled colleagues from time to time, and only briefly. Contact is irregular and depends on the department's requirements. Group B, on the other hand, was comprised of employees being in direct and constant contact with one or more colleague with a disability. They worked together, frequently working at neighboring desks, and their daily collaboration was an essential part of the department's function. The free association method of De Rosa enabled identifying a certain number or words and expressions attached to an inductive term. The results are displayed in the Annex IV. We asked both groups to respond spontaneously to the following question: "What four words come to mind when you hear the expression 'disability at work'?" For each word pronounced we asked to specify whether, for them, it had a positive or a negative connotation (+ or −). We then asked them to rank their replies in order of importance (from 1 to 4). We also noted the frequency (F) i.e. the number of times the words or expressions were articulated by the members of the groups. The first results show that, in Group A, words with a positive connotation which appeared most frequently were "adaptation" ($F = 10$), "awareness" (8), and "stigma" (5). The words with a negative connotation were "denial" (6), "embarrassment" (5) and "lack of training" (5). From group B we noted that more words with a positive connotation appeared. We heard "no difference" ($F = 5$), but also "ignorance", "openness of mind", "no hindrance" and "integration". Among the words with a negative connotation, we heard "fear" ($F = 4$) and the words "denial" and "embarrassment" ($F = 3$). To find the central core of views (CC), we then calculated the ratio between the average level (L) and the frequency (F). The closer this number is to 0, the closer the corresponding word or expression is supposed to be to the central core of the views. The ratio between the average level of importance (L) and the frequency of appearance (F) shows that the expressions closest to the central core (<1) are only slightly different between the two groups. In group A, the central core of representations comprised words and expression with positive connotations such as "awareness" (0.25), "adaptation" (0.26), and "no difference" (0.55), and those with a negative connotation such as "lack of training" (0.4) and "denial" (0.52). In group B we note, as before, a greater predominance of words with a positive connotation such as "ignorance" (0.33), "no difference" (0.4), "integration" (0.55) and "open-mindedness" (0.66). No word with a negative connotation appears in the central core with a result below 0.75.

In summary, the results from analyzing the views reveal an over-representation of words and expressions with positive connotations from the group in direct and regular contact with their colleagues with disabilities. Although the differences between the two groups are not flagrant, they nevertheless do tend to affirm positive progress in how employees regard their colleagues with disabilities when they are in a constant and close relationship.

The emergence of these two categories of views with different connotations is moreover confirmed by an analysis of informal exchanges we had during our work in immersion. The selected extracts from interviews show that, in group A, attitudes oscillate between discomfort and embarrassed silence, with disability being minimized, poorly regarded and sometimes even denied. Those interviewed expressed a lack of training, a certain level of fear, embarrassment and even a certain indifference concerning issues relating to disability. Those belonging to group B tended to show a more compassionate attitude towards their disabled work colleagues. They showed themselves to be sensitive to the situation of their colleagues with disabilities, developed a real empathy for them and claimed that their view of them had changed (Table 11.1).

It is very clear that those employees who work regularly with people with disabilities develop views that are overall more positive towards them. For them, there is no difficulty in working with disabled colleagues at their place of work. In this, our results mirror those of the national surveys carried out in recent years. Although some employees could feel embarrassment in working with people with disabilities, their misgivings seem to disappear with time. Most of the people with whom we discussed the issue claim, with a mixture of admiration and empathy, that they understand much better the everyday problems with which their differently-abled colleagues are faced.

11.3 Increase Internal Communication to Improve the Perception of Disabilities

The company's role to encourage integration of workers with disabilities is very important. The service company is making great strides in improving its policy towards disability. Taking advantage of an agreement signed with the Agefiph (the French Fund management association for providing aid to help getting people with disabilities into gainful employment), relevant flyers are distributed and events are organized. To encourage the integration of workers with disabilities, the company has created a national disability project—P.H.A.R.E. (Personnel Handicapé: Anticiper, Reclasser, Employer)*, designed to improve the welcome, integration and job protection for employees with disabilities. As one interviewee confided, this project *"helps us to adapt our working conditions for our disabled colleagues."* The national project organizes the annual 'Handy' awards. As Barnes et al. (1999) also state, disability as a social model can only evolve if disabled workers play a leading role. Here, the trophies honour the sporting achievements of disabled workers.

Table 11.1 Extracts from informal exchanges with disabled and non-disabled employees

Group A Those with an indirect and irregular contact with their colleagues with disabilities and for whom their view of them had changed little	*(2) "It's a subject that we never raise (...) I don't know if this is through embarrassment or simply out of concern for others, but we never speak about it."*
	(4) "I become embarrassed because I don't really know how to react or behave with someone who is disabled."
	(7) "Disability frequently invokes inferiority for me."
	(16) "Disability is frequently treated with indifference as long as one does not come face to face with the problem."
	(17) "Disability always seems to engender some sort of fear when one has not really been confronted by it."
	(17) Talking about disability at work is complicated—We need results and there's money at stake."
	(18) "The subject of disability remains a bit vague. We don't really want to discuss it."
Group B Those with a direct and regular contact with their disabled colleagues and for whom their view of them had changed as interactions increased	(6) "*What upsets me is to see them in that state, to see how it takes over their lives.*"
	(8) "*He comes for three and half hours every morning and it does him good, and us also. It's give and take, he needs us and we need him. I would say that there is a sort of paternal feeling that has been established to keep this contact with our disabled colleague.*"
	(9) "*My view has become more and more compassionate—He has changed and will continue to adapt as his disease evolves.*"
	(10) "*With our colleague we realize that we now have a totally different appreciation of disability.*"
	(12) "*Often, I have to go on site to do something instead of him and that is, in a way, a waste of time. But we adapt to his disability and I prefer to spend a bit of my time rather than see him suffer and think that he cannot do anything.*"
	(14) "*I think we are a plus for him because we can re-motivate and encourage him, but also don't let him overextend himself and we shield him from his disease.*"

Thomas,[7] a high-level athlete, is a case in point. His participation in the Paralympic Games in Sochi was shown live on giant screens, so that his colleagues could watch his performances. Manon (she is Engineer and paratriathlete) explains that it was through sport that she was able to create a dialogue with her colleagues. The company is also very active in the sporting arena, and every 2 years organizes a sports rally for the staff. Teams comprise both able-bodied people and those with disabilities and their colleagues are encouraged to watch the event on giant screens. *"There is a real team spirit"*, relates one of our interviewees, *"which enables us to showcase workers with disabilities to others."* The company has recently created an internal network of some 20 'Disability' ambassadors whose company-wide mission is to highlight positive experiences in terms of integration and employment of people with disabilities. It is worth noting that the company received the 2012 'Diversity' label, further emphasizing the company's commitment to equal opportunity and support for diversity. This recognition has also reinforced the company's positioning as a socially responsible organization.

Thus, implementing a determined internal policy of communication and awareness is revealed as an indispensable building block for a company to remove the barriers to an effective integration of workers with disabilities. As we have tried to show throughout this article, the presence of people with disabilities in the professional world is not something that is easily accepted. Yes, it provokes kindness, even compassion, but also embarrassment and apprehension. To overcome such obstacles the roles of inter-personal relations and a veritable internal communication and awareness policy are determinant. In our situation, sport is an indispensable asset.

11.4 Conclusion

With regard to intellectual disability, Esnard (1998) observes that social behavior is led by representations, which have an impact on the integration of those concerned. Our study provides some interesting perspectives. It shows that disability at work is incomparably better understood by their able-bodied colleagues when the latter create close and regular daily relationships with their disabled counterparts. All opportunities for creating awareness of disability at work, in particular through sport, are also extremely pertinent. Although the term disability was not well known among the general public several years ago, studies show that mentalities have changed considerably since. The employment rate for physically disabled persons is certainly still insufficient and far from the legally imposed quotas, but our article endeavors to illustrate that real advances have been made. The examples given here are evidence that it is possible to reconcile physical disability and a professional career. The employees that we met were aware that their representations

[7] Thomas is physiotherapist, visually impaired and an elite athlete. He won a medal at the Paralympic Games in Sochi.

of disability changed through contact with disabled colleagues. Our results show that they feel more related to the issue and that their perception is more positive overall.

However, our analysis includes clear limitations. The free association method presents semantic biases. The analysis of interview content cannot fully reproduce the interlocutors' thoughts and types of self-censorship are always possible. Thus, it would seem appropriate to have a better analysis of how, in the context of an organizational inductive element, interpersonal relations may contribute to optimizing acceptance and inclusion of disability in a company or organization. In-depth studies, in the form of real-life personal accounts will be, in this context, particularly useful.

Annex I. List of People Surveyed in the Pre-Survey (22)

Role	Company
National head of the disability mission	Mutualité sociale agricole (MSA)
Head of the disability and integration project	Disney
Department of Major accounts	AGEFIPH
Physiotherapist (disabled employee)	Centre de rééducation Martel
Head of the disability mission (disabled employee)	Clarins
Physiotherapist (disabled employee)	Fondation Saint Marie
Head of socio-professional supervision for elite athletes	Fédération Française handisport (French federation for disability sports)
HR and disability mission	Havas
Head of the national disability mission	GDF SUEZ Cofely Ineo
Quality technician (disabled employee)	Elissor
Sports consultant (disabled employee)	Handiamo!
PhD in economics and management	Paris town hall
Head of the disability mission	Assystem France and E&OS
Vice president for social action, health and social education, health and disability	Région Île-de-France
Head of disability mission	BUT
University lecturer, PhD in management science	École de management de Nantes
Head of training	TH Conseil
Inter-regional head of the Île-de-France disability mission	FIPHFP
Head of the disability mission	RATP
Office of career support	Social ministries
Deputy director	Diversidées
Co-founder CEO	Handiamo!

Annex II. Liste des travailleurs handicapés et sportifs de haut niveau (7)

First name	Handicap	Company position	Practised sport
Bastien	Little's disease	Quality technician	Disabled table tennis player
Olivier	Visually impaired	Physiotherapist	Cyclist
Lionel	Ankylosing spondylitis disability	Mission manager	Disabled rally driver
Michael	Paraplegic	Consultant	Tennisman
Thomas	Visually impaired	Physiotherapist	Nordic skier and bi-athlete
Manon	Functional dystonia	Engineer	Paratriathlete
Charles	Head trauma	Consultant	Swimmer

Annex III. Sex and Roles of People Surveyed in Line with the Free Association Method (30)

Sex	Role
Group A: People with indirect and irregular contact with a disabled colleague (20 employees)	
M	Design office technician
M	Business manager
M	Cryptographer (pricing study)
M	Construction site manager
M	Deputy head of maintenance and service
F	Office assistant
M	Deputy branch manager
F	Payroll administrator
F	Office assistant
M	Deputy branch manager
F	HR assistant
M	Head of shop security
M	Maintenance technician
F	Head of maintenance contract
F	Project assistant technician
F	Reception assistant
F	Office manager
M	HR manager
F	Design office manager
M	Business manager
Group B: People with direct and regular contact with a disabled colleague (10 employees)	

(continued)

Sex	Role
M	Research technician
M	Research technician
M	Research technician
M	Trade unionist
M	Research technician
F	Research technician
F	Project manager
M	Office manager
M	Office manager
M	Project manager

Annex IV: Correlation Between the Level of Importance and the Frequency of Appearance Using the Free Association Method

Group A: People with indirect and irregular contact with a colleague with a disability (20 respondents)

words / Respondents	1	2	3	4	7	16	17	18	19	20	21	22	23	24	25	26	27	28	29	30	F	L*	A+ -	CC (L/F)
Ignorance	1		1					4								4					4	2.5	+	0.62
Fear	2																				1	2	-	2
Denial	3								3					3	2			4	4		**6**	3.16	-	**0.52**
Lateness	4														3						2	3.5	+	1.75
Embarrassment		1		4						3	4						3				**5**	3	-	0.6
Mockery		2						3		4											3	3	-	1
Awareness		3		2		2				2		1		1				2		3	**8**	2	+	**0.25**
No difference		4		1				1													3	2	+	0.66
Problem						1															1	1	-	1
Difficult to accept			3	3																	2	3	-	1.5
Stigma			4						4								4	3		1	**5**	3.2	+	0.64
Tolerance					2						2	4									3	2.66	+	0.88
Admiration																					0	0	+	0
Openness of mind							3														2	1.5	+	0.75
Adaptation					1	4			2		1	3	4	4	4				1	2	**10**	2.6	+	**0.26**
Taboo subject													1								1	1	-	1
No difference					3				1								1				3	1.66	+	**0.55**
Non-issue					4												2				2	3	+	1.5
Opposition to change																					0	0	-	0
An asset for the company							1									3				4	3	2.66	+	0.88
No hindrance													3			1					2	2	+	1
Integration													2			2					2	2	+	1
Fitting out the																		1			1	1	-	1
workstation								2													1	2	-	2
Wheelchair						3				1	3	2			1						**5**	2	-	**0.4**
Lack of training							4												2		2	3	-	1.5
Bad image							3												3		2	3	-	1.5
Safety issues																								

Group B: People with direct and regular contact with a colleague with a disability (10 respondents)

words / Respondents	5	6	8	9	10	11	12	13	14	15	F	L*	A+ -	CC (L/F)
Ignorance	1	2									**3**	1	+	**0.33**
Fear		4		4					4		**4**	3	-	0.75
Denial					2	1		4			**3**	2.33	-	0.77
Lateness											0		+	
Embarrassment					3		3	3			**3**	3	-	1
Mockery											0		-	
Awareness									2	3	2	2.5	+	1.25
No difference	2	1	1	2	4						**5**	2	+	**0.4**
Problem			2								1	2	-	2
Difficult to accept											0		-	
Stigma											0		+	
Tolerance										4	1	4	+	4
Admiration		3							1		2	2	+	1
Openness of mind	3							1		2	**3**	2	+	**0.66**
Adaptation								2			1	2	+	2
Taboo subject	4								3		2	3.5	-	1.75
No difference						2					1	2	+	2
Non-issue						4	2				2	3	+	1.5
Opposition to change			4								1	4	-	4
An asset for the company											0		+	
No hindrance			3	1		3					**3**	2.33	+	0.77
Integration				3	1					1	**3**	1.66	+	**0.55**
Fitting out the workstation											0		-	
Wheelchair											0		-	
Lack of training											0		-	
Bad image							1				1	1	-	1
Safety issue											0		-	

[a]R = Rang moyen d'importance; F = Fréquence; M+/– Moyenne de la connotation; NC = Noyau central des représentation

References

Abric, J. C. (1994). *Pratiques sociales et représentations*. Presses Universitaires de France.

Abric, J. C. (2005). *Méthodes d'étude des représentations sociales*. ERES "Hors collection".

AGEFIPH. (2013). http://www.agefiph.asso.fr/Actualites/Conference-social-L-Agefiph-publie-ses-resultats. Press release, 19 June 2013.

Auerbacher, E. (2007). Politique, handicap et discriminations. *Reliance, 1*(23), 100–102.

Barbusse, B. (2002). Sport et entreprise: des logiques convergentes ? *L'Année sociologique, 52*, 391–415.

Barbusse, B. (2009). Entre sport et entreprise, une attirance réciproque. *L'Expansion Management Review, 134*, 10–19.

Barel, Y., & Fremeaux, S. (2012). Les attitudes face à la contrainte légale. L'exemple de l'intégration professionnelle des personnes handicapées. *RIMHE, 2*(2), 33–49.

Barnes, C., Mercer, G., & Shakespeare, T. (1999). *Exploring disability: A sociological introduction*. Royaume-Uni Polity Press.

Blanc, A. (2006). Handicap et insertion professionnelle: égalité et démocratie. *Reliance, 19*, 42–49.

Davin, B., Joutard, J., Moatti, P., Paraponaris, A., & Verger, P. (2006). Besoins et insuffisance d'aide humaine aux personnes âgées à domicile: une approche à partir de l'enquête Handicaps, incapacités, dépendance. *Sciences sociales et santé, 24*, 59–93.

De Rosa, P., & Sophie, A. (2003, 2ème édition 2005). Le réseau d'associations. In J. C. Abric (Ed.), *Méthode d'étude des représentations sociales* (pp. 81–118). Erès.

Esnard, C. (1998). Les représentations sociales du handicap mental chez les professionnels médico-sociaux. *Revue Européenne du handicap Mental, 5*(19), 10–23.

Gardou, C. (1991). *Le regard interrogé: Handicaps – Handicapés*. Edition ERES.

Kerroumi, K. (2007). Responsabiliser le management. In D. Poizat & C. Gardou (Eds.), *Désinsulariser le handicap* (pp. 161–167). ERES Connaissances de la diversité.

Le Dantec, J. (2004). Entre travail et handicap. *Empan, 55*, 73–80.

Le Houerou, A. (2014). *Dynamiser l'emploi des personnes handicapées en milieu ordinaire. Aménager les postes et accompagner les personnes*. Rapport parlementaire remis au 1er Ministre en septembre.
Morin, B. (2006). L'insertion professionnelle des personnes en situation de handicap- Réflexion à partir d'une pratique en entreprise. *Reliance, 19*, 62–66.
Mormiche, P., & Goillot, C. (2003). Enquête Handicap-Incapacités-Dépendances de 1998–1999. Société 22.
Point, S., Charles-Fontaine, C., & Berthélemé, G. (2010). (Re)considérer le handicap: regards croisés sur les approches en entreprise. *Management & Avenir, 38*(8), 293–305.

Chapter 12
Physical and Sports Activities Diagnosis in Brazil: Methodology to Support Policies to Improve the Population's Quality of Life

Ailton Fernando Santana de Oliveira, Antonio Mussino, Julio Brugnara Mello, and Marcelo de Castro Haiachi

12.1 Introduction

The practice of regular physical activity is associated with a series of physiological benefits at all stages of life (Warburton et al., 2006; Warburton & Bredin, 2017). However, recently, Piggin (2020) questioned how much physical activity should be observed only from the perspective of energy expenditure and effects on the body, thinking it as something quantitative. Thus, physical activity is currently understood as a human behavior, which involves, in addition to physical effort, socialization, motivation, important self-image and self-efficacy changes, which is therefore a complex behavior related to social, psychological and physiological aspects of the human being.

In this perspective, in 2020, WHO launched the update of Physical Activity Recommendations (Bull et al., 2020), which was driven by the "Every movement counts" campaign. These recommendations establish the physical activity volume and intensity that should be practiced in each age group and also in groups in which physical activity requires special attention such as pregnant women and people with disabilities. However, new WHO recommendations provide important considerations on social and public policy aspects involved in physical activity and sedentary behavior.

A. F. S. de Oliveira (✉)
Department of Physical Education, Federal University of Sergipe, São Cristóvão, Sergipe, Brazil

A. Mussino
Sapienza Universitá di Roma, Rome, Italy

J. B. Mello
Universidade Federal de Sergipe, São Cristóvão, Sergipe, Brazil

M. de Castro Haiachi
Faculdade Sogipe, Porto Alegre, Rio Grande do Sul, Brazil

P. Corvo, F. M. Lo Verde (eds.), *Sport and Quality of Life*, Social Indicators Research Series 84, https://doi.org/10.1007/978-3-030-93092-9_12

With regard to sedentary behavior, some important information related to the harms of excess of this behavior is described in some systematic literature reviews (Edwardson et al., 2012; Zhai et al., 2015). When low levels of physical activity are added to high time in sedentary behavior, health harms include muscle weakness, poor physical proficiency, indexes of inflammatory markers at risk to cardiovascular health and osteopenia earlier than usual (Ford et al., 2005).

In this sense, different strategies can be implemented to promote physical activity and decrease sedentary behavior at population level. Among these strategies, programs at providing places for the practice of sports are an important pillar within physical activity promoting public policies (Bergmann et al., 2020; Mendonça et al., 2020; Moretti et al., 2009). Although a recent study has shown that, in Brazil, despite mega sporting events that took place in the last decade, the percentage of sports practice among children and adolescents is below 40% (Mello et al., 2020). In this scenario, even with the Olympic Games, strategies to promote sports practice were not in evidence. During the period of occurrence of these sports events, of the 105 normative acts published by the Brazilian Federal Government, most (32%) dealt with the administrative structure, that is, with the internal organization of the government, such as the composition and powers of the National Council Sports and other bodies (BRASIL, 2010).

However, some other options have been demonstrated, such as the use of public spaces and the other spaces that make up the urban environment (Handy et al., 2002; Smith et al., 2017). Some studies in different cities in Brazil have shown that people at different age groups are more active when they have public spaces with quality structures available close to their residences (Hino et al., 2011; Mello et al., 2020). Some recent studies have pointed out that the relationship between physical activity and environment is dependent on socioeconomic status, pointing out that people with lower incomes depend more on public spaces to be active (Giles-Corti & Donovan, 2002). In this context, the aim of this study was to demonstrate that, based on a diagnostic protocol, the degree of development of the reality about practitioners and non-practitioners of physical and sports activities in Brazil can be identified, known and explained, aiming to subsidize public policies that can contribute to promote health and quality of life for Brazilians.

12.2 Method

Data presented here are based on the raw database (record files) of the National Household Sample Survey—PNAD-2015 in its Sports Supplement (IBGE, 2017), conducted by the Brazilian Institute of Geography and Statistics—IBGE, commissioned by the former Ministry of Sports and available on the IBGE website. This research adopted the protocol developed by Oliveira et al. (2013) with the collaboration and approval of researchers from five Brazilian Federal Universities who coordinated the Diagnosis of Sport in Brazil—DIESPORTE research and IBGE researchers.

Table 12.1 Brazil sample plan by age and gender in percentage

Age group	Gender		Total
	Male	Female	
15–19	11.5%	10.1%	10.8%
20–24	10.3%	9.1%	9.7%
25–34	20.0%	18.9%	19.4%
35–44	18.7%	18.9%	18.8%
45–54	16.3%	16.6%	16.5%
55–64	11.8%	12.9%	12.4%
65–74	7.5%	8.0%	7.8%
75+	3.9%	5.5%	4.7%
Total	100.0%	100.0%	100.0%
Number of units	32.843	38.299	71.142

The survey sample was defined by the IBGE standard criteria for this type of research, taking into account people aged 15 years or older stratified by gender, age and Brazilian state, with 71,142 interviews being carried out. In 2015, according to IBGE data, Brazil had estimated population of around 204 million people, thus, IBGE survey data had estimated focus for 161.8 million people over 15 years of age. Data collected were related to the practice of physical and sports activities performed or not by interviewees in the period between September 2014 and September 2015 (12 months).

Data were processed according to a methodology (DIESPORTE) based on international experiences, inspired by COMPASS (Coordinated Monitoring of Participation in Sports). This European project was useful to define the general guidelines of the research, indicators and the methodological steps to be followed by studies (Oliveira, 2013; Mussino, 2002). The sample was stratified by sex, age groups and federation unit (state), giving specific weights, allowing error of 2% more or less in the presentation per federation unit and a confidence index of 95 (Table 12.1).

12.3 Main Results for Practitioners and Their Practice Conditions

Data have demonstrated that, of the 161.8 million Brazilians, only a little more than 35 million (21.9%) declared to practice physical activity on a regular basis, as directed by the World Health Organization—WHO—(three or more times a week), while approximately 127 million (78.1%) of Brazilians are: sedentary, about 100.5 million (62.1%) or practice physical activity irregularly, about 26.5 million (16%), less than three times per week. Considering data by gender, women (66.6%) are more sedentary than men (57.3%). This can be explained by the double working hours that have historically been imposed on women, according to Tables 12.2 and 12.3.

Table 12.2 Practice profile according to WHO recommendation

Profile	Gender		Total
	Male	Female	
Sedentary	57.3%	66.6%	62.1%
Less than twice a week	4.0%	1.9%	2.9%
Twice a week	16.9%	9.7%	13.1%
Three or more times a week (WHO)	21.9%	21.9%	21.9%
Total	100%	100%	100%

Table 12.3 Practice profile according to WHO recommendation by age

Age	WHO classification				Total
	Sedentary	Less than 2× per week	2× per week	3× or more per week	
15–19	48.9%	4.2%	20.3%	26.6%	100.0%
20–24	53.3%	3.9%	16.7%	26.1%	100.0%
25–34	57.0%	3.5%	15.6%	23.8%	100.0%
35–44	63.3%	2.9%	12.5%	21.3%	100.0%
45–54	66.5%	2.5%	10.7%	20.2%	100.0%
55–64	68.5%	1.7%	9.2%	20.6%	100.0%
65–74	70.9%	1.5%	9.3%	18.4%	100.0%
75+	80.4%	1.1%	6.3%	12.2%	100.0%
Total	62.1%	2.9%	13.1%	21.9%	100.0%

There is a worldwide trend of greater sporting practice among young people, which decreases with increasing age. In the elderly, it was observed that practicing sports is more complex due to physical problems and diseases, which is compensated by the increase in the practice of physical activities, showing growth up to the age group of 55–64 years, decreasing in the age group of 65–74 years.

An ideal health promotion policy that directly contributes to active lifestyle and consequently to quality of life should take into account the improvement of the of **regular practice** indicator, whether by raising the sporting standard, practice qualification, or by health issues, with prevention of diseases linked to the lack of physical activities. Another option is to pay special attention to the **almost-regular** indicator, providing opportunities for democratization of access to these practices, as well as their universalization.

The most practiced Physical activities among Brazilians were (Table 12.4):

Traditional sports like Volleyball, Handball and Basketball were rarely mentioned. The Sport Atlas of Sergipe (OLIVEIRA, 2011) pointed out that these modalities were little practiced due to the lack of adequate facilities, need for guidance for adequate practice and appropriate sports equipment. Activities change their importance in the course of life. Soccer, which is the sport most practiced by teenagers/youngsters up to 24 years old, decreases in preference with increasing age. Fitness activities in gyms and on the streets, in contrast, raise preferences as people grow older. The lack of policies with projects and programs with professional guidance suitable for the practice of sports, in addition to the lack of sports facilities

Table 12.4 Most practiced sports activities

Activities	Male %	Female %	Total %
Walking	24.6%	52.2%	37.3%
Soccer/futsal	41.1%	2.7%	23.4%
Fitness activity	7.9%	18.1%	12.6%
Bodybuilding	4.9%	4.7%	4.8%
Cycling	5.9%	2.7%	4.5%
Other collective games	2.1%	3.6%	2.8%
Athletics/running	3.6%	1.4%	2.7%
Swimming/water activities	2.0%	2.8%	2.4%
Other individual games	2.0%	2.4%	2.3%
Gymnastics	0.5%	3.2%	1.7%
Martial arts/fights	2.3%	1.1%	1.7%
Dance	0.5%	2.7%	1.5%
Volleyball	0.8%	1.8%	1.2%
Small ball games	0.5%	0.06%	0.3%
Skate	0.3%	0.08%	0.2%
Basketball	0.4%	0.02%	0.2%
Sport with animals	0.2%	0.6%	0.1%
Handball	0.1%	0.3%	0.1%
Adventure sport	0.1%	0.04%	0.1%
Motorbike	0.1%	0.0%	0.1%
Cognitive games	0.1%	0.04%	0.03%
Total	100%	100%	100%

Table 12.5 Location of physical and sports activity practice

	Gender		
Practice locations	Male	Female	Total
Paid sports facilities	29.8%	32.7%	31.1%
Free sports facilities	17.2%	9.3%	13.6%
Open public space with sports equipment	21.7%	21.6%	21.7%
Open space without sports equipment	28.2%	32.3%	30.1%
Activities practiced in walled communities or at home	3.1%	4.1%	3.5%
Total	100%	100%	100%

and equipment have reduced the practice of traditional and collective sports for the benefit of running, walking and fitness activities.

As shown in Table 12.5, physical and sports activities are practiced in most cases (31.1%) in paid sports facilities, which is worrying, considering the economic conditions of large part of the population. In second place are open spaces without sports equipment (30.1%), which only allows running, walking, soccer activities, which is evidenced in the practice options. This fact corroborates the low adherence and diversification of physical and sports activities of the population, whether due the lack of financial conditions to afford paid activities or for not having adequate and safe place for this practice, being translated by the lack of sports policy that

Table 12.6 Reason for practicing physical and sports activity

Reasons	Gender		Total
	Male	Female	
By medical indication	7.2%	19.7%	13%
To improve or maintain physical performance	20%	21.7%	20.7%
To improve quality of life and well-being	24.4%	41.3%	32.2%
For enjoying competing	10.4%	2.6%	6.8%
To relax or have fun	32.7%	12%	23.1%
To socialize	4.7%	1.7%	3.4%
Other	0.6%	1%	0.8%
Total	100%	100%	100%

democratizes the access and use of sports spaces for the poorest part of the population and that allows the qualification and diversity of these practices.

Among the approximately 61 million practitioners of physical and sports activities, 2.5 million (4%) of them practice Fitness activities in gyms. When this activity is analyzed by age group, 153 000 practitioners are over 55 years of age and 61 000 over 65 years of age. This represents 1.5% (about two million) of practitioners who pay for their physical practices.

As shown in Table 12.6, Brazilians practice physical activity and sports primarily to improve quality of life (32.2%), improve or maintain physical performance (20.7%) and to relax and have fun (23.1%). It thus demonstrates that the priority of projects and actions that develop physical and sports activities must focus on quality of life and active lifestyle.

Another relevant data to understand the needs of the population are indicators of practice objectives. Thus, it was observed that of Brazilians who practice sport and physical activity, 96.2% of them do not have the purpose of participating in official competitions, with men being 93.5% and women 98.7%. It was also found that 98.7% do not represent any club, federation or league during their practice, with little difference between men and women. Of those who reported liking to compete (3.8%), the majority participate in tournaments among friends, neighborhoods and school and in municipal competitions. Thus, there is low adherence to the traditional sports organization model—with clubs, federations and confederations—and participation is more focused on quality of life (health and well-being promotion).

Important information about qualification and diversity of practice was also found, when 70% of practitioners of sport and physical activity practice without guidance from a professional or an instructor in the area. Compared to locations of practices, these data suggest that the problem of low participation is linked to financial conditions and low income of the population. As most Brazilians are unable to pay for their practices, the population uses open spaces without structure and without guidance for their practices, thus justifying the great adherence to walking. Thus, programs and actions to democratize and qualify the practice for the low-income population become essential.

12.4 Main Results for Non-Practitioners and Their Conditions

Of the sedentary 100.5 million (62.1%), who did not practice any physical or sports activity, 25.5% declared to have practiced sport at some point in their life and later abandoned it. In other words, one in four sedentary people has practiced sports in the past, showing great and worrying abandonment rate. This abandonment is greater among men (35.1%) than among women (17.9%), a fact that also occurred among younger people. In particular, the sport abandonment observed predominantly among adolescents and young people up to 24 years of age and during school is also worrisome.

Among reasons, the main ones were: "lack of time" due to studies, "work", "family" (51%), with no significant differences between men and women; being followed by "health or age problems" (20.3%), more prevalent in men, "for not liking or not wanting (13.9%) to continue"; "due to the lack of accessible sports facilities nearby" (3.4%).

The survey also investigated opinions on municipal policies and 67.4% of interviewees reported that the government should promote more programs and actions to favor physical and sports activities aiming at guaranteeing health, democratizing access and qualifying sports and leisure practices (sport for all). Only (5.8%) reported "prioritizing the training of high-level athletes or professionals in general", others (26.7%) reported other priorities such as health, education, safety.

Summarizing the profile of practitioners and non-practitioners, it appears that about 61 million citizens declared to practice sport and/or physical activity, and approximately 39 million (24%) practiced sports while around 22 million practiced physical activities (13.9%), and about 100.5 million (62.1) are sedentary.

Results were also controlled in relation to schooling: schooling had a discriminatory role, concluding that the highest levels of sedentary lifestyle are among individuals with low schooling, demonstrating that sport is in fact a cultural phenomenon.

With regard to spending on sports, studies carried out by DIESPORTE 2014 point to the following monthly spending on sports in 2013: (61.2%) of Brazilians practiced sports for free, (29.1%) spent up to R$ 10,000 (one hundred reais) and (9.7%) more than R$ 10,000 (one hundred reais). As for physical activities, it was found that (78.2%) performed physical activities for free (16.8%) spent up to R$ 10,000 (one hundred reais) and (5.0%) more than R$ 10,000 (one hundred reais).

12.5 Concluding Remarks

A synthesis of obstacles found for the democratization of access and qualification of practice of physical and sports activities of the Brazilian population aiming at contributing to quality of life was presented: (a) lack of time for practice due to the workday, training and/or professional qualification; (b) problems related to urban mobility (reduction of free time); (c) abandoning the practice of sports and physical activity among young people (unhealthy habits and life routines and non-appropriation of sports culture); (d) soccer culture, whether in the imaginary, in practice or as a spectator, creating sports monoculture; (e) low female participation in sport, either due to the double workday or to historical and cultural barriers to sports practice among women (limiting women's access to the sports environment); (f) restriction to the practice of systematic and oriented physical and sports activities (self-determination and quality of practice); (g) absence of programs and actions developed by public authorities aimed at the poor population (sport for all).

However, the practice itself already produces some inclusion walking, for example, that is one of the preferred choices of practitioners of both genders and in all regions—and that is often unstructured, uncompetitive and disorganized, sometimes leads to the meeting of people of different genders and age groups. It is noteworthy, therefore, that about (80%) of older adults interviewed in the survey were practitioners of this activity.

In these terms, the knowledge and identification of the reality found about practitioners and non-practitioners and their practices allows a better understanding of the situation and its development and the identification of obstacles to the universalization of physical and sports activities, with development indicators that point out what is required for the construction of habits and routines that promote quality of life and well-being for citizens.

In this sense, analysis and evaluation of public policies need to be understood with in-depth and evidence-based studies, offering suggestions for overcoming obstacles; thus, the application of a study as proposed by Oliveira et al. (2013) and validated by researchers from six Brazilian universities, adopting standard methodology that can capture information about individuals who practice or not sports and physical activity, in its generality and particularity, capturing their movement and specificities and that is applied over time and space, will serve as important assessment tool to know the degree of development of the active lifestyle of a given population, as well as the effectiveness of implemented policies.

Finally, it seems important to analyze other elements of the system such as financing, infrastructure and legislation to have a complete analysis for governments to improve the quality of life of the population.

References

Bergmann, G. G., Streb, A. R., Ferrari, M., Alves, D. C. C., Soares, B. A. C., Ferreira, G. D., et al. (2020). Barriers for the use of outdoor gyms in adults and elderly from a southern city of Brazil. *Revista Brasileira de Atividade Física & Saúde, 25*, 1–8.

Brasil. (2010). Lei n° 7.258 de 8 de maio de 2010. Cria a empresa brasileira de legado esportivo S. A—Brasil 2016. *Diário Oficial da República Federativa do Brasil. Brasília DF*, 8 de maio de.

Bull, F. C., Al-Ansari, S. S., Biddle, S., Borodulin, K., Buman, M. P., Cardon, G., et al. (2020). World health organization 2020 guidelines on physical activity and sedentary behaviour. *British Journal of Sports Medicine, 54*(24), 1451–1462.
DIESPORTE. (2014). Relatório do financiamento do Esporte: dados 2013. UFBA.
Edwardson, C. L., Gorely, T., Davies, M. J., Gray, L. J., Khunti, K., Wilmot, E. G., et al. (2012). Association of sedentary behaviour with metabolic syndrome: A meta-analysis. *PLoS One, 7*(4), e34916.
Ford, E. S., Kohl, H. W., Mokdad, A. H., & Ajani, U. A. (2005). Sedentary behaviour, physical activity, and the metabolic syndrome among US adults. *Obesity Research, 13*(3), 608–614.
Giles-Corti, B., & Donovan, R. J. (2002). Socioeconomic status differences in recreational physical activity levels and real and perceived access to a supportive physical environment. *Preventive Medicine, 35*(6), 601–611.
Handy, S. L., Boarnet, M. G., Ewing, R., & Killingsworth, R. E. (2002). How the built environment affects physical activity: Views from urban planning. *American Journal of Preventive Medicine, 23*(2), 64–73.
Hino, A. A. F., Reis, R. S., Sarmiento, O. L., Parra, D. C., & Brownson, R. C. (2011). The built environment and recreational physical activity among adults in Curitiba, Brazil. *Preventive Medicine, 52*(6), 419–422.
IBGE. (2017). *Práticas de esporte e atividade física: 2015.* IBGE.
Mello, J. B., Duncan, M., Dias, A., Bergmann, G., Gaya, A., & Gaya, A. (2020). Biological and urban environmental variables as correlates of adolescents' physical activity. *Revista Brasileira de Atividade Física & Saúde, 25*, 1–10.
Mendonça, R., Lopes, M. S., Carvalho, M. C. R., Freitas, P. P., & Lopes, A. C. S. (2020). Adherence to healthy lifestyles in the program academia da Saúde. *Revista Brasileira de Atividade Física & Saúde, 25*, 1–9.
Moretti, A. C., Almeida, V., Westphal, M. F., Bógus, C. M., et al. (2009). Práticas corporais/ atividade física e políticas públicas de promoção da saúde. *Saúde e Sociedade, 18*, 346–354.
Mussino, A. (2002). *COMPASS 2002—Progress report.* CONI.
Oliveira, A. F. S. (2011). *Atlas do Esporte em Sergipe.* SESI.
Oliveira, A. F. S. (2013). *Diagnóstico Esportivo no Brasil: desenvolvendo métodos e técnicas* [Dissertação de Tese]. PPGE/UFBA.
Oliveira, A. F. S., Haiachi, M. C., Matta, G. B., & Taffarel, C. N. Z. (2013). Sport diagnosis in Brazil: In-depth analyses. *FIEP Bulletin, 83*(1), 358–361.
Piggin, J. (2020). What is physical activity? A holistic definition for teachers, researchers and policy makers. *Front Sports Act Living, 2*, 72.
Smith, M., Hosking, J., Woodward, A., Witten, K., MacMilan, A., Field, A., et al. (2017). Systematic literature review of built environment effects on physical activity and active transport—An update and new findings on health equity. *International Journal of Behavioural Nutrition and Physical Activity, 14*(1), 158.
Zhai, L., Zhang, Y., & Zhang, D. (2015). Sedentary behaviour and the risk of depression: A meta-analysis. *British Journal of Sports Medicine, 49*(11), 705–709.
Warburton, D. E., Nicol, C. W., & Bredin, S. S. (2006). Health benefits of physical activity: The evidence. *CMAJ, 174*(6), 801–809.
Warburton, D. E., & Bredin, S. S. D. (2017). Health benefits of physical activity: A systematic review of current systematic reviews. *Current Opinion in Cardiology, 32*(5), 541–556.

Part IV
Physical Activity and Quality of Life

Chapter 13
Social Fitness and *Gamification*. The Impact on Body Health and Physical Activity

Loredana Tallarita

13.1 Introduction[1]

This article is an in-depth study of the research conducted in Palermo in the year 2018/2019 (Tallarita, 2019) through a *case study* (Glaser & Strauss, 1967; Yin, 2014). There, using the Parkrun community, have been analyzed the relationship that has been established[2] between the use of social networks and *digital fitness* applications with an open-*air* fitness. There have been verified the role of active participation in Parkrun events on health and well-being (Grunseit et al., 2018; Russo, 2011, 2013; Stevinson & Hickson, 2014) and the impact of social networks on motivation in open-air sports practices. The choice of the type of workout is related to the significance attributed to the value (Geertz, 1973) of sport, well-being and body health (Martelli, 2010; Porro, 2010), and the results that you want to achieve (Tallarita, 2013, 2017). The community shares workout results on social network, and park is one of the most appropriate relational contexts to create new friendships and establish new connections. The further exploration of the research conducted in 2018/2019 (Tallarita, 2019) confirmed already hypothesized consolidation of some cultural forms (Schütz, 1982) in the community and their relation to the observed social environment: the propensity of community members to pursue health and well-being goals.

[1]The article is an in-depth analysis of *KeepFit* research. *Ben-essere attivo e nuove tecnologie:* Tallarita L. (2019), *Sport, corpo e nuove community. Il fitness open air è sempre più social,* Angeli, Milano

[2]Parkrun was born in 2004 in London thanks to Paul Sinton-Hewitt's idea to impose to a group of friends to have a 5 km run together on Saturday morning in one of London's parks- Bushy Park-Richmond

L. Tallarita (✉)
"Kore" University of Enna, Enna, Italy
e-mail: loredana.tallarita@unikore.it

P. Corvo, F. M. Lo Verde (eds.), *Sport and Quality of Life*, Social Indicators Research Series 84, https://doi.org/10.1007/978-3-030-93092-9_13

13.2 Methods and Techniques

The research includes the full interview with the manager of Parkrun in Italy: Giorgio Cambiano and Parkrun data updated in 2020.The in-depth analysis of this case has allowed to know further community's values, symbolic and cultural meanings (Geertz, 1973). Moreover, this inquiry has revealed an interest in body health and well-being, social fitness and social ties (Glaser & Strauss, 1967; Yin, 2014). Performed exploration highlighted the existence of emerging cultural forms (Schütz, 1982) within the community, consolidated on the web as well as critical issues and good practices put in place for the spread of the phenomenon in Italy. The most peculiar community's aspects (Geertz, 1973) that have emerged: actual body health (Grunseit et al., 2018; Tallarita, 2019), well-being (Russo, 2011, 2013) and physical activity (Borgna, 2005; Martelli, 2011; Porro, 2010) benefits. The data available on Parkrun's website (www.parkrun.it) have allowed to investigate the case (Stake, 1995; Yin, 2014) and to identify aspects related to lifestyle and time devoted to sport.

13.3 Results

Open-air sport is the new catalyst for today's sporting needs and Parkrun experience is a witness to it: a phenomenon is spread across the world. 5 km of timed and non-competitive race that takes place on Saturday mornings in parks around the world. Parkrun is the occcurence expanded on the web and is a global event presented in all countries. The event testifies to the positive impact of *outdoor* running on body health, physical activity and well-being (Grunseit et al., 2018; Tallarita, 2019) and the formation of a digital community that unites lovers of running and fitness through the web. The events are coordinated by *ex-marathon* runners and *running champions* in order to promote health.

13.4 Parkrun Community Between Health, Aesthetics and New Trends

Parkrun has achieved an enormous success thanks to the proliferation on the web and social networks, involving a wide statistical population: walkers or former marathon runners, young and adults, people with disabilities (Tallarita, 2019). The first circuit in Italy was born in 2014 in Palermo from the initiative of Giorgio Cambiano, ex-marathon runner. Parkrun is a free of charge event and park is one of the ideal places to give substance to the *individual health project* and to maintain active lifestyles. Italy offers as many as 16 circuits but it is a *digital* community that unlike other *sports* communities offers reliable quantitative data on the frequenters, thanks to the site members registration. Regular visitors, their nationality, gender, age, health status and attitude to the fitness are known. Parkrun is a non-competitive sports practice model (Grunseit et al., 2018; Stevinson & Hickson, 2014; Tallarita, 2019). Participants receive a *barcode* that calculates running times. Statistics in Italy is always up to date. The information available on the website (www.parkrun.it) is communicated to community members through a monthly newsletter. Parkrun opens unprecedented scenarios in the field of health and well-being (Grunseit et al., 2018; Tallarita, 2019). In England the National Health shows the positive impact on many diseases: diabetes and obesity, heart failure, Parkinson's disease. Among the research questions there was an attempt to analyze the news compared to the initial experience. In this regard, Giorgio Cambiano, interviewed in April 2020 during COVID-SARS-19 lockdown, to the question about the community's evolvement in Italy, answered:

> During the first 5 years we grew in the direction of health. Today we have the same approach: on Saturday morning at 9.00 am there are 5 km of timed and non-competitive race. The participation of adults and people with physical problems has grown and hosting for less performing, those who prefer to walk rather than run, has also developed. Parkrun engages the disabled who participate in the wheelchair edition. In Milan, before the COVID-SARS-19, a paraplegic boy with the exoskeleton has also participated, performing the route in 2 h. During events there is no the last or the first. There are precise figures: *the tail walker* and *the tail runner*. No one is the last. Parkrun has generated a model of sport not based on performance but on health, adapting itself to the needs of the participants. Well-being comes from running or walking and from relationships. The idea that after the race there is a socialization, offers the opportunity to meet people and to make friends. Friendship is the most important thing in the community. You are part of a family and wherever you are, you find the same spirit and create your own circle of friends. The moments of personal life are shared, birthdays or celebration of those who participated in the 50 editions of Parkrun. In England the environment is more international but community of Palermo is characterized by a constant presence of people whose age range varies from 40 to 50 years. There are beginners: young people between 30 and 35 and senior citizens, 65–75 years old. There are 80 year olds. Equal numbers of men and women. In the last two years, the presence of women has increased. These are women who have lived a sedentary lifestyle because they have taken care of their family and children and want to get back in shape and relate to a new environment. The men tackle the route running and have a history within the running groups. They participated in numerous marathons running 75 km compared to 5 km (from the interview with Giorgio Cambiano, the manager of Parkrun in Italy).

From the community's values (Geertz, 1973; Schütz, 1982) emerges the typological profile of the parkrunner: the sedentary individuals who aim to improve their quality of life adopting an active life-style; ex-professional athletes who want to remain fit and attend sports environments (Tallarita, 2019). The youngest train after 5 km of running with isometric-postural exercises guided by digital applications. Older people participate in events with the aim to prevent or control eventual cardiovascular diseases, diabetes, obesity and finally to make friends. The age *range* varies from 25 to 65. Women and young people attend the community more assiduously. The disabled- with discontinuity (Tallarita, 2019). Social inclusion is one of the goals of the community. It offers participants an opportunity to find a health space and mature an attitude of resilience to diseases or disability condition (Russo, 2011,

2013, Russo & Bagnini, 2019; Tallarita, 2019). The age group from 25 to 34 is seduced by body aesthetics and publishes *on social networks* the images of the results obtained. The 35–44 year olds are sport and fitness fanatics: ex-marathon runners, ex-cyclists and ex-professional athletes of various sports disciplines, who consider Parkrun as an opportunity to train and be timed. The 45–54 year olds see the event as a chance to fight stress. The 55–65 year olds are quite sedentary and for them Parkrun is an opportunity to keep fit, lower blood pressure and cholesterol levels. Foreigners aged 35–55 are former athletes and professionals and fans of sports tourism. T*he not-regular* runners, approached the events with curiosity, become regular visitors (Tallarita, 2019). The community is frequented by individuals attentive to the body (Turner, 2014) and prevention and protection of it, as explained by the Italian manager of Parkrun:

> Health means disease prevention and maintenance of active and healthy lifestyles. This is one of the community's priority values. Health communicates being well from the physical and mental point of view. Sharing interest in events is important because you feel part of the community. Pakrunner's motto is: "We work together for a healthier and happier world". Health is a social issue. Parkrun is an event that reactivates and educates the body, also referring you to other sports. If you have some physical problems it is a healthy way to exercise, because it respects everyone's timing. The cardiopathics, the diabetics and those who have to recover after fractures do participate. There were editions in Milan for the people affected by Parkinson and Alzheimer diseases, for autistics. Sponsoring events like those of Parkinson's or other diseases is a nice showcase. A space of social inclusion. In Ireland the community offers concrete benefits to body health and receives financial contributions from the state. Parkrun has an agreement with the medical association. The family doctors recommend Parkrun to the sick people. The idea is to bring the culture of fitness and wellness to health management and make agreements with the medical-hospital associations. Health comes first and is associated with prevention and well-being and fun (from the interview with Giorgio Cambiano, *the manager of* Parkrun in Italy).

Parkrun is a busy community with health and well-being goals. To the ethical motivations are added those of aesthetics (Grunseit et al., 2018; Lane et al., 2012; Tallarita, 2019) that involve communication and display on the web of body muscles, physical beauty and sensuality. This trend engages people of all ages (Tallarita, 2013, 2019). Through images of bodies advertised within the community individuals are confronted with new widespread body models (Tallarita, 2013, 2017). This affects the approach to sport and social relations. The individual expresses on his body an identity project of health and well-being, aesthetics and performance. Digital applications have carved out a wider space in the field of body care policies (Maturo & Moretti, 2018). The other aspect that emerges is vanity and self-satisfaction: expressed by the images that circulate on the web and that testify to the new values. The body exhibited and shared on social networks triggers a system of perception/interpretation that induces the most active members of the community to want to achieve that result and to reproduce the pattern of the proposed advertised image. The *culture of narcissism* (Cesareo & Vaccarini, 2012; Lasch, 2005; Tallarita, 2013) satisfies those expressive needs of the body which are centered on gratification through the sharing of images on the web. Beauty is a form of power and the practices spread on the web constitute a new symbolic language (Tallarita,

2019; Volli, 2002) that distinguishes Parkrun community on which the social relations of the members are built. Social networks facilitate the emergence of mechanisms of adhesion and identification towards images, responsible for unprecedented forms of protagonism on the web (Tallarita, 2019).

13.5 Active Lifestyles and Social Fitness

In Italy, the *performance* of open-air running is shared by community members thanks to the site (www.parkrun.it), the YouTube channel and social networks. The web is the bonding agent of the community, whose values are health, well-being and care for the aesthetic dimension of the body (Tallarita, 2013, 2019). The community promotes the concept *of high quality of life* (Fabris, 2003; Featherstone, 1994; Franchi, 2007) and physical activity is a social therapy (Stevinson & Hickson, 2014; Tallarita, 2019). Digital sports communities and web connections (Boccia Artieri, 2012, 2017; Bennato, 2011) generate the evolution of sub-cultures (Maffesoli, 2004, 2009) created around the concept of health, physical activity and friendship. The *connective relationships* on the web (Boccia Artieri, 2012, 2017; Martelli, 2011) constitute the new social space, used to exhibit own trained, seductive and desirable body and to share a passion for open-air running. The combination of sport and the web has created an unprecedented emerging structure (Boccia Artieri, 2012, 2017; Bennato, 2011; Martelli, 2011) and the sharing the obtained results on Social Media expresses an individualist and narcissistic trend (Cesareo & Vaccarini, 2012; Tallarita, 2013, 2019) involving the world of sport. The web is a generator of iconic trained bodies (Porro 2010; Tallarita, 2013) that testify to the active lifestyle that penetrates the imagination of individuals and establishes their identity and behaviors. In the community, the youngest continue the training with the support of digital applications: Strava, Fitocracy and Freeletics that, inspired by the mechanics of fitness gaming, allow members to improve their training after the race. The frequent body check (Matteucci, 2019) confirms the narcissistic process of body privatization (Cesareo & Vaccarini, 2012; Tallarita, 2013) through sports practice. Social fitness embraces this latter objective, which is combined with the use of fitness *gaming* mechanics that act on individual needs at a psychological level (Zichermann & Cunningham, 2011) pushing to change their habitus (Bourdieu, 1983). *Fitness gaming* facilitates the development of a positive approach to sport (Deterding et al., 2011). The principles of play applied to fitness promote *engagement* and loyalty of potential followers by offering workouts characterized by different levels of difficulty. Gaming applied to fitness (Groh, 2012; Luminea, 2013) involves the growth of engagement and loyalty of digital users. To the question addressed to Parkrun's manager in Italy about the importance of technology in an after race training, he replied:

> Our parkrunner use digital apps to complete their training. After the 5 km of the circuit, the workouts continue with Runtustic or Strava: the two most used in our community apps. We have stopped due to COVID-SARS-19 and we continue on Social. At the moment there are

> 21 countries in which the editions have been blocked due to the lockdown imposed by COVID-SARS-19. The reopening of the circuits and risk planning will depend on the UK Department for Digital, Culture, Media and Sport (DCMS). Awaiting the reopening of the circuits, we organize weekly individual meetings dedicated to training with social media. You train together using Strava or Runtustic and share postural isometric exercises on the web. Technology is fundamental and we as a community can be reached at the following link: www.parkrun.it. We use Facebook and Youtube to advertise events and share images of each of our events. Since March, due to COVID-SARS-19, editions have been suspended all over the world and the community remains interconnected on the web. Social networks allow to keep Parkrun family together. On the website, on the Facebook page and on the Youtube channel we organize physical-motor training with the instructors who attend Parkrun. We simulated the circuit on some of the community members' terraces that reproduced 5 km of running, exercising on Saturday morning, as per weekly appointment. There are those who created the path of the circuit within the condominium garden fencing. Thanks to social networks and the community website, the event directors are in constant contact with the event curators and with the participants. This is a period when a social distance decreases thanks to the support of web technology (from the interview with Giorgio Cambiano, the manager of Parkrun in Italy).

After the first worldwide experiences, the community has grown in two directions: health and dimension of digital communication. Digital communication (Bennato, 2011; Meyrowitz, 1995; Mirzoeff, 2012) is a precious "cultural and value capital" (Bourdieu, 1983; Franchi, 2007) which exerts its regulatory functions in the non-gaming sport context of the community, thanks to the symbols and information always available online.

13.6 Relationships, the Impact on Physical Activity and Physical Activity and Critical Issues

The community is a relational network (Martelli, 2011; Boccia Artieri, 2012, 2017) that has a significant impact on the health and well-being of the body (Russo, 2011, 2013) and on the improvement of the attitude towards physical activity (Villard & Moreno, 2012). Friendship and community values tie members while digital connections strengthen the bonds built. The park is one of the most appropriate socio-cultural and relational contexts to create new friendships. The social bonds created (Granovetter, 1993) assume a binding regulatory effect (Boccia Artieri, 2012, 2017) which motivates the attendance of events. Parkrun combines two socio-relational aspects: the sense of community that motivates "adults" and "youngsters" not to miss a workout and to share the results on the web (Maffesoli, 2004) and digital connections, which are also cogent on attitudes and behaviours implemented in the sports environment. The latter aspect has intensified due to COVID-SARS-19 which has brought to the knees all areas of our society, especially that of sport. The lockdown imposed by governments worldwide has allowed individuals to experiment with new forms of communication and to pursue, as in the case of Parkrun, the 5 km path in their own backyard or on the roofs of buildings and the connections on the web have documented the experiences developed in this period. The connections between community members have intensified and being interconnected through the virtual space has made it possible to spread values globally and exchange information (Boccia Artieri, 2012, 2017; Martelli, 2011) while continuing to measure results and performance. The dialogues held during the three-month lockdown continued on social networks and on the website. COVID-SARS-19 has helped to form new digital communication spaces. Parkrun's manager clarifies the matter:

> Parkrun has grown globally thanks to the web and social networks. In the Parkrun environment friendships have been born between those members who after training use Runtustic and Strava: two apps used by running groups, who often or out of curiosity take part in our editions. Parkrun offers many chances to athletes, former marathon runners and to ordinary sedentary people with health problems or disabilities because those who participate according to their physical and health conditions can decide whether to walk or run. In the community, the exercises after running on the terrace of the house or in your garden associated with the use of digital applications for fitness made it possible not to stop due to COVID-SARS-19. The results of this attitude and the continuity of the workouts were certainly tiring but the commitment and dedication of the organizers made it possible to train during the lockdown. In times of COVID-SARS-19 the community has grown further (From the interview with Giorgio Cambiano, Parkrun's manager in Italy).

Parkrun members constitute real and proper social groups structured on the web. The meaning given to the sport and physical activity and the thematic discussions within the digital community have changed the way in which sports experiences are fruited and practiced. To the question asked to the manager of Parkrun in Italy, on what are the points of strength or criticality, he replied:

> The critical issues depend on the fact that Parkrun is little known from the point of view of the benefits it offers to health. When we ask an Administration for authorization to open the circuit in a Park it is difficult to make understand the importance of the phenomenon. The difficulties are bureaucratic and the City Hall clerk grants permissions for footraces, marathons and mini-marathons: isolated events that last only one day and have no continuity as Parkrun. If we ask to use the Park on Saturday morning the city manager answers: "Do you want an authorization for the whole year?" "Every Saturday morning?" That depends on the lack of openness. We have found the same problems in the province of Milan, Sardinia and Sicily. In Montelepre (PA) the mayor not only gave us permission to activate the circuit and use the park but also advertised events. It is difficult to find adequate resources to organize events. Another critical point is the distrust towards Parkrun of many running clubs because it triggers a mechanism of competition. Parkrun is neither a race nor a competition. Those who come from Parkrun and have no health problems often start to love the race and then join a running club. As for the strengths: Parkrun is free and every Saturday morning offers the opportunity to train and be outdoors, to be monitored, event after event, and achieving the progress, to have photos of events and to make friends. If you participate in 50 editions you have the opportunity to have the 50th edition T-shirt and a bracelet and a water bottle with our logo. Parkrun is good for everyone: for professional athletes and beginners or people with physical problems or disabilities because it spreads the culture of health quality of life. Some people have overcome depression, disabling illnesses and have felt welcomed and included as part of a community (from the interview with Giorgio Cambiano, the manager of Parkrun in Italy).

Outdoor running and training with Strava, Runtustic, Freeletecs and the use of social media distinguish the Italian community. The interweaving of social media and sport has further multiplied opportunities for knowledge and participation in other digital communities (Tallarita, 2019). The community testifies to the birth of a new cultural model in today's sports universe that is centered on the well-being of the body as an *expressive resource* to be built and protected.

13.7 Discussion

The interview with the manager of Parkrun confirmed the strengths that have made the community known all over the world. Parkrun has become a worldwide phenomenon able to attract all social categories. It is not a running club but a digital community that puts health and well-being first, consenting to adults and the elderly to keep under control certain diseases (cardiovascular disease, diabetes, obesity, Parkinson's and Alzheimer's). The in-depth analysis of the case (Glaser & Strauss, 1967, Yin, 2014) allowed to delineate more clearly the characteristics of the community and the positive impact on lifestyles and health (Grunseit et al., 2018; Lane et al., 2012; Tallarita, 2019). The relational dimension established among community members is extended through social networks and to the site (www.parkrun.it) where the results of training, the passion for open-air running and working out guided by applications are shared (Tallarita, 2019). The community has an extraordinary impact on the health and use *of* the web and gaming applications for fitness, by the youngest, has made it possible to raise awareness of the phenomenon worldwide. Parkrun did not stop during the lockdown imposed by the COVID-SARS-19. It is re-proposed again in the net in a new light, representing in all the countries of the world the 5 km race, to practice individually in the terraces and in the gardens of own homes. In England, Ireland and the United States it is considered a tool for the prevention of pathologies and is recommended by primary care providers to counter sedentary lifestyles. The four micro-dimensions explored in the previous research (Tallarita, 2019) were confirmed and the interview with the manager of Parkrun Italia highlighted the importance of the phenomenon in the sphere of health. The critical issues were also emerged in Italy, due to bureaucratic and slow administrative systems, which hindered the opening of circuits not taking into account the positive impact on health.

13.8 Conclusion

Parkrun is a known worldwide free of charge sport event. Today it is a digital community that shares through its website (www.parkrun.it) and social media its members' sporting experiences and the passion for open-air running. Here, using qualitative research methods, we have tried to get a deeper understanding of community's impact on body health and well-being and on the approach to physical activity (Grunseit et al., 2018; Lane et al., 2012; Tallarita, 2019). From the interview with Giorgio Cambiano there has emerged a solid proof that despite the lockdown, imposed by the COVID-SARS-19, the phenomenon has grown thanks to the use of social networks. The community has developed further and the "being together" virtually, while practicing individually a 5 km race in the gardens adjacent to the homes or on the terraces of the house, showed the strength of Parkrun. The community attendance and the use of digital *gaming applications for* fitness have further confirmed the positive impact on health and psycho-physical well-being. In the urban metropolises that were stopped by the COVID-SARS-19, Parkrun continued its activity thanks to the network, positively influencing lifestyles and safeguarding the body from diseases with training. Parkrun is a space of health and health has become a trend, a lifestyle aimed at excellence in every aspect that leads individuals to stay in contact with nature, spend moments of well-being and training. Social fitness has become an increasingly large part of the community and the impact of digital fitness applications on health and physical activity (Grunseit et al., 2018; Lane et al., 2012; Tallarita, 2019) has been further confirmed.

References

Bennato, D. (2011). *Sociologia dei media digitali. Relazioni sociali e processi comunicativi del web partecipativo*. Laterza.

Boccia Artieri, G. (2012). *Stati di connessione. Pubblici, cittadini e consumatori nella (Social) Network Society*. Angeli.

Boccia Artieri, G. (2017). *Fenomenologia dei social network. Presenza, relazioni e consumi mediali degli italiani online*. Guerini e Associati.

Borgna, P. (2005). *Sociologia del corpo*. Laterza.

Bourdieu, P. (1983). *La distinzione. Critica sociale del gusto*. Il Mulino.

Cesareo, V., & Vaccarini I. (2012). *L'era del narcisismo*. Angeli.

Deterding, S., Dixon, D., Khaled, R., & Nake L. (2011). From game design elements to gamefulness: defining gamification. *ACM Other Conference*. https://doi.org/10.1145/2181037.2181040.

Fabris, G. (2003). *Il nuovo consumatore verso il post-moderno*. Angeli.

Featherstone, M. (1994). *Cultura del consumo e postmodernismo*. Seam.

Franchi, M. (2007). *Il senso del consumo*. Mondadori.

Geertz, C. (1973). *The interpretation of culture*. Basic Book.

Glaser, B., & Strauss, A. (1967). *The discovery of grounded theory: strategies for qualitative research*. Aldini; (trad.it. (2009). La scoperta della grounded theory. Strategie per la ricerca qualitativa (a cura di) Strati A. Armando, Roma).

Granovetter, M. (1993). The strength of weak ties. *American Journal of Sociology, 78*(6), 1360–1138.

Groh, G. (2012). *Gamification: State of Art Definition and Utilization*. In N. Asaj, B. M. konings, F. Poguntke, B. Schauh, M. Wiedersheim, & Weber M. (Eds.), *Proceedings of the 4th seminar on research trends in media informatics* (pp. 39–46). Institute of Media Information, University of Ulm.

Grunseit, A., Richards, J., & Merom, D. (2018). Running on a high: parkrun and personal well-being. *BMC Public Health, 18*, 59.

Lane, A., Murphy, N., Bauman, A., & Tien, C. (2012). Active for a day. Predictors of relapse among previously active mass event participants. *Human Kinetics Journals, 9*, 48–52. https://doi.org/10.1123/jpah.9.1.48
Lasch, C. (2005). *The Culture of Narcissism*. Norton & Co. (*trad. it. La cultura del narcisismo. L'individuo in fuga dal sociale in un'età di disillusioni collettive*, Bompiani, Milano, 1981).
Luminea, C. (2013). Gamification. *Financial Management, 42*(2), 13.
Maffesoli, M. (2004). *Il tempo delle tribù. Il declino dell'individualismo nelle società postmoderne*. Guerini e Associati.
Maffesoli, M. (2009). *Icone d'oggi. Le nostre idolatrie post-moderne*. Sellerio.
Martelli, S. (2010). *La comunicazione per lo sport e la salute*. Angeli.
Martelli, S. (2011). *Sport, media e intrattenimento. Emozioni in/controllate e struttura sociale emergente*. Angeli.
Matteucci, I. (2019). *La palestra digitale: i nuovi modelli di consumo per il fitness. KeepFit. Ben-essere attivo e nuove tecnologie*. Angeli.
Maturo, A., & Moretti, V. (2018). *Digital health and the gamification of life. How apps can promote a positive medicalization*. Emerald Publishing.
Meyrowitz, J. (1995). *Oltre il senso del luogo. Come i media elettronici influenzano il comportamento sociale*, Baskerville.
Mirzoeff, N. (2012). *Introduzione alla cultura visuale*. Meltemi (*ed. orig.:* 2000).
Porro, N. (2010). *Corpi e immaginario. Memoria, seduzione e potere dal Milite ignoto al Grande Fratello*. Bonanno.
Russo, G. (2011). *La società della wellness. Corpi sportivi al traguardo della salute*. Angeli.
Russo, G. (2013). *Questioni di Ben-Essere. Pratiche emergenti di cultura, sport, consumi*. Angeli.
Russo, G., & Bagnini E. (2019). *Fitness e wellness nella società digitale: tecnologie smart e ben-essere attivo. KeepFit. Ben-essere attivo e nuove tecnologie*: Angeli.
Schütz, A. (1982). *Life forms and meaning structure*. Routledge & Kegan Paul.
Stake, R. E. (1995). *The art of case study research*. Sage.
Stevinson, C., & Hickson, M. (2014). Exploring the public health potential of mass community participation event. *Journal of Public Health, 36*(2), 268–274. https://doi.org/10.1093/pubmed/fdt082
Tallarita, L. (2013). *Lusso e narcisismo. Erotizzazione e deisderabilità dei corpi, Euno Edizioni. Unikore Press.*
Tallarita, L. (2017). Uno sguardo esplorativo sul pilates: moda, attività fisico-riabilitativa o luogo di socialità? *Salute e Società* (pp. 118–135. Fasc. 3-Suppl.) Angeli. https://doi.org/10.3280/SES2017-SU3008.
Tallarita, L. (2019). *Sport, corpo e nuove community. Il fitness open-air è sempre più social. KeepFit. Ben-essere attivo e nuove tecnologie*: Angeli.
Turner, B. S. (2014). *The body and society* (III ed.). Sage.
Villard, H., & Moreno, M. A. (2012). Fitness on Facebook: Advertisements generated in response to profile content. *Cyberpsychology, Behaviour and Social Networking, 15*(10), 564–568. https://doi.org/10.1089/cyber.2011.0642
Volli, U. (2002). *Figure del desiderio: corpo, testo mancanza*. Cortina.
Yin, R. (2014). *Case study research. Design and methods*. Sage.
Zichermann, G., & Cunningham, C. (2011). Gamification by design. Implementing Game Mechanics. *Web and Mobile Apps, O' Reilly Media*, Sebastopol CA 95472.

Chapter 14
A Running Enemy: Jogging at the Time of Covid-19 Pandemic

Michele Filippo Fontefrancesco

14.1 Introduction

Since the 1970s, sports have been at the centre of social research. Anthropologists and sociologists analysed sportive practices, from boxing (Wacquant, 2003), to football (Barba, 2016; Giulianotti & Robertson, 2009) and cricket (Appadurai, 1996), as a subject through which to study the emergent complexity of contemporary society (Besnier & Brownell, 2012). Sports were studies to understand the structure of local and global societies, as well as issues such as identity, embodiment, and economic and political struggles. Within this rich context, since the 1980s, scholars have explored jogging to understand the cultural roots of this practices as well as the reasons of its global success (Latham, 2015), and the particular spatial relationship that generates within an urban setting (Cook et al., 2016), with particular attention on themes such as the one of mobility and liveability of the urban space (Bodin & Hartig, 2003; Karusisi et al., 2012). Jogging is an intrinsically non-agonistic form of running: it is famous the definition of Sheehan (1978), who suggested the only distinction between jogging and running was "a signature on a race application." Jogging is described as a slow run, less than 15 km/h, and is largely practised in urban contexts, along less trafficked roads, or sidewalks, pathways, and dirt roads. Most of the joggers' practice on an everyday or week bases, being jogging a constituent part of their everyday life (Certeau, 1984).

This physical practice was codified in the United States of America in the 1960s, being suggested as an activity aimed at improving the quality of life of the urban middle class (Latham, 2015). Since the 1980s, jogging has reached a global success becoming one of the most practised sportive activity in the West. In Italy, jogging is the most practices sport: about half of the active population jogs at least once a

M. F. Fontefrancesco (✉)
Cultural Anthropology, University of Gastronomic Sciences, Bra, Italy
e-mail: m.fontefrancesco@unisg.it

P. Corvo, F. M. Lo Verde (eds.), *Sport and Quality of Life*, Social Indicators Research Series 84, https://doi.org/10.1007/978-3-030-93092-9_14

month, and by the 10% on a weekly (Patucchi, 2017). Despite the success, jogging can be considered quite a recent phenomenon. It was introduced at the end of the 1970s (Gervasoni, 2010). It is only in the past decade that jogging reached its prominence, being considered one of the most important sportive activities to improve the quality of life in an urban environment (e.g. Health City Institute, 2016).

In light of the current debate concerning jogging in the social sciences and the prominence of this physical practice in Italy, the chapter looks at the experience of joggers to understand further the relationship between sports and quality of life in an exceptional context, such as the one of the Covid-19 pandemic in Italy in 2020. The chapter explores the impact of the first lockdown (March–April 2020) among joggers in North-western part of Italy, and how the lockdown transformed their understanding of jogging and the one of the urban surrounding, impacting on their quality of life.

The chapter presents the research and its context. Then, focusing on the history of the life of the joggers, it explores the impact of the lockdown.

14.2 The Field and the Research

The research was completed during the first semester of 2020, including the so-called Fase 1, "Phase 1", of the lockdown followed the outbreak of the Covid-19 pandemic in Italy. The early cases of infection were recorded on the 30th of January 2020 in Rome. However, the first hotspot was found in Lombardy: on the 20th of February, 16 cases were identified in Codogno (LO). After a few hours, the first Covid-19 victim died. The contagion spread fast across the region. In face of the emerging crisis, on the 25th, the national government adopted the extraordinary measure, restricting the mobility on a local and international level: from suspending all the direct flight to and from China, to the institution of quarantine zones, the so call Zone Rosse, "Red Zones", to isolate the municipalities of the hotspots. The access to the red zone was precluded from the outside, and the people in these areas were forbidden to leave the houses but for matters of necessity (such as for work or doing quick shopping) or sport; moreover within the red zone, all public offices and shops were closed or worked on restricted hours.

These measures did not stop the contagion. On the 7th of March, the Government announced the extension of the mobility restrictions experimented in the red zones to the territory of 14 provinces in the Northern part of the country. On the 11th, the lockdown was extended to all Italy: it was the beginning of Phase 1, which ended after 2 months, on the 4th of May.

During phase 1, all retail trade was suspended, with few exceptions such as food stores and news agencies. Schools, restaurants, bars, theatres, and cinemas, most of the industries and public offices were closed. Only those firms working in strategic sectors, such as health and care, food business and agriculture, could continue their activities. Mobility was restricted. People could move outside home only for quick shopping, medical treatment or to reach their workplace. The severe national measures were further intensified by the Regional government, in the North, to cope with the ramping medical emergency.

During the lockdown, the political debate posed great attention on the theme of sport, and in particular to jogging. While parks, gyms and swimming pools were closed, and biking was banned, the only sportive proactive allowed was jogging, but only in the proximity of one's home. Regional governments adopted specific acts to fix the maximum range within which the jogger could move (e.g. 200 m, 500 m, 1 km), and the use of personal protection devices (such as face mask). While the public institutions posed new limits to jogging, since the very beginning of the lockdown, media started reporting cases of abuses committed against joggers, as in the case of the soubrette Elisa Boscolo attacked in Adria (https://www.ilgazzettino.it/nordest/rovigo/coronavirus_insulti_minacce_aggredita_jogging-5121212.html) or the marathon runner Alessia assailed in Milan (https://www.lastampa.it/topnews/primo-piano/2020/03/22/news/coronavirus-la-runner-alessia-e-la-caccia-alle-streghe-a-milano-1.38624382).

The research moved after these cases and the many other reported by the press and in the social media, expanding an ongoing work concerning the perception of the urban space during lockdown (Fontefrancesco, 2020). It investigated the transformation in the perception of the urban surrounding experienced by joggers during the lockdown. To provide an ethnographic account of the change, the research involved a campaign of in-depth interviews conducted between March and May 2020 with joggers living in Alessandria, one of the largest cities in the Northern Italy and one of the most severely hit by the pandemic in Piedmont (Fontefrancesco, 2021). The interviews were conducted in Italian on phone or through VOIP service (e.g. Messanger, Skype, WhatsApp). All the interviewees were selected among the recurrent participant to a charity run that is yearly held in Alessandria (namely Stralessandria, http://www.stralessandria.it/) and active in the local online groups about jogging and running. The interviews were conducted according to the life-history method (Bertaux, 1999), paying attention to the meanings given by the jogger to the sportive practice and their experience during the lockdown.

This chapter focuses on the experience of four joggers: Luca, a bank clerk in his 40s; Francesco, an engineer in his 50s; Maria, a teacher in her 50s; and Laura, a professional in the restaurant sector in her 30s.

14.3 The Meaning of Jogging

The birth and spreading of jogging in the USA are linked with the success of fitness movements in raising awareness about the link between sportive practice and expectation of better health (Latham, 2015). It connects also with a deeper sense of redemption felt by a generation and a class during a period of economic and political insecurity. "Running had appealed to politicians and businessmen in the sixties as a means to cardiovascular health. But exercise had also been seen by some as part of a program in better living that was to be the first step towards the spiritual renewal of America." (Gillick, 1984, p. 380).

Forty years after Gillick, in Italy jogging is linked to strong demand for wellbeing felt by a large part of the active population in a context of reduction of physical activity at work (Cialdea & Michelini, 2019). As Luca put it:

> I started jogging a few years ago. It must have been 2015. Since then my daily run has become an indispensable part of my day. Every morning I run my 5 or 6 km. It is often the only real physical activity I do [. . .]. I work in an office. Hours in front of the computer. The best I do is the way to the garage and from the parking lot to the office. I need to run; it's freedom and well-being for me.

To jog is a bodily practice (Alan, 2004). It is embedded in a hierarchy of values (Herzfeld, 2004) in which the individual's wellbeing is linked to one's fitness. However, the opportunity to practice sports are limited due to work and family duties. Thus, to go to the gym or to practice other sports which requires specific facilities appear difficult. As Laura clearly explained:

> I started jogging 5 or 6 years ago when I changed jobs. Before I worked in a shop and with shifts, I managed to go to the swimming pool most days. Since I started working in the restaurant sector I started commuting with [a nearby town]. There is no swimming pool there and I could not put the times together to go every day to the swimming pool in Alessandria. So, I decided to start running every day. For better or for worse, I manage to go running every day in the morning, one hour. It makes me feel good and I don't have big-time problems . . . .

Despite jogging is, first of all, an individual activity, it does not preclude the opportunity for socialization, making the run a moment of gathering and chat among friends. This is crucial for Maria:

> I started jogging 15 years ago. I was twenty or so. From jogging then I started to participate in some non-competitive races, such as Stralessandria. Jogging is my way to relax after a day in the office. Taking part in these competitions amuses me because I team up with friends. To get with friends for running is important. Every week, before the pandemic, on Saturday afternoon, I and other friends went for a run. Sometimes just outside the city, we took the car and went to some new places in the countryside. For me, at the end of the day, jogging is to live the space of the city and the countryside and share the emotion with the people who run with me.

For Luca and Maria, jogging is mostly an urban experience. However, jogging from my interviews is also a way to escape from the city and immerse into nature. This is the case, for example, of Francesco:

> I work in the city, but I live outside it. My house is a farmhouse. My wife and I renovated it in the 1990s. The best thing about the house is that you are in the middle of the fields and 15 minutes from the freeway. Our closest neighbour is, I think, a good ten-minute walk far from us, even if you can see her house from the window. My wife and I are both professionals and, in the evening, when we are back from the office, we go for a run in the countryside. We both run. It is something we do mostly two or three times a week and it is our way to escape from the city and it makes us feel good.

In their interviews, jogging is first of all about a different use of the urban space: a functional alternative to the ordinary use of the urban space, as suggested by Camy et al. (1993), that is deeply social and moves through an ideal appropriation and a signification of the surrounding. By jogging, the individuals can use the urban space, making it feel homey, and, at the same time, they can foster their social relationship with friends and acquaintances, pursuing and fulfilling the tacit duty of fitness, felt by the interviewees, that characterizes contemporary society (Bauman, 2005). Thus, jogging is a fundamental element in the embodied perception of wellbeing, which was deeply undermined by the lockdown.

14.4 The Experience of Lockdown

Jogging, such as walking (Olwig, 2008), is a creative act through which individuals makes sense of their environment. Through the fruition of space, they understand the risks of the environment and associate meanings to the objects and people they encounter. In so doing, they create their mental image of the world, the society that lives it, and the ongoing transformation that takes place (Porter et al., 2010). In this respect, jogging is not only a fundamental element of everyday life (Certeau, 1984) but also a key method through which joggers, among which the informants, live in the world. The lockdown imposed strong limitations on this physical and mental practice, and this affected the joggers' very perception of the world during the pandemic. This emerging new world is a hostile environment, but the sense of danger is not linked to the spreading of the virus, but rather to a stiffening sense of social control lived by the informants that emerged in form of insults and assaults experienced for the first time:

> "Since May, I feel alive again," Luca exclaimed when asked about his jogging experience during the pandemic. "I run alone. I live almost in the countryside, so my ride is more or less always the same. I leave the house, go to a farmhouse about three kilometres from home and go back. I run at 6.00/6.30. If I meet someone it is some animal or possibly someone of my condominium (I live in a condominium). March and April were tough. Even before the most stringent obligations, people have changed. It didn't matter if I had a mask or whatever. For the first time, I realized that people were looking at me. A neighbour, one day, started shouting at me from the balcony: 'Bastard! you want to kill us all!' The thing repeated for someday. Then, I started going to run earlier; at 5.00, in order not to meet anyone, but still I did not feel well. I felt like they had put me in a cage. In the end, I bought a treadmill and for almost a month days I didn't put my nose out of the flat."
>
> "My jogger quarantine experience?" Exclaims Laura. "A bucket of cold water at the beginning of March. I don't speak metaphorically. It was still more or less allowed to go for a run. I leave the house to do my usual run. I go under various condominiums and shops. I usually go around 7.00 in the morning and it's not like there are all these people. Well . . . I ran and: 'splash!'. From the second floor, a man threw me a bucket of water. A bad thing! I had almost a heart attack. A joke? No. He shouted at me: 'You should be ashamed running these days! Stay at home!' I didn't do anything. I didn't say anything. I left, running. What do you want to do? Do you denounce him? For what? After that day, I hung up the boots once and for all after that episode. Well, more or less. Sometimes I got up before dawn and went around a few blocks . . . but I felt moving in a hostile landscape; not because of the virus. For the people around me."

As Augé (1986) suggested, the everyday experience of the urban space is often linked to the sense of anonymity. A common affection often described in the literature is to feel alone in the crowd (Coleman, 2009). Despite a lockdown is about isolation and detachment from the social space, the joggers associate it to an increase in social control; a rise in social pressure that leads to a compulsory domiciliation. The control becomes evident in the attacks suffered by Laura and Luca, which are underpinned by a villainization of the jogger in the public space. In this process, police controls played a part, as it was remarked by Francesco:

> During the lockdown, well, we worked mostly from home and, given where we live, we could also afford to go out, staying well inside the fields of our farmhouse. Yet, for the first time in twenty years, we have seen police patrols go through these streets. Once, twice, three times in a few days. Never, never seen them before over here. They came in the hours when we are used to taking our run. I believe that our neighbours called them. We go out in the dark now. We felt like criminals even if we moved around our fields. However, when I think about the blue cars of the police going down these dirt roads, I do not feel secure... I feel as if there, in that house, there are no more neighbours, but enemies ready to make us arrested...

Thus, the increasing social control is what limits the possibility of jogging and precludes even those space the lockdown policies would allow. In front of this limitation, the practice changes and is conducted in new, interstitials times, as in the cases of the previous interviewees, and spaces, as in the case of Maria:

> During the lockdown, I continued to work. My company continued its activity. Tension and fear were high. A dozen colleagues were affected by the disease or had close relatives affected. Staying in the office was so anything but reassuring. When I got home, I needed to be distracted. I needed to move. As far as I could, I kept running. I went in the evening. I follow my usual route. Sometimes, some neighbour shout. I ignored them. When they put the obligation to run within a few meters from home, I started going around the block. I felt like an idiot, but I continued for a few days. Then the police stopped me. They were about to fine me because I was jogging. We discussed for a good ten minute before they understood I was jogging just around my block. I read about other joggers being stupidly fined on the internet and I read about people who were starting to run up and down the stairs of their buildings. I live in a ten-story building. I started doing it too: up and down, up and down. I did not use my shoes because I did not want to bother too much my neighbours. I ran with two pairs of socks to do men or noise. There was certainly someone else in the building who run on the stairs during the night because I could hear the rushing up and down. In the end, I made the stair go well. In May, the first time I was able to run on the street again without fear of being fined or insulted, I started to cry with happiness.

14.5 Jogging and the Experience of an Enemy Space

The lockdown is a period of alterity that shakes the social and spatial normality of the joggers. This alterity, however, is not the one of the communitas, as theorized by Van Gennep (1960) and Turner (1967), in which the suspension of normality creates fundamental solidarity between comrades of fortune. While the human condition is open to a diversity of practices (Kapferer, 2019), the period of lockdown ushered into an anticommunitas in which the social norms, usually in place, are intensified and the social fabric is further individualized. In the context of the anticommunitas the individual's is forced into the boundaries of their houses and workplaces, while a growing control and pressure are exercised on these boundaries. Obliged in this emergent, new landscape, the jogger is faced to choose whether to stop the physical activity, as in the case of Laura, or explore new spaces for practice, in the house, as in the case of Luca, or in places where the control is loose, as in the case of Francesco and Maria. In any case, the result is the intensification of a claustrophobic sense of control, which further exacerbates the experience of the pandemic and dumpers the quality of life of the joggers.

The analysis confirms physical activity has an impact on the perception of individual well-being, even during the lockdown. Where in normal conditions jogging can improve the perception of wellbeing, during the period of maximum limitation, the relationship is inverse, reinforcing the sense of insecurity. Significantly, the research points out, the sense of insecurity is not (just) generated by viral threat, but rather by the people surrounding the joggers and controlling them.

Overall, the research confirms the general trend reported by the media concerning the hostility towards the joggers. In so doing, it shows the role of this pressure in defining a new geography of jogging that pushes the practitioners to a path of appropriation of new places and times, which are remote to most of the population.

In light of this, the research opens up to new reflections linked to the social study of jogging after the crisis and to the legacy that the lockdown can have both in the relationship between joggers and urban space and between individuals and the urban community. In fact, where the lockdown has been narrated mainly as a measure linked to the well-being of the social body of a nation, it is clear that not only this collective well-being was achieved through the sacrifice of individuals' well-being, but above all, also in the case of joggers, the lockdown has called into question the liveability of the urban space as a whole, drawing attention to the central role played by the difficult negotiation of everyday practices that exists between the individuals and the community.

References

Alan, T. (2004). Pierre Bourdieu and the sociological study of sport: Habitus, capital and field. In R. Giulianotti (Ed.), *Sport and modern social theorists.* (pp. 161–172). Palgrave Macmillan.

Appadurai, A. (1996). *Modernity at large: Cultural dimensions of globalization.* University of Minnesota Press.

Augé, M. (1986). *Un ethnologue dans le métro.* Hachette.

Barba, B. (2016). *Calciologia. Per un'antropologia del football.* Mimesis Ed.

Bauman, Z. (2005). *Liquid life.* Polity Press.

Bertaux, D. (1999). *Racconti di vita. La prospettiva etnosociologica.* Franco Angeli.

Besnier, N., & Brownell, S. (2012). Sport, modernity, and the body. *Annual Review Anthropology, 41*, 443–459.

Bodin, M., & Hartig, T. (2003). Does the outdoor environment matter for psychological restoration gained through running? *Psychology of Sport and Exercise, 4*, 141–153.

Camy, J., Adamkiewics, E., & Chantelat, P. (1993). Sporting uses of the city: Urban anthropology applied to the sports practices in the agglomeration of Lyon. *International Review for the Sociology of Sport, 28*, 175–185.

Certeau, M. D. (1984). *The practice of everyday life* (Vol. 1). University of California Press.

Cialdea, L., & Michelini, M. (2019). L'intensità dell'attività fisica degli occupati. In E. di Bella, F. Maggino & M. Trapani (Eds.), *AIQUAV 2018. V Convegno Nazionale dell'Associazione Italiana per gli Studi sulla Qualità della Vita. Fiesole (FI), 13–15 Dicembre 2018. Libro dei Contributi Brevi* (pp. 83–90). Genoa University Press.

Coleman, L. (2009). Being alone together: From solidarity to solitude in urban anthropology. *Anthropological Quarterly, 82*, 755–777.

Cook, S., Shaw, J., & Simpson, P. (2016). Jography: Exploring meanings, experiences and spatialities of recreational road-running. *Mobilities, 11*, 744–769.

Fontefrancesco, M. F. (2020). The urban disease revealed in Italy. *Anthropology News*.

Fontefrancesco, M. F. (2021). Jogging during the lockdown: Changes in the regimes of kinesthetic morality and urban emotional geography in NW Italy. *Societies, 11*(4), 124. https://doi.org/10.3390/soc11040124

Gervasoni, M. (2010). *Storia d'Italia degli anni Ottanta: quando eravamo moderni*. Marsilio.

Gillick, M. R. (1984). Health promotion, jogging, and the pursuit of the moral life. *Journal of Health Political Policy Law, 9*, 369–387.

Giulianotti, R., & Robertson, R. (2009). *Globalization & football: A critical sociology*. SAGE Publications.

Health City Institute. (2016). *La salute nelle città: Bene Comuneb*. Associazione Nazionale Comuni d'Italia.

Herzfeld, M. (2004). *The body impolitic: Artisans and artifice in the global hierarchy of value*. University of Chicago Press.

Kapferer, B. (2019). Crisis and communitas: Victor Turner and social process. *Anthropology Today, 35*, 1–2.

Karusisi, N., Bean, K., Oppert, J.-M., Pannier, B., & Chaix, B. (2012). Multiple dimensions of residential environments, neighborhood experiences, and jogging behavior in the RECORD study. *Preventive Medicine, 55*, 50–55.

Latham, A. (2015). The history of a habit: Jogging as a palliative to sedentariness in 1960s America. *Cultural Geographies, 22*, 103–126.

Olwig, K. (2008). Performing on the landscape versus doing landscape: Perambulatory practice, sight and the sense of belonging. In T. Ingold & J. L. Vergunst (Eds.), *Ways of walking*. Ashgate.

Patucchi, M. (2017, June 3). Running "partito di maggioranza", il 51% degli italiani corre almeno una volta al mese. *La Repubblica*.

Porter, G., Hampshire, K., Abane, A., Munthali, A., Robson, E., Mashiri, M., et al. (2010). Youth transport, mobility and security in sub-Saharan Africa: The gendered journey to school. *World Transport Policy and Practice, 16*, 51–71.

Sheehan, G. (1978). *Running and being: The total experience*. Simon and Schuster.

Turner, V. W. (1967). Betwixt and between: The liminal period in rites of passage. In V. W. Turner (Ed.), *The forest of symbols: Aspects of Ndembu ritual* (p. 405). Cornell University Press.

Van Gennep, A. (1960). *The rites of passage*. Routeledge and Kegan Paul.

Wacquant, L. (2003). *Body and soul: Notebooks of an apprentice boxer*. Reaktion.

Chapter 15
Aging and Quality of Life in the Elderly: Role of Physical Activity

Ivana Matteucci

15.1 Introduction. The Challenges of Aging

People aged 60 and over represent the fastest growing segment of the world population (UN-United Nations, 2017): across the globe this age group is growing faster than any other.[1] The steady increase in the elderly population and the goal of improving the quality of life and psycho-physical well-being of this age group represents a major challenge with important social and cultural repercussions (Censi and Minetti Zavaritt, 2012). Hence, there is a need to bring about changes to meet the needs of a growing older population with higher expectations with regard to their well-being.[2] Common ideas regarding the role and opportunities afforded by physical activity and sport in the lives of the elderly need to be carefully re-examined in light of changing populations and social processes. Indeed, a challenge for sports sociologists involves the need to question the dominant perceptions of aging (Pike, 2015; Pike et al., 2015) which assert that most sports activities are unsuitable for the

[1]According to data from *World Population Prospects* 2017, the number of older people—aged 60 and over—should more than double by 2050 and more than triple by 2100, going from 962 million in 2017 to 2.1 billion in 2050 and 3.1 billion in 2100. https://population.un.org/wpp/Publications/Files/WPP2017_KeyFindings.pdf. Accessed May 13, 2020.

[2]For example, the research *Over 65: Life in Color (Over 65: Una vita a colori)* commissioned in Italy by BNP Paribas Cardif and carried out by AstraRicerche on a sample of over 700 seniors aged 65–85, provided a picture of an elderly population that has changed its lifestyle and habits becoming more active and positive in a variety of areas: from their health to their relationship with technology, from their family to their social life and leisure activities. https://bnpparibascardif.it/-/bnp-paribas-cardif-i-nuovi-over-65-la-prima-generazione-senior-digitale-che-progetta-un-futuro. Accessed May 13, 2020.

I. Matteucci (✉)
Department of Communication Science, Humanistic and International Studies (DISCUI), Carlo Bo University of Urbino, Urbino, Italy
e-mail: ivana.matteucci@uniurb.it

P. Corvo, F. M. Lo Verde (eds.), *Sport and Quality of Life*, Social Indicators Research Series 84, https://doi.org/10.1007/978-3-030-93092-9_15

aging body. This is a fundamental challenge, because denying or limiting the opportunity to engage in physical activity means restricting the ability of the elderly to fuse a range of different skills and to maintain a good level of quality of life.

Old age is accompanied by the onset of a series of limitations, including deterioration of health, a reduction in functionality and diminishing vital energy. Difficulty walking, sensory limitations, and from a mental standpoint, a reduction in the breadth of their intellectual capacities, often drive the elderly towards self-isolation and limit their mobility. Inactivity affects both their physical and mental health, usually causing a general deterioration. On the other hand, older athletes have been found enjoy a broad range of physiological benefits unlike their sedentary peers (Chodzko-Zajko et al., 2009; Marcos-Pardo et al., 2019; Vitulli et al., 2012). In addition, physical activity has been shown to play an importan role in the treatment and management of anxiety-depressive disorders (Blumenthal et al., 1999; Chodzko-Zajko et al., 2008; Alves Apóstolo et al., 2019; Dongwook & Sae-Hyung, 2019). Indeed, regular age-adjusted physical activity can yield significant improvements in overall psychological well-being (Folkins & Sime, 1981; McAuley & Katula, 1998; Blair et al., 2001; Mather et al., 2002; Netz et al., 2005; Rejeski et al., 2008; Notthoff et al., 2017).

Although physical activity appears to be positively associated with quality of life, the exact nature of this relationship is still not well understood. In a review of the literature concerning the relationship between physical activity and the quality of life in the elderly, several scholars (Rejeski & Mihalko, 2001) conclude that, based on available scientific evidence, physical activity appears to be positively associated with many, but not all aspects of quality of life, both in terms of physical well-being (physical fitness, health and self-sufficiency), and psychological well-being (affectivity, self-esteem, satisfaction, cognitive function). Engagement in physical activity has been identified as a predictor of enhanced quality of life, which is connected to an increase in social relationships and a reduction in feelings of loneliness (McAuley et al., 2000; McAuley & Katula, 1998). Other studies have focused on the relationship between social capital and the health and well-being of the elderly, pointing out the mediating role played by physical activity (Boen et al., 2019; Yu et al., 2018): the specific indicators of social capital were positively, though modestly, related to health and well-being. The experience of coming into contact with their peers has emerged as the strongest predictor of health and well-being in the elderly: physical activity mediated and facilitated social relationships by making a sense of belonging to a group emerge as a determining factor.[3]

[3]The World Health Organization considers the promotion of physical activity among the five priority interventions in the aging plan for Europe 2012–2020 (WHO, , 2012). In support of priority area number one of Health 2020 called "Investing in healthy aging throughout the course of existence", the prevention of risk factors for the elderly, namely isolation and social exclusion, is recommended, particularly in the absence of family networks or support. Indeed, social exclusion affects every aspect of well-being in the elderly, from mental health including the development of dementia, to the risk of emergency hospitalizations due to avoidable diseases such as serious cases of dehydration or undernutrition.

Environment and social conditions are strongly linked to the opportunities one has to engage in physical activity and sport in one's leisure time. A study carried out in Scotland (Crombie et al., 2004) showed that the strongest deterrent to doing physical activity was lack of interest. Other factors included the lack of daily availability of a car, poor health, having an aversion to go out alone or in the evening, a perceived lack of vital energy, and doubts regarding the benefits of exercise. A study on the participation of the elderly in sports and physical activity in Germany, examined the socio-demographic variables (gender, age and social class) of the population and analyzed how they came into play (Tischer et al., 2011). A relationship between age group and engagement in sports was shown: namely, engagement appeared to decrease with increasing age. The study also highlighted the important effect of social stratification: with older women from the lowest socio-economic level engaging in sports the least of all. Furthermore, a direct correlation was observed between engagement in sports activities and educational level and cultural capital. This correlation was found to be more significant than the correlation between engagement in sports activities and socio-economic conditions.

The aim of this study was to examine physical activity, whose frequency, duration and intensity were assessed, and the quality of life of the elderly in terms of sensory perception, autonomy, satisfaction with opportunities, and social participation. Two fundamental questions were posed:

(a) What specific kinds of physical activity do the elderly engage in?
(b) Are there relationships between the amount and type of physical activity and the measured quality of life of the elderly?

15.2 Materials and Methods

A 2019 study conducted by the Italian National Institute of Statistics (ISTA) focusing on older people, aged 65–75, in the province of Pesaro/Urbino in the Marche region of Italy, showed that this area had high levels of perceived well-being as well as high longevity and good health. Before the start of the study, the minimum sample size was calculated. To determine the sample size of the resident population (Table 15.1), as a first approximation we adopted the formula $n = 1/e^2$,

Table 15.1 Resident population on 1 January 2018 by age and municipality—Marche Region

	Age		
Province	65–74	65–75	Tot. pop
Pesaro Urbino	**40.549**	**43.795**	**360.125**
Ancona	53.732	58.199	472.603
Macerata	35.409	38.325	316.310
Ascoli Piceno	23.798	25.820	208.377
Fermo	19.452	20.932	174.338
Marche region	**172.940**	**187.071**	**1.531.753**

Source: ISTAT—Statistics for the Marche Region

which, by accepting a 10% margin of error for the estimates, provides a minimum value of 100 units, amply ensured by the sample that was actually measured.

The subjects, all volunteers, met the following eligibility criteria:

(i) being between 65 and 75 years old
(ii) residing in the selected province
(iii) having no signs of dementia
(iv) the absence of any self-reported medical diagnoses that involve functional impairment

Two questionnaires from the literature were used: the Physical Activity Scale for the Elderly (PASE) (Washburn et al., 1993; Washburn & Montoye, 1986) for measuring physical activity, and the questionnaire of the World Health Organization on quality of life (version for the elderly) WHOQOL-OLD (WHO-World Health Organization, 2006). The questionnaires were administered online in September 2019. The study group consisted of 192 subjects recruited through random sampling, of whom 124 were female and 68 male. Participants assessed their usual physical activity using the Physical Activity Scale for the Elderly. This scale was chosen because it had been validated for people over 65, for whom even simple daily movements or short walks cannot be overlooked in calculating the amount of exercise. PASE is a 12-item scale that measures the average number of hours per day spent doing recreational sports, domestic and work activities in the previous 7-day period. The same items are then attributed to three categories: *leisure time activity*, *household activity*, and *work-related activity*.

In the "leisure time activity" category, the frequency and duration of engagement in the following five activities were evaluated: *walking*, *light sports*, *moderate sports*, *strenuous sports*, *muscle strength/endurance exercises*. In order to ensure that the participants correctly classified their sports and recreational activities as light, moderate, vigorous, or high, examples of specific activities were provided (for example walking the dog, playing tennis, dancing ...).

The frequency of the activity was assessed by asking respondents how often they had engaged in the activity in the previous week. The following four-point scale was used in the answers: 0 = never; 1 = rarely/1–2 days; 2 = sometimes/3–4 days; 3 = often/5–7 days. The duration was assessed by asking participants how many hours a day they had spent on average doing the activity. The answers were indicated using a four-point scale: 1 = less than 1 h; 2 = between 1 and 2 hrs; 3 = 2–4 hrs; 4 = more than 4 hrs. These categorical frequency and duration indices were used to calculate the average daily engagement frequency for each activity. Using a standard procedure, the ordinal categorical methods were converted into numerical scales.

In the "household activity" category, engagement in six activities was assessed: *light houseworks*, *heavy houseworks*, *home repairs*, *lawn work or yard care*, *outdoor gardening*, and *caring for another person*. Using a binary scale (1 = no, 2 = yes) the respondents indicated if they had engaged in any of these activities in the previous 7 days. These scores were then converted to indicate frequency. If a domestic physical activity had been carried out in the previous 7 days, an average

PASE ACTIVITY	PASE WEIGHT
Walking*	20
Light sports*	21
Moderate sports*	23
Strenuous sports*	23
Muscle strenght/Endurance*	30
Light houseworks°	25
Heavy houseworks°	25
Home repairs°	30
Lawn work or yard care°	36
Outdoor Gardening°	20
Job involving standing or walking*	21
Caring for another person°	35

**Determine average hours per day over the pas 7-day period,*
and multiply the average number of hours of the PASE activity by the PASE weight.
°Scored 1 = engaged in that activity or
0 = did not engage in that activity during the previous 7 days.

Fig. 15.1 The PASE activities and their PASE weights

daily frequency of 1 was assigned. If it had not been performed, the assigned daily average frequency was 0.

Under the category "work-related activity", the participants indicated whether they worked for compensation or as volunteers (1 = no, 2 = yes). Those who answered affermatively were also asked to indicate the number of hours they had worked and to characterize their work as: (1) *mainly sitting with some slight arm movement*; (2) *sitting or standing with some walking*; (3) *walking with some handling of materials generally weighing less than 50 pounds*; (4) *walking and heavy manual work often requiring the handling of materials weighing over 50 pounds*. If a respondent's job was characterized as "sitting mainly with slight arm movements", the average daily frequency for the work-related physical activity assigned was 0 hrs. For all other types of work, the average daily frequency was calculated by dividing the number of hours of work in the previous week by 7 (days).

In order to make the different activities comparable, Washburn et al. (1993) designed a set of activity weights for each of the 12 PASE items. These weights reflect the amount of energy spent by the elderly person engaged in that particular activity. The scores of the PASE items were calculated by multiplying the weight of the activity by the average daily frequency of the activity. The PASE items were then summed to create an overall PASE score (Fig. 15.1). Washburn et al. reported that PASE scores can range from 0 to 400 or more.

The quality of life of the subjects was assessed using the World Health Organization (WHOQOL-OLD) quality of life test. The WHOQOL-OLD test is composed of 24 items measured using the Likert scale assigned to six distinct categories (Facets): (1) *Sensory abilities* (SAB); (2) *Autonomy* (AUT); (3) *Past, present and future activities* (PPF); (4) *Social participation* (SOP); (5). *Death and Dying* (DAD); 6. *Intimacy* (INT) (Fig. 15.2). Each category includes four indicators.

Facet I – Sensory Abilities (OLD-SAB)
OLD-01 Impairments to senses affect daily life
OLD-02 Loss of sensory abilities affect participation in activities
OLD-10 Problems with sensory functioning affect ability to interact
OLD-20 Rate sensory functioning
Facet II – Autonomy (OLD-AUT)
OLD-03 Freedom to make own decisions
OLD-04 Feel in control of your future
OLD-05 People around you are respectful of your freedom
OLD-11 Able to do things you'd like
Facet III – Past, Present and Future Activities (OLD-PPF)
OLD-12 Satisfied with opportunities to continue achieving
OLD-13 Received the recognition you deserve in life
OLD-15 Satisfied with what you've achieved in life
OLD-19 Happy with things to look forward to
Facet IV – Social Participation (OLD-SOP)
OLD-14 Have enough to do each day
OLD-16 Satisfied with the way you use your time
OLD-17 Satisfied with level of activity
OLD-18 Satisfied with opportunity to participate in community
Facet V – Death and Dying (OLD-DAD)
OLD-06 Concerned about the way you will die
OLD-07 Afraid of not being able to control death
OLD-08 Scared of dying
OLD-09 Fear pain before death
Facet VI – Intimacy (OLD-INT)
OLD-21 Feel a sense of companioship in life
OLD-22 Experience love in your life
OLD-23 Opportunities to love
OLD-24 Opportunities to loved

Fig. 15.2 WHOQOL-OLD: Facets and items

For each of the categories, the total score of all the items can range from a minimum of four to a maximum of 20, provided that all the items in a category have been completed. The scores of these six categories or the values of the 24 individual items of the WHOQOL-OLD questionnaire can be summed to produce a general score (GQOL) relating to the quality of life of the elderly subject, indicated as the "total score" of the WHOQOL-OLD questionnaire. Higher scores indicate higher quality of life and a greater sense of well-being.

15.3 Results and Discussion

Table 15.2 shows the socio-demographic characteristics of the respondents (numerical and percentage values) divided according to gender.

Table 15.2 Participant characteristics, stratified by gender

Characteristic	Males $n = 68$	Females $n = 124$
Education (completed)		
Elementary	n.4 (5.9%)	n.20 (16.1%)
Middle school	n.16 (23.5%)	n.0 (0%)
High school	n.4 (5.9%)	n.0 (0%)
University	n.44 (64.7%)	n.104 (83.9%)
Employment status		
Retired	n.36 (52.9%)	n.80 (64.5%)
Unemployed, looking for work	n.0 (0%)	n.0 (0%)
Never employed	n.0 (0%)	n.0 (0%)
Employed	n.32 (47.1%)	n.44 (35.5%)
Living arrangements		
Live alone	n.0 (0%)	n.52 (41.9%)
Live with his/her partner	n.28 (41.2%)	n.52 (41.9%)
Live with others	n.0 (0%)	n.20 (163%)
Senior's housing	n.40 (58.8%)	n.0 (0%)
Gross monthly household income[a]		
<€ 686.91	n.8 (11.8%)	n.16 (12.9%)
>€ 686.91	n.60 (88.2%)	n.108 (87.1%)
Health conditions Chronic diseases:	n.24 (35.3%)	n.24 (19,4%)
(Cardiovascular disease, Arthritis, Diabetes, Asthma) Cancer	n.4 (5.9%)	n.0 (0%)
Hypertension	n.0 (0%)	n.24 (19,4%)
Obesity	n.8 (11.8%)	n.0 (0%)
Other diseases	n.32 (47%)	n.16 (12.9%)
None of these	n.0 (0%)	n.60 (48.3%)

Source: Istat (National Institute of Statistics). https://www.istat.it/it/dati-analisi-e-prodotti/contenuti-interattivi/soglia-di-poverta. Accessed May 13, 2020

[a]*Value of the absolute poverty threshold relating to a person aged 60–74 residing in a small town in Central Italy–year 2018*

Most of the respondents were university graduates, more than half were retired but a considerable percentage reported that they were still busy at work. A rather high percentage of the males reported living in residential homes for the elderly, while this was not the case for any of the females, who mostly reported living with their spouse or alone. Income in most cases exceeded the poverty line, but over 10% of both gender groups reported living below that threshold. Females appeared to enjoy better health than males.

The physical activity scores of the sample under study were then determined by calculating the average for each item (Table 15.3). In PASE, the scores of the 12 items ranged from a minimum of 0 to a maximum of about 200 depending on the amount of physical activity that was performed (Fig. 15.3).

The average value of the PASE score was mostly determined by domestic activities such as taking care of the house or the garden, gardening or taking care of a person, and a little less so by leisure activities such as walking, cycling or doing

Table 15.3 PASE scores—average values per item and overall

PASE activities	N	Mean	Std deviation
PASE 1	192	20.90	18.855
PASE 2	192	8.02	18.680
PASE 3	192	1.71	5.838
PASE 4	192	1.35	4.275
PASE 5	192	2.29	7.644
PASE 6	192	21.88	8.355
PASE 7	192	18.23	11.227
PASE 8	192	1.25	6.058
PASE 9	192	10.50	16.536
PASE 10	192	7.08	9.666
PASE 11	192	6.56	13.805
PASE 12	192	0.44	3.031
PASE Total	192	100.19	40.312

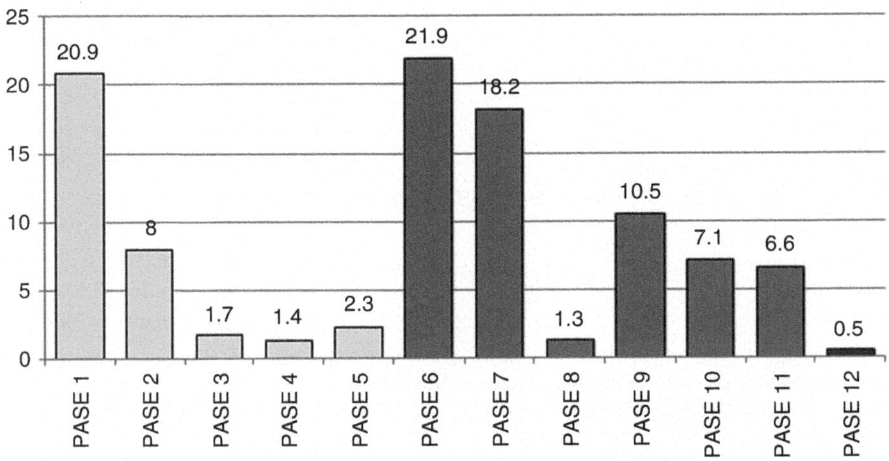

Fig. 15.3 Average values of the weighted indicators of physical activity (light gray: leisure activity, intermediate gray: domestic activities, dark gray: work-related activities)

structured physical activities. Walking outside the home was the most common activity among leisure activities. Indeed, more than half of the interviewees reported having taken a walk or gone for a bike ride in the week preceding the interview, but overall even more reported having engaged in a structured leisure activity, mostly light activities such as soft gymnastics; fewer reported engaging in moderate physical activity such as dancing or hunting, or heavy activity such as swimming, running, or aerobic or equipment activity. Domestic activities were performed by most of the interviewees. Housework (from cleaning to the heaviest activities) as well as gardening and caring for another person were engaged in more frequently by female, while doing minor repairs or caring for the garden were performer more frequently by men. Among the work activities that were esamined, some were

Table 15.4 WHOQOL-OLD scores—average values of FACET indicators

Pase Facet	N	Mean	Std. deviation
FACET I	192	16.10	3.429
FACET II	192	14.06	2.869
FACET III	192	14.65	2.356
FACET IV	192	14.50	2.154
FACET V	192	12.79	3.555
FACET VI	192	13.13	3.330

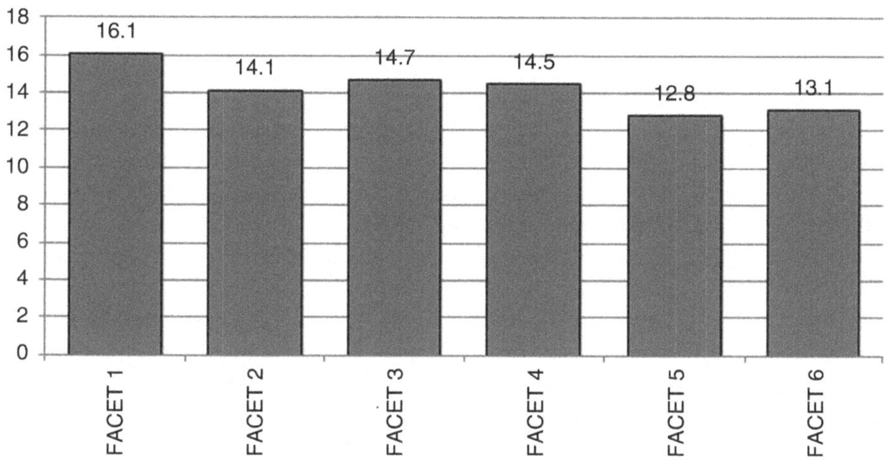

Fig. 15.4 Average values of quality of life indicators

considered physical activity if they involved dynamic movement. It was found that the lowest percentage of interviewees performed this sort of activity involving walking or considerable physical effort. The PASE score decreased significantly with age, it was lower among women, those who had many economic difficulties and those with a low level of education, and those living alone.

In the QDV-OLD test relating to the quality of life of the elderly, the scores of the 24 items result in a scale ranging from 4 to 20 points (Table 15.4 and Fig. 15.4).

Regarding quality of life, the values do not appear to differ significantly from one another This similarity among the values may be attributed to the type of questionnaire that was used in the study. Since the questionnaire was designed to evaluate the quality of life of the elderly, it aimed to investigate related aspects of feeling and perception, elements that tend to be less objective and more difficult to measure. The subjects of the sample generally had a high level of quality of life. In particular, they seemed satisfied with their sensory abilities. This result is likely related to the generally good health reported by the subjects in the final part of the questionnaire dedicated to health. Interesting values were also found for items regarding subjects' satisfaction with what they have achieved so far in life, social recognition, as well as future opportunities. Subjects were found to be satisfied with their social engagement at a community level, and with the level of autonomy they enjoy in performing daily activities.

The wealth of information that was collected on multiple issues related to the subjects' engagement in activities as well as their quality of life, allowed us to investigate possible links between the various indicators and the effect of several contextual variables on these indicators. Since at this stage we will limit ourselves to a bivariate analysis, the first queries we have tried to answer concern any possible gender differences and the role played by age.

Regarding the PASE indicators, there were 12 items (one for each activity) as well as an overall score (sum of all the items). Five of the items: 1, 3, 5, 6 and 9 (*walking*, *moderate sports*, *muscle strenght/endurance*, *light houseworks*, *lawn work or yard care* respectively), varied significantly according to gender (t test for independent samples, $p < 0.05$). If we also consider that two other items (eight-*home repairs* and 12-*caring for another person*) were, at least in our sample, exclusively female activities, the number of gender-based differences rises to eight. Specifically, with the exception of item six (*light housework*), in all other comparisons that yielded significant differences, the males were characterized by a greater quantity of activity, pointing to a gender differences stemming from the 'clear' separation of domestic duties and leisure time activities along gender lines. As regards relationships with age, although in many cases the data seem to suggest a decrease in the amount of activity with increasing age, in no case did the relative measures reach significance (correlation coefficients).

The relative WHOQOL-OLD assessment tool adopt a similar scheme with six facets indicating quality of life. In this case, none of the indicators showed significant differences between genders, while in two cases (FACET III—OLD-PPF and FACET VI—OLD-INT) there was an indirect relationship with age. Specifically, with increasing age the subjects were found to be less satisfied with the past (opportunities in life, recognition received, and achievements), the present (daily work) and the future (happiness with things to look forward to). We should bear in mind that in this case the questions that were asked were not as 'objective' as those relating to the evaluation of activities, and may therefore have yielded less precise assessment, which might not exactly reflect the subject's actual situation.

Finally, if we look at the two blocks of indicators, we discover how the summary indicator of the performed activities (overall PASE) shows a significant relationship with FACET III—OLD-PPF, which is also characterized by the agreement among the relative values. Hence, although satisfaction with the past, present and future, generally decreases with age, it nevertheless increases with the overall amount of physical activity performed. If we examine the individual components of PASE, two significant relationships emerge (PASE 1/FACET IV—OLD-SOP and PASE 12/FACET VI—OLD-INT) indicating a generally positive correlation between the amount of physical activity performed and quality of life indicators. Indeed, there is a correlation between the activity designated *walking* and satisfaction with social participation, indicated with satisfaction with the use of one's time, the level of activities carried out, and opportunities to participate in community life. Likewise, there is a correlation between the activity defined as *caring for another person* and the possibility of experiencing companionship and giving and receiving affection.

15.4 Conclusions

The results of this study regarding the physical activity of the elderly in a province of a region in Central Italy, show that gender differences persist among the elderly popolation, with males found to be engaged in a greater amount of leisure and domestic work activities, while females were shown to be more involved in light household activities, and exclusively involved in caregiving. With respect to the relationship between age and physical activity, in many cases there was a decrease in the amount of activity with increasing age; however significant levels of activity were often maintained.

In conclusion, positive relationship between physical activity and quality of life in older people was confirmed. The results of the study confirmed statistically, show that the amount of physical activity had an impact on the various measures of the quality of life of the population under study. In particular, these relationships concern the measures of quality of life in terms of social participation, highlighting the role that physical activity can play in maintaining social interactions and strengthening social integration. Also relevant from a social standpoint is the relationship between physical activity and finding companionship and giving and receiving affection.

References

Alves Apóstolo, J. L., Dos Anjos Dixe, M., Campos, E., & Areosa, T. (2019). Effectiveness of a combined intervention on psychological and physical capacities of frail older adults: A cluster randomized controlled trial. *International Journal of Environmental Research and Public Health, 16*(17), 3125. https://doi.org/10.3390/ijerph16173125

Blair, S. N., Dunn, A. L., Marcus, B. H., Carpenter, R. A., & Jaret, P. (2001). *Active living everyday: 20 weeks to lifelong vitality*. Human Kinetic.

Blumenthal, J. A., Babyak, M. A., Moore, K. A., et al. (1999). Effects of exercise training on older patients with major depression. *Archives of Internal Medicine, 159*(19), 2349–2356. https://doi.org/10.1001/archinte.159.19.2349

Boen, F., Pellsers, J., Scheereder, J., Vanbeselaere, N., Vos, S., Hurkmans, E., Smits, T., & Fransen, K. (2019). Does social capital benefit older adults' health and Well-being? The mediating role of physical activity. *Journal of Aging and Health*. https://doi.org/10.1177/0898264319848638

Censi, A., & Minetti Zavaritt, A. (2012). La sfida della grande vecchiaia: tra legami fluidi e riconversioni identitarie. The challenge of old age: Between fluid relationships and identity adaptations. *Quaderni di Sociologia, 58*(2012), 89–106. https://doi.org/10.4000/qds.595

Chodzko-Zajko, W., Schwingel, A., & Hee Park, C. (2008). Successful aging: The role of physical activity. *American Journal of Lifestyle Medicine, 31*(1), 20–28. https://doi.org/10.1177/1559827608325456

Chodzko-Zajko, W. J., Proctor, D. N., Fiatore-Singh, M., Minson, C. T., Nigg, C. R., Salem, G. J., & Skinner, J. S. (2009). American College of Sports Medicine (ACSM). Exercise and physical activity for older adults. *Medicine and Science in Sports and Exercise, 41*(7), 1510–1530. https://doi.org/10.1249/MSS.0b013e3181a0c95c

Crombie, I. K., Irvine, L., Williams, B., McGinnis, A. R., Slane, P. W., Alder, E. M., & McMurdo, M. E. T. (2004). Age and ageing. Why older people do not participate in leisure time physical activity: A survey of activity levels, beliefs and deterrents. *British Geriatrics Society, 33*(3), 287–292. https://doi.org/10.1093/ageing/afh089

Dongwook, C., & Sae-Hyung, K. (2019). Health capability and psychological effects of regular exercise on adults: Middle-aged and older. *The International Journal of Aging and Human Development*. https://doi.org/10.1177/0091415019882009

Folkins, C. H., & Sime, W. E. (1981). Physical fitness training and mental health. *American Psychologist Journal, 36*(4), 373–389. https://doi.org/10.1037//0003-066x.36.4.373

Marcos-Pardo, P. J., Orquin, F. J., Garcia, G. M. G., & Menayo Antúnez, R. (2019). Effects of a moderate-to-high intensity resistance circuit training on fat mass, functional capacity, muscular strength, and quality of life in elderly: A randomized controlled trial. *Scientific Reports, 9*(1), 7830. https://doi./10.1038/s41598-019-44329-6

Mather, A. S., Rodriguez, C., Guthrie, M. F., McHarg, A. M., Reid, I. C., & McMurdo, M. E. (2002). Effects of exercise on depressive symptoms in older adults with poorly responsive depressive disorder: Randomised controlled trial. *British Journal of Psychiatry, 180*, 411–415. https://doi.org/10.1192/bjp.180.5.411

McAuley, E., Blissmer, B., Marquez, D. X., Jerom, G. J., Kramer, A. F., & Katula, J. (2000). Social relations, physical activity, and Well-being in older adults. *Preventive Medicine, 31*(5), 608–617. https://doi.org/10.1006/pmed.2000.0740

McAuley, E., & Katula, J. (1998). Physical activity interventions in the elderly: influence on physical health and psychological function. In M. P. L. R. Schulz, & G. Maddox (Eds.), *Annual review of gerontology and geriatrics* (pp. 115–154). Springer.

Netz, Y., Wu, M. J., Becker, B. J., & Tenenbaum, G. (2005). Physical activity and psychological Well-being in advanced age: A meta-analysis of intervention studies. *Psychology and Aging, 20*(2), 272–284. https://doi.org/10.1037/0882-7974.20.2.272

Notthoff, N., Reisch, P., & Gerstorf, D. (2017). Individual characteristics and physical activity in older adults: A systematic review. *Gerontology, 63*(5), 443–459. https://doi.org/10.1159/000475558

Pike, E. C. J. (2015). Assessing the sociology of sport: On age and ability. *International Review for the Sociology of Sport, 50*(4–5), 570–574. https://doi.org/10.1177/1012690214550009

Pike, E. C. J., Jackson, S. J., & Wenner, L. A. (2015). Assessing the sociology of sport: On the trajectory, challenges, and future of the field. *International Review of the Sociology of Sport, 50*(4–5), 357–362. https://doi.org/10.1177/1012690215574127

Rejeski, W. J., King, A. C., Katula, J. A., Kritchevsky, S., Miller, M. E., Walkup, M. P., Glynn, N. W., & Pahor, M. (2008). Physical activity in prefrail older adults: Confidence and satisfaction related to physical function. *The Journal of Gerontology B, 63*(1), 19–26. https://doi.org/10.1093/geronb/63.1.p19

Rejeski, W. J., & Mihalko, S. L. (2001). Physical activity and quality of life in older adults. *The Journals of Gerontology A, 56*(2), 23–35. https://doi.org/10.1093/gerona/56.suppl_2.23

Tischer, U., Hartmann-Tews, I., & Combrink, C. (2011). Sport participation of the elderly: The role of gender, age, and social class. *Europen Review of Aging and Physical Activity, 8*, 83–91. https://doi.org/10.1007/s11556-011-0087-8

UN-United Nations Department of Economic and Social Affairs/Population Division. (2017). *World population prospects: The 2017 revision, key findings and advance tables.*

Vitulli, P., Femminella, G. D., Ciccarelli, A. L., Rengo, F., Lombardi, A., Cellurale, M., Aruta, S. F., Kamici, K., Allocca, E., de Lucia, C., & Rengo, F. (2012). Exercise training and aging. *Journal of Gerontology and Geriatrics, 60*, 172–181.

Washburn, R. A., & Montoye, H. J. (1986). The assessment of physical activity by questionnaire. *American Journal of Epidemiology, 123*(4), 563–576. https://doi.org/10.1093/oxfordjournals.aje.a114277

Washburn, R. A., Smith, K. W., Jette, A. M., & Janney, C. A. (1993). The physical activity scale for the elderly (PASE): Development and evaluation. *Journal of Clinical Epidemiology, 46*(2), 153–162. https://doi.org/10.1016/08954356(93)90053-4

WHO- World Health Organization. (2006). *The WHOQOL-OLD module—manual*. Retrieved May 15, 2020, from https://www.who.int/mental_health/evidence/WHOQOL_OLD_Manual.pdf?ua=1.

WHO-World Health Organization. (2012). *Strategy and action plan for healthy ageing in Europe, 2012–2020*. Retrieved May 16, 2020, from http://www.euro.who.int/__data/assets/pdf_file/0008/175544/RC62wd10Rev1-Eng.pdf

Yu, C. Y., Hou, S. I., & Miller, J. J. (2018). Health for older adults: The role of social capital and leisure-time physical activity by living arrangements. Journal of Physical Activity and Health, 15(2): 150–158. http://doi:https://doi.org/10.1123/jpah.2017-0006.

Chapter 16
Physical Activity as Daily Practice "Active Ageing" between Social Needs, Technology and *Quality-of-Life* Improvement

Luca Benvenga and Elisabetta Trinca

16.1 Introduction

This essay aims to highlight how, in contemporary modernity, an increasing number of collectivities share a set of practices that redefine daily activities and social communities. Pursuing shared interests and lifestyles among persons of different class and age is the central issue of a growing panorama of new cultural habits linked to physical activity.

Modern science has traditionally agreed on the idea that regular physical activity could help reduce risks for the human body and favor socialization in different frameworks (family, friends, acquaintances). In this respect, scientists consider the association between movement and health as important due to:

(a) the proper psychological and physical development of the subject;
(b) the opportunity to shift the stress biologically experienced in family and/or workplace contexts onto physical activity, with fundamental health benefits of persons, and, by extension, on their surrounding social environment. In fact, the condition of well-being contributes to improve relational criteria in family and professional circles that represent the vital network of each person.

In recent years, there has seen a growing institutional debate on the pair physical activity and health. The WHO Regional Committee for Europe, in 2011, on the

---

The chapter is the result of a reflection and a common work of both authors, as far as the writing of paragraphs two and four is to be attributed to Luca Benvenga, the writing of paragraph three to Elisabetta Trinca and the writing of paragraphs one and five to both.

L. Benvenga (✉)
University of Salento, Lecce, Italy
e-mail: luca.benvenga@unisalento.it

E. Trinca
Roma, Italy

P. Corvo, F. M. Lo Verde (eds.), *Sport and Quality of Life*, Social Indicators Research Series 84, https://doi.org/10.1007/978-3-030-93092-9_16

occasion of its 61st session, confirmed its mandate to the Regional Office for Europe to develop a new health policy framework, namely *2020* (Salute, 2020). In order to achieve this goal—as stated in the document—*sound policies for healthy ageing are indispensable, in response to fast demographic ageing in the European region* (Salute, 2020, *passim*). This reference to healthy ageing, as well as its planning, are related to physical activity as a guidance throughout all life stages; its positive impact is proved by the preventive potential it generates, especially in fostering proactive behavior of subjects who often identify physical activity as a framework in which they can interact, confront between each other and reduce degenerative diseases and social atomization.

In the following pages, this paper will aim to understand to what extent the role played by physical activity ensures individual and social well-being. It will be focused on the fundamental elements listed below:

(a) *daily actions* that in this sense promote behavioral regularities improving quality of life and the relation established with urban spaces;
(b) *physical activity* as an opportunity of experiencing socialization, as well as the role played by technologies in evaluating biological functioning of social actors in promoting physical exercise, calling for commitment and sharing results and objectives with other users, in which there is a tangible translation and hybridization of the (*off-line* as well as *on-line*) dynamics of sociality;
(c) the concepts of *healthy ageing* and *active citizenship*, as well as European intervention strategies aimed at creating a virtuous chain which originates within and from institutions.

The present paper will systematize the viewpoints that pivot on the combination among individual responsibilization, physical activity and well-being. Through this mixture the authors will critically analyze "active ageing", the participation of older people in social life and the importance of physical activities; in the concluding remarks, there will be a short reasoning on the enhancement of agency on the basis of physical activity through the self-awareness of a *sui generis* lifestyle, the social networks and the capabilities of rehabilitation to life scenarios of the same period.

16.2 Daily Life and Urban Spaces

For decades, physical activity has been evolving to become an indisputably important phenomenon at a social, cultural and economic level. Today, more than in the past, within the complex framework characterizing the subject who faces the challenges of *performance society*, individuals, public and private institutions recognize a primary role to sports and physical activity in conveying health values and well-being, thus attributing to them a privileged status that improves daily activities.

A *proactive* lifestyle, capable of tackling ageing at a psychological and physical level, is based upon the individual external and internal resources. Practicing physical activity every day is fundamental in itself to gain self-confidence and strengthen communities of interactions. A social network enthusiastically promoting physical activity improves the quality of life as well as social and professional performances of active subjects, provides real opportunities to dialogue between bodies, and integration for those who have a circumscribed social capital (older persons, for instance), and is also an opportunity for the new *city-users* to benefit from the regeneration of functional spaces and territories.

For that reason, the promotion of a regular lifestyle has to envisage a balance between the primary need of the subject and a city planning in terms of urban policies (Dorato & Montera, 2015). In fact, the urban space planning impacts not insignificantly on the scope of social behaviors. Citizens are encouraged to make healthy choices and to lead more balanced and active lives, if public response to these needs is devoted to promote and preserve green spaces, recreational areas accessible to everyone, pedestrian areas, cycle tracks, etc. (*ibidem*), and everything that is concerned with mobility preparatory to physical exercise and to the creation of relational exchanges.

A possible innovation practice, which binds together sports or physical activity with new criteria of urban inclusiveness and inter/infra-generational sociality, is represented by the so-called *community hubs*.

Community hubs are physical spaces that, in recent years, have taken a dominant role in the public debate on integrationist policies (Calvaresi, 2018; Foth et al., 2008; Zeigler et al., 2014). They are *re-signified* spaces, that center around the relation between persons and their community. These are re-used buildings (like, for instance, industrial disused premises), where a set of different activities can be delivered, so as to allow a qualitative development of the host neighborhood and a mind-body network. In these spaces, leisure courses addressed to subjects of different age groups could coexist with aggregation opportunities as well as with cultural and physical activity programs for older persons, basic welfare services. Community hubs, therefore, foster and exponentially increase relational exchange, where opportunities for proximity between individuals and groups, and, by extension, between individual, social and urban spheres, are more likely to intertwine.

In these contexts, what is prevailing is undoubtedly the need to feel part of a wider group, to socialize life experiences during leisure time, recreational and cultural activities. The Community hub has to be considered as the fundamental example if the focus is on public health and "healthy body" (both physical and social). In fact, the assumption of this paper is the territorial enhancement of this and other types of practices emphasizing the central role of the community (Maddocks, 2014). In these places, and more generally, from the *tout court* regeneration practices inscribed in them, it is possible to create a synergy between social and urban policies, between recreational activity—physical activity being nothing but an expression of it -, and daily interaction, but above all between vulnerable and/or inactive subjects, well-being and collectivity.

It must be also reviewed and underlined that technology—especially *AI-oriented technology*—has a supportive power in active ageing processes. The scope which keeps the needs of older persons into due consideration is receiving unprecedented attention by developers and major companies. The objective of these technologies is firstly to improve the perceived quality of life, and also to stimulate older persons to engage in new activities, thus stimulating the subject's proactivity. Thus, planning these technologies does not only deals with usability and accessibility to devices: it is about providing response to the needs of elderly persons also in terms of health protection, management of domestic spaces, entertainment and social relations.

16.3 Assistive Technology for the Elderly: From "Design for All" to Custom-Made Devices

This paragraph aims at discussing the link between ICT-based applications, Artificial Intelligence and active aging. This focus intends to offer hints on a series of very useful applications for active ageing, both in the field of health and sports or home automation. The attempt is to spur further scientific debate on the development of technologies designed for older users.

As underlined in literature by Cabrera and Malnowski (2009), technologies aimed to meet the needs of older persons in terms of quality of life in highly developed countries should be classified according to five categories: *health*, comprising technologies that ensure a good functional status and an adequate system of social support for the older individual; *safety*, through devices that guarantee physical inviolability of the persons, especially in domestic as well as in reconverted spaces; *independence*, regarding the possibility for the elderly to stay in their own homes for longer and avoid to move to living/nursing homes; *mobility*; *participation*, i.e., the possibility to have friendship relations and exchanges with other people and implement them in specific fields, such as third-age universities or senior citizens clubs.

The production of technologies oriented to these features is part of what literature defines as *silver economy*, that is the market share centered around the over-1965s and caters to their needs. This kind of market has notably changed in the last years, especially because of the fast technological progress brought about by the development of web 2.0, and also artificial intelligence, machine learning and natural language processing that, in the last few years, have made an unprecedented leap forward.

Technologies oriented to the elderly aim to recreate environments and life conditions where older people can feel at ease and face new challenges.

In Europe, for a number of years already, the European Commission has started the Active and Assisted Living Programme (that was launched in 2008 as Ambient and Assisted Living), oriented to finance ICT for silver economy, since it involves both technological and social innovations, and also a wide range of products (Enste et al., 2008). In Italy, where the ageing population is a constant problem and gives rise to significant costs for the national health care and pension systems, silver economy is not particularly developed and older persons are not widely represented neither by the media nor by policy makers, as stated by the Active Longevity Institute (ALI).

This paper cannot offer an in-depth analysis of medical products, or products having a financial, *age management* or residential nature (Cabrera & Malnowski, 2009)—which are part of silver economy—: instead, there will be an overview of devices that, resorting to digital and artificial intelligence, can support active ageing above all at a mobility and physical activity levels. These are technological equipments that provide older persons and their caregivers with services, but they are not specifically designed for this market: these are *design for all* technologies (Moore, 2009), but substantially respond to elderly persons' needs and support them in daily activities that facilitate active ageing.

For some years, literature has already dealt with technological systems defined as Ambient Assisted Living (AAL) that envisage the utilization of auxiliary sensors making the independent life of a person more comfortable and easier in the home environment (Demir et al., 2017). In many cases, the AAL makes use of robots in the home environment, thus requiring a definitely complex development as well as considerable economic costs. In recent years, however, this type of functions, usually linked to a "system", are carried out by much cheaper and affordable technologies that result in only one user-friendly device.

As mentioned before, although they have not been originally designed for the elderly market, the devices that will be described below fit three important functions which affect them directly:

- Monitoring psychological and emotional health status of the older person;
- Companionship or entertainment and physical activity;
- Anomaly detection and release of alert signals.

In this respect, increasing importance has been gained by the recent role played by *Voice User Interfaces* (VUI) and *Vocal Social Agents* (VSA), voice-user interfaces which enable human interaction with computers, using voice recognition to understand voice commands, reply to questions and reproduce an answer (Gehl & Bakardijeva, 2017). Conversational agents can provide cognitive and emotional assistance to older users or persons with disabilities who are often not able to organize their day or follow some basic steps of their routines (Kopp et al., 2018). As a result of the significant growth of the comprehension of natural language in the last few years, the VUIs are now a reliable tool to interact with computers and, in the case of persons with reduced mobility, they are proving to be a low-cost, yet very functional, technology. Successful examples of this aspect are Amazon Echo and Alexa, Google Home, Siri and Cortana for mobile versions. These technologies are normally used in different ways by elderly persons for some tasks of daily life.

Alexa and Google Home are cloud-based artificial intelligences presented in the form of voice assistant, a software that can be integrated in speakers and other smart devices. By interpreting natural language, they can interact with humans. These VUIs can perform very simple but also very complex actions; nevertheless, they can provide the older person with a beneficial support and greater agility in daily life.

They can provide companionship, becoming a familiar voice in a home setting, and provide entertainment, i.e., reading sections of text, audiobooks or newspapers to all those who are visually impaired or cannot read. They can schedule simple daily training activities, encouraging the older person to do physical and muscular activity in order to stay healthy and in good shape.

They can remedy minor inconveniences linked to age, such as localizing the smartphone within the house and let the owner easily find it. VUIs, in their specific meaning of voice agents included in smartphones, can also be very assistive in controlling the smartphone through a voice command. It is undeniable that technology can be a source of uneasiness, a great concern for the elderly, who, especially passing from the traditional telephone to mobile/smart devices, have not been able to adjust to the rapid change very easily.

These voice assistants can also provide voice reminders for important routine commitments or appointments, such as taking medicines at a given time.

There is also the field linked to home automation. In fact, a further improvement in VUI skills is obtained by connecting them with home automation devices that can give the elderly the real feeling to take back control of their life: this is the case of controlling the heating by a voice command, switching on the lights or activating the alarm and security systems. For instance, *Ask my Buddy*, available on Alexa, allows to immediately alert a planned list of contacts by a simple voice command, functioning as if the older person living alone can hit the panic button, hence conferring a certain autonomy. In fact, the beneficial psychological effect of these devices is represented by the fact that the elderly can stay in their homes autonomously but knowing that they are monitored (Lee et al., 2013).

Definitely, not all older people enjoy excellent health. In the case of serious diseases, the VUIs can prove to be even more efficient. In patients with dementia or Alzheimer's disease, these devices can unquestionably improve their health status. By providing a constant presence, they can answer the repetitive and orientation questions that patients with these pathologies repeatedly ask, thus offering relief to caregivers who meanwhile can carry out other tasks.

Certainly, no technology will ever replace the importance of human caregivers; however, beyond serious pathologies or severe disabilities, they can embody assistance, support for those who, despite their age, wish to foster social relations, autonomous living but are also willing to cope with new technological tasks, developing an aptitude to the new world outlined by technology.

Obviously, as it is well known, all these active background devices are raising many doubts on ethical and privacy matters involved in their use (Lau et al., 2018) and the debate over coming years will provide new suggestions on the cost-benefit relation related to them.

16.4 Healthy Ageing, Active Citizenship and New Intervention Strategies in Europe

Literature on the issue of welfare systems is plentiful and in broad agreement with the assumption that the crisis of a model based on wealth distribution and the compromise between workers and capital dates back to the 1970s. Most of the State policies on wage and labor market regulations that guaranteed the right balance between supply and demand, and kept the market relatively stable, have given way to new standards of social security. The automation of the production processes, the central role of knowledge, the progressive segmentation of the labor market and the redefinition of gender relations have consequently shown the inadequacy of state interventions in the past, unable to provide immediate response to the ongoing economic and productive as well as historical and social changes (and crisis). Moreover, in the same perspective, "Fordist" welfare policies aimed to develop forms of social regulation between conflicting groups and generations, to prevent disaggregation, to propose solutions that allow inclusion and mediation among social actors.

In this transitional stage, demographic structures have, in turn, suffered propound transformations and, as a knock-on effect, impacted on social and healthcare services. As a result, there has been a fall in fertility rate due to the impossibility to plan the future because of the reduction of life chances, altering the balance of the "generation pact" on which the whole structure of the Fordist welfare state was based, exacerbating the existing severe financial problems. Anthony Giddens (2006) poses that the problem of welfare regulation is intertwined with the demographic crisis and population change according to age groups: this is one of the major issues that the European welfare systems have had to face since the early twenty-first century. Furthermore, the transition towards a service and knowledge economy, the transformation of family relations and population ageing due to a better efficiency of the health and long-term care systems, have originated a series of troubles in demographic, productive, employment structures and, more generally, in infragenerational relations all over Europe.

Although demographic changes in European countries have not been homogeneous, generally speaking the decrease in mortality rates in the European Union (EU) during the last century has led to an increase in life expectancies, whereas, in the last decades, since the 1970s, the EU has recorded once again a decline in fertility rates (Struttura e invecchiamento della popolazione, 2020). Since then, all over the EU there was a shift from a mainly young society to a society constituted by a significant and growing percentage of elderly people (by 2050, more than a quarter of the population—27%—is expected to be 65 or over 65). If the population ageing is an indicator of longevity, conversely it is very challenging at a European level, with reference to the planning of new social and cultural policies oriented to the empowerment of this segment of citizens; raising their awareness to be proactive is essential, since, after all, an expensive welfare state based on the twentieth-century model is no longer feasible. Rather than health assistance and care, the preventive medicine measures do minimize costs and increase personal and community benefits.

In order to cope with these challenges, the road map proposed by the European Union with the Lisbon Agenda in 2000 and ratified by the new Europe 2020 strategy has set out several complementary objectives, coherent with the “active welfare state paradigm” that is prevailing in debates on European social policy (Garavaglia & Lodigiani 2013, 385). In this perspective, the factors facilitating active ageing are focused on the promotion of programs and services of individualization, on the investment in human capital (Ibidem) and on the concept of “active citizenship”.

In addition to measures that encourage the employability of older workers who embrace a pluriverse ageing process (Ottaviano, 2012), and whose social utility is underlined by their participation in educational programs and their non-sedentary lifestyle, an educational tool for “active citizenship” is also physical activity (Libro Bianco sullo Sport, 2007). Therefore, it not only helps individuals to be active in the labor market as long as possible, but prepares social systems to the needs of the ageing population, circumscribing it into experiences of urban and rural regeneration, into projects of territorial and heritage enhancement, and, last but not least, encouraging it to promote a healthy lifestyle characterized by physical activity.

The subjects should be aware of the influence of physical exercise on health for two reasons. The first one is the quality-of-life improvement and the possibility to carry out daily tasks during their ageing process: in this sense, apart from facilitating the preservation of independence, physical activity reduces the risk of hospitalization (Erikson et al., 2011; Bowen, 2012; Almeyda et al., 2014) as well as of degenerations of the cognitive system, stimulating practical and relational intelligence. The second reason can be measured through the contribution that these virtuous practices ensure to the sustainability of national healthcare systems: the ever growing flows of applications for hospital care provision linked to chronic illnesses and undesirable conditions would lead to the collapse of the delivery of healthcare services already doomed to weakness.

A recent document outlines the bases of a new European policy framework supporting a cross-sectoral action plan across government and society for health and wellbeing (Strategia e piano d’azione per l’invecchiamento sano in Europa, 2012–2020); in this document, the European Regional Committee and the WHO commented on the promotion of physical activity practiced by older people, investing in healthy ageing throughout their life-course through the development of local context and social activities. According to the WHO, priority interventions to be undertaken *strictu sensu*, whose appropriate implementation—as proved by scientific evidence—can bring about important achievements (Strategia e piano d’azione per l’invecchiamento sano in Europa, 2012–2020), are listed below:

- foster cooperation and sharing of experience and good practice on effective measures to increase physical activity levels among older persons, in order to support their implementation and evaluation;

- develop and implement community programs for physical activity targeted to older people, including a combination of individual and group-based behavior change approaches, with support and follow up;
- provide advice about physical activity in all health and social care settings for older people, specifically targeting sedentary people, with a special focus on moderate-intensity physical activity (particularly walking), providing ongoing support;
- support local governments in creating motivating environments and infrastructures for physical activity (in particular active transport) for all ages (Strategia e piano d'azione per l'invecchiamento sano in Europa, 2012–2020).

16.5 Concluding Remarks

What emerges from the present study on active ageing is a multifaceted scenario. According to the authors, such a framework offers a reflection on the importance of a lifestyle conducive to physical activity, that matches perfectly and prospectively with national, European, and technological innovation policies. In fact, active ageing is deeply rooted in a social context that can facilitate the possibility to practice physical activity in an urban space and encourage to build adequate environments—the example of community hubs is explicative—through public policies aimed at achieving individual and collective well-being.

Obviously, many challenges undermine the implementation of a virtuous path combining active ageing—concept meant as a tool of disease prevention and health promotion—with legislative and institutional framework. In this respect, there is an urgent need for institutional investments in the technological aspects connected to artificial intelligence and ICT, that should be integrated in public—national and European—policies as a supportive element, essential for active ageing. Furthermore, a healthy lifestyle may not disregard the subject's fulfillment of some qualitative standards—pursuit of psychological and physical balance, regular physical activity, active participation in social life -, that are fundamental to create forms of individual activeness, leading to direct benefits on society as a whole. In fact, among the manifold reasons to promote active ageing, besides quality-of-life improvement, the demographic feature gains a special mention: the trend curve of the European population has shifted towards the over 1965s in the last years, with consequent economic implications in terms of care and assistance of inactive older people (ibidem) and deprivation of essential social services for other citizens.

References

Almeyda, Osvaldo P., Khan, Karim M., Hankey, Graeme, J., Yeap, Bu B., Golledge, Jonathan and Flicker, Leon. 2014. 150 minutes of vigorous physical activity per week predicts survival and successful ageing: A population-based 11-year longitudinal study of 12,201 older Australian men. British Journal of Medicine 48: 220-225. https://doi.org/10.1136/bjsports-2013-092814.

Bowen, M. E. (2012). A prospective examination of the relationship between physical activity and dementia risk in later life. *American Journal of Health Promotion, 26*(3), 333–340. https://doi.org/10.4278/ajhp.110311-QUAN-115

Cabrera, M., & Malnowski, N. (Eds.), 2009. *Information and communication technologies for active ageing: Opportunities and challenges for the European union* (Vol. 23). IOS Press.

Calvaresi, C. (2018). Agenda Urbana e community hub. *Territorio, 84*, 105–110. http://doi:10.3280/TR2018-084016

Demir, E., Köseoğlu, E., Sokullu, R., & Şeker, B. (2017). Smart home assistant for ambient assisted living of elderly people with dementia. *Procedia Computer Science, 113*, 609–614.

Dorato, E., & Montera, G.. 2015. *La città attiva*. Retreived June 2, 2020, from http://sociale.regione.emilia-romagna.it/anziani/par/materiali-delle-conferenze/brochure-citta-attiva.

Enste, P., Naegele, G., & Leve, V.. (2008). The discovery and development of the silver market in Germany. In *The silver market phenomenon* (pp. 325–339). Springer.

Erikson, K., Voss, M., Prakas, R., Shaurya, B., Chandramallika, S., Amanda, C., Laura, K., Jennifer, S., Heo, S., & Alves, H. (2011). Exercise training increases size of hippocampus and improves memory. *Proceedings of the National Academy of Science, 108*(7), 3017–3022. http://doi:10.1073/pnas.1015950108

Foth, M., Choi, J., Hee, J., Bilandzic, M., & Satchell, C. (2008). *Collective and network sociality in an urban village*. In *Proceedings of the 12th international conference on Entertainment and media in the ubiquitous era* (pp. 179–183).

Garavaglia, E., & Lodigiani, R. (2013). Active welfare state and active ageing. Inertia, innovations and paradoxes of the Italian case. *Transformacje (Transformations), 3-4*(78-79), 285–410.

Gehl, R. W., & Bakardjieva, M. (Eds.), (2017). *Socialbots and their friends: Digital media and the automation of sociality*. Taylor & Francis.

Giddens, A. (2006). *Europe in the global age*. Polity Press.

Kopp, S., Brandt, M., Buschmeier, H., Cyra, K., Freigang, F., Krämer, N., & Straßmann, C. (2018). Conversational assistants for elderly users–The importance of socially cooperative dialogue. In *Proceedings of the AAMAS Workshop on Intelligent Conversation Agents in Home and Geriatric Care Applications co-located with the Federated AI Meeting* (Vol. 2338).

Lau, J., Zimmerman, B., & Schaub, F.. (2018). Alexa, are you listening? privacy perceptions, concerns and privacy-seeking behaviors with smart speakers. In *Proceedings of the ACM on Human-Computer Interaction, 2(CSCW)* (pp. 1–31).

Lee, J. V., Chuah, Y. D., & Chieng, K. T. (2013). Smart elderly home monitoring system with an android phone. *International Journal of Smart Home, 7*(3), 17–32.

Libro Bianco sullo Sport. (2007). Retrieved May 30, 2020, from https://eur-lex.europa.eu/legal-content/IT/TXT/PDF/uri=CELEX:52007DC0391&from=EN.

Maddocks, I. (2014). *The community hub: A proposal to change the role of residential aged care facilities* (RACFs). *Family Medicine and Community Health, 2*(4), 20–25. http://doi10.15212/FMCH.2014.0139

Moore, P. A. 2009. *Design for All: A practitioner's view*. In C. Marcelino, & N. Malanowski (Eds.), *Information and communication technologies for active ageing: Opportunities and challenges for the European union* (Vol. 23). IOS Press.

Ottaviano, C. (2012). Invecchiare attivamente: nonni e nonne nella società dell'ambivalenza. *Studi di Sociologia, 4*, 379–401.

Salute. (2020). *Un modello di politica europea a sostegno di un'azione trasversale al governo e alla società a favore della salute e del benessere*. Retrieved May 25, 2020, from http://www.salute.gov.it/imgs/C_17_pubblicazioni_1819_allegato.pdf.

Strategia e piano d'azione per l'invecchiamento sano in Europa, 2012–2020. Retreived May 29, 2020, from http://www.salute.gov.it/imgs/C_17_pubblicazioni_1847_allegato.pdf.

Struttura e invecchiamento della popolazione. Retrieved May 31, 2020., from https://ec.europa.eu/eurostat/statistics-explained/index.php?title=Population_structure_and_ageing/it.

Zeigler, B. P., Redding, S. A., Leath, B. A., & Carter, E. L. (2014). Pathways community HUB: A model for coordination of community health care. *Population Health Management, 17*(4), 199–201.

The manufacturer's authorised representative in the EU is Springer Nature Customer Service Centre GmbH, Europaplatz 3, 69115 Heidelberg, Germany. If you have any concerns regarding our products, please contact ProductSafety@springernature.com

Printed and bound by CPI Group (UK) Ltd, Croydon, CR0 4YY
30/09/2026
02225498-0009